Wild Mares

Wild Mares

My Lesbian Back-to-the-Land Life

DIANNA
HUNTER

University of
Minnesota Press
Minneapolis
London

Published by the University of Minnesota Press
111 Third Avenue South, Suite 290
Minneapolis, MN 55401-2520
http://www.upress.umn.edu

Printed in the United States of America on acid-free paper

The University of Minnesota is an equal-opportunity educator and employer.

24 23 22 21 20 19 18   10 9 8 7 6 5 4 3 2 1

Library of Congress Cataloging-in-Publication Data
Names: Hunter, Dianna, author.
Title: Wild mares : my lesbian back-to-the-land life / Dianna Hunter.
Description: Minneapolis : University of Minnesota Press, [2018]
Identifiers: LCCN 2017056765 (print) | ISBN 978-1-5179-0266-7 (pb)
Subjects: LCSH: Farm life–United States. | Women farmers–United States. |
   Lesbians–United States.
Classification: LCC S521.5.A2 H86 2018 (print) | DDC 630.86/643–dc23
LC record available at https://lccn.loc.gov/2017056765

Contents

PROLOGUE vii

1 The Great Man and the Dead Cow 1

2 MAD, MAD, MAD, MAD World 12

3 They Can't Kill Us All (Can They?) 19

4 A Room of My Own 28

5 Getting There 39

6 The First Lesbian Conference 48

7 Country Lesbian Manifesto 58

8 The Trouble with Land 64

9 Suzanne Takes You Down 74

10 Family of Woman 80

11 Women, Horses, and Other Embodied Spirits 85

12 Lurk-in-the-Ditch 92

13 Another Dance and a Funeral 96

14 At the Speed of Hooves 104

15 Rising Moon   117

16 Making Hay   125

17 Mel's Place (Dick Pulls Us Through)   138

18 Del Lago   151

19 Thundering Ice, Talking Spirits   164

20 Ravenna's Refuge   174

21 Dancing Leads to This   190

22 Divorce and Dispossession   207

23 Going, Going, Gone   219

    ACKNOWLEDGMENTS   235

    RESOURCES   237

    ILLUSTRATION CREDITS   239

Prologue

I grew up in an unlikely place for a utopian. So it seems, though I wonder if some wild seed wasn't in the air or tucked deep inside the double helices of our DNA, because the people of Minot, North Dakota, elected a Socialist mayor in 1912, and the forebears of our state's present-day farmers dreamed big enough around that time to wage an economic revolt and create a state-owned bank, mill, and grain elevator meant to ensure decent prices and interest rates for farmers. Things had changed by the 1960s, when the government built a Strategic Air Command base north of town, with B-52 bombers, hydrogen bombs, and missiles that could reach the Soviet Union. Minot became a nuclear target, and H-bomb explosions entered my dreams. I was thirteen when the Cuban Missile Crisis threatened to kill us all, but I didn't know what a queer was until my mother warned me to watch out for a few who might be playing on a women's softball team I admired. In the aftermath of my parents' own war—the most violent one ever, World War II—they both worked at union jobs for hourly wages, and they managed to save enough to send me nearly five hundred miles away to study at an up-and-coming liberal arts school in St. Paul, Minnesota. I felt out of place at first among the cultured professors and mostly middle-class students at Macalester. When I asked my smart and hardworking parents for advice, they didn't know what to tell me.

Self-doubt and homesickness almost sent me slouching back

to Minot before I made friends with Karen. A couple of dorm-lounge card sharks and news junkies, we spent many evenings comparing notes about our war, the one the Vietnamese call the American War. I saw that the stories coming from government and military sources didn't seem to square with facts uncovered by reporters. I remember improbable body count numbers of Vietnamese identified as Vietcong, repeated reports of American field successes while our overall position never seemed to improve much, stories about American dissidents under surveillance by the FBI, and many more bits of information that conflicted with the official "truth." As a citizen, I felt duty-bound to parse through it all, to find the facts if I could, and to act, so I participated in sit-ins, marches, and demonstrations for peace. The war traumatized us and called us to action, and then the wave of women's liberation writing hit us.

The ideas of Simone de Beauvoir, Kate Millett, Sidney Abbott, Martha Shelley, and other feminist writers entered my consciousness at a deep, transforming level. In response, as a student I designed and taught a class on feminism during a one-month experimental term at Macalester. The following spring, friends and I started a consciousness-raising group. Once we opened up about our experiences, we began to see how we had been socialized as girls and women, and we made connections between our personal lives and the politics that drove our subordination. It seemed to me that we couldn't separate sexism from the oppressive forces that led to the war. White supremacy, male dominance, repression of dissidents, and a self-congratulating pride had combined to perpetuate a cycle of violence rooted in our history and our social norms. Sexual harassment, sexual assault, domestic violence, discrimination, racial violence, violence against lesbians and gay men, lack of childcare and women's health care, and many other problems identified by women's liberation activists screamed for attention in 1971.

I soon surprised myself by coming out and then realized that my friends had figured out my sexual identity long before I did.

Karen led the way, coming out after she met a lesbian at work. The coworker and her partner invited us to dinner in their apartment near Loring Park. We were both single and available, and they introduced us to other lesbians and showed us the gay bar scene in Minneapolis and St. Paul. We found Gay House, a gathering place for organizing and gay community education, in one of the substantial hillside houses above the Walker Art Center. Soon Karen applied for a grant to open an alcohol-free center where lesbians could gather and organize for change. She got the grant, rented a run-down storefront near Twenty-second and Lyndale in South Minneapolis, and started the Lesbian Resource Center (LRC) a few blocks from the Harriet Avenue apartment where I lived.

More lesbians showed up than I imagined ever finding. We checked each other out, shot pool, flirted, argued politics, and planned political actions and a trip to the nationwide West Coast Lesbian Conference of 1973. Jane started the LRC's journal *So's Your Old Lady* and put my drawings on the covers of the first two issues. In the second one, I read "Country Lesbian Manifesto" by two Wisconsin women, Martha and Marea, and then my friend Lena, who knew them, drove me to the farm they'd named Haidiya (an Arabic word for gift, since they raised Arabian horses). After two attempts at living with women on other pieces of land, I found myself living at Haidiya Farm with Martha, Marea, Shirley, Summer, and the three-year-olds, Sara and Trent, plus dogs, cats, horses, goats, chickens, ducks, rabbits, and a cow named Beauty. My lover, Molly, and many other lesbians came to visit from Minneapolis, and I soon bought a half-blind red gelding named Dick.

When we struggled over finances and personal boundaries at Haidiya Farm, my friend Shirley and I decided to move to Rising Moon, an old farm that Jane of *So's Your Old Lady* owned and declared, as we heard it, "women's land, open to all women." When we arrived with Shirley's daughter, Sara, five other women already lived at Rising Moon in tents, tipis, and an old shed.

In all, I spent most of a decade living and working with other lesbians on hardscrabble, back-to-the-land collectives in

Wisconsin and Minnesota. At farms we called Haidiya, Rising Moon, Mel's Place, Del Lago, and Pliny, we worked the land with hand tools, antique machinery, and horse-drawn implements. Our dream was utopian by definition, both idealized and perfectionistic. We wanted to change the world by establishing women's land, spaces where we could slip through the cracks of patriarchy, militarism, and capitalism, in order to live in peace, feed and care for ourselves, and sustain our values as well as our lives.

Our methods were a lot like those of many sustainable farmers today: do it yourself and make it up as you go. To move our horses, Shirley and I rode them more than two hundred miles because we craved the adventure and we couldn't afford to hire a truck. Along the way, we camped and met people who welcomed and helped us—and some who mistrusted whatever it was that they saw in our low-budget, dykey demeanor. We couldn't always avoid homophobia, but we did our best to act as if it didn't matter.

As we tried to lay the groundwork for our pro–woman, green, sustainable, and nonviolent social experiments, we always seemed to find ourselves short of one needed thing or another. Sometimes it was patience with another woman's politics, or tolerance of a lover's straying romantic interests, but most often it was resources. We found that we needed to connect with the broader rural community in order to survive and thrive. The summer that Shirley and I arrived at Rising Moon on our horses, some of us made hay with a neighbor in exchange for a share of his crop. In the fall, another neighbor invited us to glean his cornfield behind his mechanical picker. We harvested the leftover ears by hand and threw them into the bed of Summer's old pickup. We found part-time jobs and helped neighbors in exchange for other things we could use, like firewood or mechanic's labor. Much of the time, I felt frustrated by money—or, rather, by lack of it. I could see what needed to be built, fixed, or bought, but we could almost never afford to make the progress we imagined.

To address that problem, I took a job with a local dairy farmers' organization, and after six years of working with them, I got a large loan from the government to buy a dairy farm. My lover at the time had just finished some deferred college courses and started a new job in Duluth, and we were full of ideas for continuing our life together. After years of struggling, I saw the dairy farm as a place where we could make a living on the land while taking care of the Earth, the animals, and each other. We knew that weather could divert and stymie our best-laid plans, but as farmers we expected to dance with nature and let her call the tune. The funny thing is that other kinds of systems damaged us most—systems under human control. We couldn't know that the farm crisis of the 1980s would soon overtake us.

In the face of plummeting farm prices, debt, and divorce, I found my way, step by step, to new relationships, a network of farm activist allies, graduate school, and an academic career. Like the Fool in the tarot deck, I have stepped off many cliffs and yet somehow managed to land upright most of the time. In my sixties, I still hold in my visual memory that sunny summer afternoon when I rode my old red gelding down the road behind Shirley on her broad-backed mare, Cheyenne. We were headed toward our dream and our vexation: Women's Land, Open to All Women.

Wild Mares tells the story of my journey.

1 The Great Man and the Dead Cow

On a map, Lake Superior pointed like a giant finger at our farm, directing rain, snow, and fog from the east. Winds off the lake sometimes pinned a weather system in place right over us, until we couldn't drive our tractors into the fields because of too much water in one form or another. Each morning at six a.m., I walked from the house to the barn, hung my coat on a nail inside the door, and went to work feeding and milking thirty Holsteins. I dressed to survive and thrive in coveralls, jeans, shirts, and rubber boots that I bought from the men's clothing sections of local farm stores. My men's clothes were made with stouter fabric, heavier zippers, bigger pockets, and more generous seam allowances than the clothes in the women's section. Mine stood up to barbed wire and other farming stresses, and they fit me. I was blessed with muscles and a waist that bore little resemblance to the connecting tube of an hourglass. At the Lesbian Resource Center in the 1970s, we used to say that any clothes a woman chose to wear became women's clothes. By the spring of 1986, I had been out of the closet for fifteen years, and I didn't care if the wrong people thought I looked like a dyke as long as the right people recognized me for exactly who I was.

Thirty Holsteins turned their heads and bellowed greetings when I stepped into the barn.

I yelled back, "Hello, Girls!"

A timer had already switched on the lights. I adopted this low-cost, low-tech innovation after I read in a farm magazine that more hours of light stimulated cows' hormone production, which in turn increased milk production.

"That's using your noodle," the electrician said when he installed the timer. "'Course, my dad would say it's crazy. You know how set in their ways some of the old-timers can be."

I did. And I do, from both sides now. I was thirty-six then. Now I'm sixty-eight.

The more I age, the more I think about memory. This strange mental power of ours can be sketchy and unreliable, but it lets us bring the dead back to life and travel in time through multiple pasts. Through memory, I picture and feel the farm concretely. Even though I last saw it more than thirty years ago, I still go there in memory and dreams. I understand now that the nostalgia of "old-timers" comes from wanting to hold on to things we love. The tragedy of nostalgia is that we can't hold on and have to be prepared to let go. We may take comfort in the idea that scary times and repulsive people will pass, but we also have to learn to accept that everything we love is destined to transform into something else: $e=mc^2$—you know? We are in constant flux.

Of course, I wasn't thinking that way when I switched on the radio and entered the milk room, a clean compartment, walled off from the rest of the barn. More or less on autopilot, I started the system that sucked sanitizer and fresh water through the milking equipment. While it ran, I scrambled up the ladder to the loft and threw down the cows' morning snack—five forty-pound hay bales.

After I climbed back down, I saw my lover standing at the end of the feed aisle, ready to drive to work in her red wool coat and polyester slacks. No gloves. No hat. Slightly frazzled hair. A round, kind face. What was with the bare hands and head? I didn't get it.

Cedar said a little nervously, "You're going to milk early tonight, right?"

"Yeah, that's the plan," I answered, breaking bales over my

knee and spreading chunks down the feed aisle. That sounded a little qualified, I realized right away. I knew she worried that I worked too much and we didn't do enough fun things together. "Your idea of a good time," she once complained, "is going to the farm supply store in Moose Lake." I felt like I needed to sell her on my commitment to actually making tonight's plan happen, so I added, "I really do want to see this guy!"

The cows were reaching and stretching to get each other's hay by then, except for Lena, who stood oddly still and disengaged. Or was it my imagination?

"Norman Myers," Cedar said.

Because of my earlier forgetfulness, it occurred to me she might think I didn't remember anything she'd told me about this expert she'd booked to speak at a nearby environmental learning center.

"I haven't forgotten," I told her. "I'll be ready."

I did want to hear this guy. Cedar said he knew as much as anybody about biodiversity, the destruction of ecosystems, and the loss of species that depend on them. The northern volunteers for the Minnesota Environmental Education Board (MEEB) were all coming together to hear Myers. Booking him had been a coup for her. She put in long hours regularly, coordinating the northern region for MEEB, a state agency with a few paid staffers like her who helped volunteers plan and run programs in their local districts. I wanted her to know that I couldn't wait to see my girlfriend basking in their appreciation.

After Cedar left for the office, I got the milking machines ready and fed the cows the first of three daily rations of grain. After eating and letting down their milk, they lay in their stalls and ruminated—literally. Looking as stoned as lotus-eaters, they regurgitated and rechewed their food. "Chewing their cud" farmers call this process. Cows' rumens, the first of their four stomachs, act like forty-five-gallon brewery vats, breaking down food with the help of bacteria. I had to learn that when feeding cows I fed microorganisms as well, and the best way to keep a healthy fermentation going was to feed small, alternating amounts of hay and grain throughout the day. Feeding this way took time but saved thousands of dollars in veterinary bills.

When I got to Lena, I noticed that she hadn't touched her grain. Her neighbor knelt in the next stall, reaching with a long tongue to steal it. I tapped the neighbor on the flank. She scrambled to her feet, and I squeezed between the two of them. This neighbor cow was a graceful scamp with a wild topknot and sharp eyes. At nineteen, she was the oldest cow in the herd and also the wiliest rule-breaker. Whenever I let the cows loose to walk to and from the pasture, she watched for me to get busy. When she saw her chance, she sneaked into the feed aisle to eat whatever she found there. The man I bought the cows from had given most of them numbers instead of names. He liked this one enough to call her Punkin. When she annoyed me, I called her the Punk Rocker.

After milking, I phoned the veterinarian and got his mother.

"I'll give him your message," she assured me.

When he called back, he said he would come after lunch. I fed another round of hay and then went outside to the other sheds to feed and water the calves, horses, chickens, and larger young cows called heifers. After a small second breakfast, I went out to "clean the barn." This euphemistic expression actually means taking out the manure and soiled bedding. The barn cleaning has to be done every day and normally feels as mundane and repetitive as housework, but when I got to the barn, I saw Lena lying awfully still in her stall. She was dead, and I felt sick. Until Lena, no cow of mine had ever fallen sick and died in the same day. I dialed the vet and got his mother again. She said she expected him home for lunch soon. While I waited, my anxiety got ahead of me.

When he called I let my worst fear slip: "This is just so weird. Could she have had some kind of big, bad, contagious disease that the rest of the herd might come down with too?"

"I doubt it," he said, and I felt some relief. I'd come to trust this hometown prodigal with shoulder-length hair and a long, serious face that reminded me of David Carradine playing the drifter Caine in the '70s TV western series *Kung Fu*. Like me, the vet was in his midthirties and making a delayed stab at a career meant to provide some financial security. "Doesn't sound like anything I can think of," he reassured me. "I'll come by later in the afternoon."

"Not after lunch?"

"Well, I've got some other calls to make."

"The sooner the better," I told him. "I've got to milk early tonight."

After a long, inscrutable pause, he said, "I'll do my best."

I knew I couldn't ask more. I understood why he wouldn't rank my dead cow ahead of other people's living animals. I needed to do what I could to move things along so that whenever he showed up I was ready. Usually, I rested for a couple of hours after lunch before starting afternoon chores, but not that day.

I cleaned the cows' stalls, scraping the manure and dirtied bedding into the gutter behind them, where I could use the barn cleaner to convey it up a ramp and into my manure spreader. As I worked around Lena's body, I felt sad. She was a decent cow, easy to work with. Beyond that, my inner pragmatist kicked in and my eulogy lost a little steam. She hadn't distinguished herself from the others as much as the Punk Rocker had. Lena produced about the average amount of milk for my herd (seventeen thousand pounds, or $1,870 worth of milk per year). She probably weighed about the average, too—fourteen hundred pounds or so. And as she was now, with the spirit that had animated her departed, she'd become dead weight while I'd become the problem solver who needed to get her out of the barn.

I thought about leaving her until the next day, and I weighed that option against having to work around her body. There was also the unfortunate coincidence that my loan officer, the Farmers Home Administration supervisor, was due to make a visit in the morning. I didn't want to make a bad impression. He must have known that any livestock farmer had to deal with death from time to time, and I hoped he knew that I hadn't dealt with much of it.

I'd managed to keep my cows healthy and raise enough of my own heifer calves to increase the herd by a third in the years since I'd bought the farm. Still, I knew that nothing sent the mind spinning in as many ghastly directions as a corpse.

I decided on a plan involving a rope, a tractor, a chain, and a come-along that I hoped would prove stout enough for the job. As a woman farmer, I'd learned to use jacks, levers, and other force-multiplying tools like come-alongs, because they helped me do things I couldn't do with body strength alone.

The Punk Rocker watched with her neck cranked and the whites of her eyes showing as I approached with a stout, short chain. I wrapped it around Lena's back legs, above the hock joints. The thing clanked like hell, and I wanted to cry. I didn't, though, because I knew that I had too much to do, and I couldn't afford the loss of control.

I hooked one end of the come-along to the chain. I attached the other end to the upright post held tight to the barn floor by a ceiling beam and the weight of the hay in the loft. I pumped the handle, hoping for the best. I needed to use most of my strength, and I was afraid the cable might snap, but it didn't. I saw Lena slide ever so slightly into the aisle in the center of the barn. I kept on pumping, and she kept on moving a fraction of an inch at a time.

The Punk Rocker still cranked her neck and looked disturbed, with lots of white showing around her pupils. "You better watch out," I told her in the most ominous voice I could muster. "This could happen to you."

As I worked, all of the cows went strangely quiet. I caught a breath and reset the come-along, since the cable wasn't long enough to finish the job in one pull. When I started ratcheting again, I kept at it until I got her into the center of the aisle. I thought I could slide her through the barn doors from there, so I got the tractor and a thick, manila rope. Using a Girl Scout knot, I tied the rope to my tractor and to the chain around Lena's legs. Then I eased the John Deere forward, feathering the throttle and looking back and forth, checking and rechecking Lena's trajectory

Cows in the dairy barn

and mine. Once she cleared the barn doors, I stopped and undid the rope. I planned to drag her out of the farmyard after the vet came and finished his work.

While I waited for him, I drove into the hayfield to make a path for later. The snow came almost to the belly of the John Deere, and the going was tough, even with chains on the tires. I quit when I saw the vet pull into the yard. I walked him over to Lena just a few minutes ahead of Cedar's arrival. She rushed over to us, looking both horrified and fascinated as he started the postmortem exam. He exposed Lena's rumen and the rest of her digestive system with a sweeping incision and then stared at her viscera for a long time without saying anything, like an augur. Finally, he proclaimed, "I'll take some samples, but I think this is just going to be one of those mysteries. Cows die sometimes."

The bill for his services, I assumed, would be in the triple digits. Six weeks of Lena's milk could have paid it, but as it was, I didn't have the cow or her milk. The timing wasn't good for losing more money. My income hadn't exceeded my expenses for more than a year, not since the Reagan administration cut farm price supports and milk slid from around fourteen dollars a hundred pounds to eleven.

"At least we have work," one of my neighbors joked when the talk turned to farm politics.

I did indeed have work. So I connected the chain to my hitch and restarted the tractor. With Cedar standing beside the tractor seat, we dragged Lena into the hayfield. I planned to cover her with snow for the time being, but this plan, like so many others before it, went awry. The drive wheels started spinning, and I couldn't back up because I had Lena tied behind me. So I untied her again, slipped into first gear, and used the front-end loader to claw the tractor forward. After a few tries, I knew we were stuck for sure, so we walked back and got shovels. Cedar helped me dig the snow from around the tractor wheels. We moved a lot of snow by hand, and once we got going in our old tracks again, I was able to cover Lena with snow, as I'd planned.

I was milking by 4:45.

Cedar stood in the aisle and said with a dreamy look in her eyes, "You're incredible."

I've never learned to take a compliment graciously, so I made a joke. "Oh, well, you know, what would old Master Kan have said to Caine on *Kung Fu*?" Before she could even begin to answer, I followed up with a bad imitation of the Kung Fu teacher's voice, "Grasshopper, the inner strength outlasts every winter."

She shook her head and said with an irony that sounded surprisingly loving, given her actual words, "You ass!"

I was not feeling incredible or strong but tired, financially stressed nearly to the point of breaking, and bent on getting off the farm for a change, learning something, and pleasing my partner. In the house after milking, I washed up and changed into my best jeans and sweater. We got into Cedar's Grand Am and miraculously got started only fifteen minutes later than we had originally planned. She drove fast, and as I sat beside her in the passenger seat, I felt my body at rest for the first time in hours. We talked, and I didn't tell her how much I hoped that her expert in biodiversity would be able to keep me awake.

At the reception that preceded the speech, I speed-fed on hors d'oeuvres and she introduced me to what seemed like a blockbuster's cast of colleagues, including a retired heterosexual couple in their early seventies. The wife was the president of their local MEEB council, and the husband a retired-businessman-turned-hobby-farmer. They were nice, cordial people who looked healthy and relaxed as they told me about the joy they found in developing their small farm.

When the speaker took the stage, I thought he looked like the professor he was, with a neatly trimmed moustache and small beard, glasses, and a precise way of talking. He told us about the clear-cutting and burning of the Amazon rain forest and how it lowered the price of burgers at fast-food restaurants in America. He laid out a complicated story that started with the cutting and burning and progressed to the plowing of thin forest soils, the subsequent loss of fertility, the intertwined extinctions of plant and animal species, the related loss of ecosystems, and the hastening of climate change through the loss of the trees that function as the lungs of our planet, capturing and storing carbon and exhaling oxygen. Worst of all, he connected all of it to our American appetite for fast-food burgers. He still remains famous for making what people call "the hamburger connection," the idea that the rain forest had to burn so that fast-food companies could buy ground beef from Brazilian exporters for five cents a pound cheaper than they could buy it from American farmers.

When the speaker called for questions, my new acquaintance, the hobby farmer, asked how small-scale farmers could interact with the northern woods in positive ways that protected our indigenous plants and animals. I don't recall how Myers answered the question, but for some reason I recall that he began by flattering the man, saying essentially, "I see by your ruddy complexion, sir, that you are a man of the land."

I waited through a few more questions before I asked what should be done for the small farmers who turned to cutting the forests out of financial desperation. I'd read that they were caught up in global economic pressures, often squeezed out of better farmlands by large landowners who hired gunmen to scare the small farmers and kill the ones who didn't comply. I don't recall that Myers mentioned my winter-reddened face or that he could see I was a woman of the land, and I felt a little stung by what I took to be a sexual double standard. What he answered, as I remember it, was that the Brazilian government should subsidize shoe factories and encourage small farmers to move to the cities and go to work in the factories. Didn't he understand, I wondered, that the land was not just a place of production for farmers, not a factory, but a hoped-for refuge from violence, a place to grow food, and a home that, in a fairer, saner world, the farmer could be allowed to nurture and preserve?

In the car on the way home, I told Cedar what I was thinking. She told me that she was disappointed that I didn't have more positive things to say about her program. I told her that I was entitled to my thoughts. She reminded me how much this event meant to her. The car got awfully quiet for a few miles, and I knew that it would stay that way until I thought of some positive things to say. My inability to do that right away, I thought, had sprung from my exhaustion, not from my feelings about her program. So I complimented her on how many people came, how much I learned, how hard she had worked on the event, and how people had liked it.

When I finished, she sighed. "It's been a long day for both of us."

At the time, our relationship was just a few months old. We didn't know each other's sweet spots and psychological buttons as well as we would in years to come. We also didn't know if we would last as a couple. As it turned out, we would have the closest thing two women could get to a marriage in the 1980s and '90s. We would do our best to care for each other, and we would stick together for nine years while the religious right learned how to use our love as a wedge issue to get out the conservative vote. But that was only starting to happen that night back in 1986. When we got home, we went almost straight to bed, and I fell asleep as soon as we slipped our arms around each other.

2 MAD, MAD, MAD, MAD World

Long before the dairy farm and all the other incarnations of women's land, as early as I can remember my world was the small, stucco house that my grandfather built in Minot, North Dakota. In the same inexorable way that one step leads to another and then to others much farther down the road, my life in that little house set the course for everything that would come later.

My grandfather died before I was born of some sort of mysterious health problems that I suspected were related to alcohol. After I was born, my parents bought the house from my grandmother. As part of the deal, she got to live with us, and because of it we never had peace. She stood about four-foot-ten with a wren's build and a cantankerous, steely will. From photographs, I could see that my dad had his father's build. I have it, too, broad-backed and powerful. My dad and his mother argued over politics and memories. Neither could concede a thing to the other, and Dad blamed my grandfather for leaving him to deal with Grandma and that funky, old house. While he worked on it, he groused regularly, "The goddamned floors aren't level. Nothing's square. He just threw stuff together any old way. He didn't care."

When Dad got that way, there was nowhere for me to go but inward. Grandma had her own bedroom. My parents had the other one, and my brother, Dave, had the couch. He got his own room in the basement when I was about five or six, after he'd grown strong enough to help Dad enlarge the coal cellar by hand with shovels and pails. He took his teenager's gear to the basement then, and I moved from a small bed in my parents' room to the hide-a-bed where Dave had been sleeping. After television arrived, I fell asleep to the soundtrack while my family looked across my body to watch their evening programs. I often woke and realized I had incorporated dialogue from *The Twilight Zone* or *Perry Mason* into my dreams.

By the time I finished grade school, both of my parents had managed to get jobs with the Great Northern Railway—laboring jobs with some of the best pay and benefits in town. Our house sat half a block from the GN's switching yard, and I used to cross the tracks and walk another mile or so to the park to watch a really good women's team play softball. One afternoon when I was eleven or twelve, I watched the third baseman, a wiry, boyish girl, chase a pop fly so doggedly that she fell over the other team's bench and landed on her back with the wind knocked out of her. When the coach trotted over to see if she was okay, she lifted her glove and showed us that she still had the ball. I thought it was the most heroic thing I'd ever seen!

I liked two other players on the team, too—lookalike sisters with trim, athletic bodies. I didn't recognize my feelings as sexual attraction. I just knew that I could hardly talk to them because I got so nervous. At the end of the season, the *Minot Daily News* published a team photo, and I asked Dad if he could draw a sketch of the sisters from it. He was a self-taught artist and a good one. He drew head-and-shoulders sketches for me, and I put them on my dresser.

Even now, I have never quite made peace with Dad's contradictions. He could be elusive, hard drinking, quick to anger, and emotionally abusive at times. He could also be funny, creative, and solid, both physically and as a provider, and I have to admit that I resemble him in many ways.

When Dad lay incoherent and dying at eighty-five, one of his nurses asked me what he'd done for a living. I said he'd been a

truck driver, and she asked if he'd ever had an accident. "He keeps talking about a wreck," she said, but I didn't remember one. Only later, when my anxiety and the first numbing edge of grief gave way, I recalled the story he told of being dispatched as a newly arrived Army medical corpsman to help a soldier who'd rolled a truck in Algeria in 1943. He found the driver dead in the wreck. Whatever else influenced Dad, war shaped him to the end. The man had been his first corpse of World War II.

Not long after Dad drew me those sketches of the softball players, I came home to find Mom alone in the living room. In those summer days before air conditioning, we drew the shades to keep the house cooler, and I thought the atmosphere felt stuffy and dark. My mother was pretty and fit and, like me, in nearly constant doubt of her beauty and her abilities. "Come and sit with me," she said, and we made small talk a while before she dropped her voice low and asked, "Do you know what a queer is?"

"I think so." I guessed: "Somebody who acts kind of weird or strange?"

"Not just that," Mom said. "It means a girl who likes to be with other girls."

Her subtle, investigating eyes plumbed mine, and I don't know what she saw. The next ten years might have been so much easier if I had been alerted to some inner truth right then, but perhaps just knowing there were girls like that was enough. Maybe it carried me through somehow, much as Alison Bechdel claims to have been sustained by the sight of a butch truck driver delivering packages to a diner where she lunched with her father.

"I want you to be careful," Mom said. "I've heard that some of the players on that softball team you like are queers. If one of them asks you to go somewhere alone with her, don't go."

"I won't," I promised, though I wasn't worried and felt completely safe around them. I don't know whether any of them actually loved other women in the way that my mother warned me against. If they did, I hope they were able to lead happy, safe, and unashamed lives, though that seems almost impossible in the

Dianna at eight with her grandmother, Pearl Iowa Galusha Hunter, and Queenie socially conservative North Dakota I knew. The best I can say for myself is that I was not put off by the idea of women loving each other, and I knew that I wouldn't like to be called *queer,* at least not in the derogatory way that everyone used the term then.

. . . . .

Soon, I had a bigger problem. Minot had become a nuclear target, and it looked like the adults were trying to kill us. The government had built a Strategic Air Command (SAC) base north of town, and I grew up watching B-52 bombers lumber over our heads. When a new, supersonic fighter jet was about to crack the sound barrier on a schedule we saw in the paper, my grandmother and I waited in our yard together, faces turned to the sky.

"My!" she exclaimed as I felt the sonic boom in my ribs and knew she must have felt it too. I learned from her that wars never end but reverberate throughout our lives. She was born in Iowa in 1880, knew people who'd lived through the Civil War, and held a grudge against Franklin Roosevelt because he broke his promise to the "mothers of America" to keep their sons out of World War II. Her grudge against the Copperheads, Iowans who'd supported the South in the Civil War, felt every bit as fresh and bitter. She was a Lincoln-style, reformist Republican and couldn't change, even when Dad's experience of the Great Depression, the Civilian Conservation Corps, the New Deal, and the Second World War made him a union man and a Democrat. Through her, I began to understand how remnants of our experiences remain with us throughout our lives, just as the consequences of 1962 would ripple through my adolescence and set my coming of age on a tumultuous track.

Just after my thirteenth birthday, we watched John Kennedy on live television as he showed those iconic reconnaissance photos that proved the Soviets had placed ballistic missiles in Cuba. We heard him warn that he would respond to any missile attack launched from Cuba with a "full retaliatory response on the Soviet Union." That meant nuclear war. Forty-some years later, one of my teaching colleagues, an Asian historian, told me that his father said, "If there's a nuclear war, we don't want to survive it. We should just drive up to North Dakota and go out in the first wave."

Did we know that we were in such danger?

I remember telling my dad, "I'm scared."

"Of what?" he replied, as if he had no clue what I was talking about.

"Dying," I said.

"Oh," he answered. "Those missiles aren't all that accurate. They might aim for us and hit the base."

The air base was thirteen miles away, and I knew from writing school reports that thirteen miles would not be enough to shield us from the effects of a hydrogen bomb blast. Besides, Dad's hypothetical case made no sense. It seemed much more likely that the Russians might aim for the base and hit us.

We didn't learn until decades later, after top-secret government records were released, that the day that Soviet ships approached the U.S. Navy blockade around Cuba, SAC went to DEFCON 2, a state of alert in which they launched the B-52s and kept them airborne, ready to head for their targets. These preparations followed a defense plan known by the acronym MAD, which stood for mutually assured destruction. MAD's rationale rested on the idea that neither side would launch a nuclear attack if they knew they might be destroyed by the other side's counterattack. That day in Minot, work and school went on as usual, and it wasn't until much later that I began to understand that the adults felt as powerless against the war planners as I did.

At seventeen, I couldn't see it all clearly or sort out what was happening, so I set a goal of getting into a college where I might meet some people who could help. I thought it should be at least a full day's drive from Minot. With those sketchy ideas in mind, I found my college by way of the sort of accidents through which some other girl might have found a boyfriend, got pregnant, and married. I met a perky college recruiter. She handed me a well-designed brochure and planted the idea that at a small liberal arts college with a progressive reputation I could take classes like the History of the Middle East taught by someone who actually grew up there. Once I got to Macalester College, after twelve years of boredom and chasing grades, I expected to feel on the verge of a budding awakening, but to my surprise I mainly felt homesick. When I placed my weekly collect calls to Mom and Dad, I couldn't keep from sobbing into the receiver. I hadn't anticipated how uprooted I would feel in the company of professors and students who seemed so much more urbane and sure of themselves than the people I'd left behind.

I took the train home that first winter break with a keen longing for Christmas as my mom made it happen for us—with a real tree, home-baked cookies, and visits to our extended family. Looking through Mom and Dad's Christmas cards, I saw a letter from an uncle who was an FBI agent in California. His son was in Vietnam with the First Airborne, and my uncle said that my cousin was doing okay and knew that he had a job to do. My cousin and his fellow soldiers would be the leaders of our country in the future, my uncle said, not the goofy protesters at the universities, whom he condemned for their scruffy looks and for being "different."

He meant the midwestern, pejorative sense of *different,* I knew, and his letter hit me like a slap. By then, I was looking like the protesters, with long, straight hair. I listened to Joan Baez and acid rock and followed the news of the war skeptically. At the same time, I loved my uncle. I knew him as a family man, a jokester, and a veteran of World War II who survived shrapnel wounds from exploding treetops in the horrific Battle of the Hurtgen Forest.

When I told my mother how insulted I felt by his letter, she answered, "Oh, honey, he knows things we can't know."

And so my alienation from family began. She was only going along with the popular idea that people in authority knew best, but she disappointed me. As I grew in confidence and found my footing in the broader world, my parents saw my skepticism as disloyalty and my changing self as an embarrassment. At one point, my father told me in exasperation, "We never should have sent you to that damn Macalester." He was on to something there. My education gave me the tools to question, pay attention to nuance, and think enough to realize that I needed to look out for my precious, authentic self.

3 They Can't Kill Us All (Can They?)

I drank my first vodka and Coke in the dorm room of my new friend Karen. A sophomore, she seemed so sophisticated that I could hardly believe I'd found a friend like her. Slight, agile, and fiercely intelligent, she was a dangerous adversary at cards and political arguments. We followed politics, kept up a running commentary on current events, and shared ironic table talk during games of hearts, bridge, and pinochle.

In the spring, Minnesota Senator Eugene McCarthy announced that he would run against Lyndon Johnson as a peace candidate. Many Macalester students worked for McCarthy's campaign. They cut their hair and went "clean for Gene," as the press dubbed it, but I liked the other antiwar candidate, Robert Kennedy. In the television lounge at the end of March, Karen and I watched Johnson's speech on the state of the war. She yipped aloud when he said, "I shall not seek, and I will not accept, the nomination of my party for another term as your President." I was slower to grasp the meaning of his words. His abdication came as such a surprise it didn't sink in until I heard her celebrating.

Unlike me, she had a boyfriend, but she never abandoned plans with me to do some last-minute thing with Richard. That might have been a clue to us if we'd known a thing about baby dykes, but we didn't. Lots of times she made a plan that included

Karen outside Dianna's door at Macalester late in the fall of 1967

all three of us, like marching against racial discrimination after a neighborhood landlord refused to rent to a black couple who were students at Mac. We were eating together in the dining commons the day before spring break in 1968 when a friend of Richard's came and told us that Martin Luther King Jr. had been shot. We could read in his face that King was dead.

"I can't believe it," Karen said.

Richard frowned and grumbled, "I can." He had grown up middle class in a Denver suburb but with a black man's experience in America. He was slender and sensitive with close-cropped hair and a huge talent for playing guitar. Later he would grow an Afro and King Tut–style goatee, but before all the tumult of 1968 to '70, his face looked soft and smooth as a boy's.

I took the train to Minot the next evening. One of the benefits Mom and Dad earned as employees of the Great Northern was a free pass for their college student daughter. The next morning, I woke to a loud voice behind me trash-talking King. When the woman announced in a shrill drawl, "He was not a man of peace," I'd had enough.

I turned and answered, "He most certainly was. He won the Nobel Peace Prize."

She frowned and shook her head. "He was in Memphis, and there was violence!"

I told her that proved nothing, and we went back and forth for a while. When I sat down, my seatmate leaned over and whispered so that only I could hear, "I'm glad you said something." She looked to be about the age of my maternal grandmother, with the same sweetness and heart-rending passivity that comes from stuffing your thoughts for decades.

When I told Mom about my argument, she disappointed me by saying, "I'm not so sure that King was a good man." She added that my FBI agent uncle had told her about "dirty things" that King had done with women. She said the agency had them on tape. Now we know that FBI Director J. Edgar Hoover used his public office to orchestrate a surveillance program against King and other African American leaders as part of the COINTELPRO project. The declassified documents are available on the FBI's own website. Much later, I would read Seth Rosenfeld's account of the conspiracy between Hoover and Ronald Reagan, then the governor of California, to brand student activists as "subversives." Citing FBI documents obtained through Freedom of Information Act requests, Rosenfeld lays bare how the two used the FBI for political purposes, influencing public opinion and government policy through eavesdropping, targeted investigations, defamation, and disinformation.

In June 1968, I had just settled into the second year of my summer job as a reporter for the *Minot Daily News*. I was dressing for work when my mother knocked on the door and said, "Robert Kennedy's been shot."

Kennedy had just won the California primary. In my mind, he was destined to be our next president. My brain short-circuited as I asked, "Is he dead?"

"No," Mom said. "He's alive, but it doesn't look good."

I shrieked, "I hate this society!"

"Oh, honey!" my mother said. "It's not the whole society." In her voice I could hear concern and grief, not just for the Kennedys or for our country but for the daughter who was changing into someone she feared she didn't know.

That summer we watched the chaotic Democratic convention, the protests and police riots in Chicago, and Hubert Humphrey's nomination for president. People like my parents loved Humphrey for his pro–labor and civil rights work as mayor of Minneapolis and as a U.S. Senator from Minnesota, but Humphrey never repudiated Johnson's war policies. In the fall, a majority of the voters went for Richard Nixon and his "secret plan" to end the war. After the election, Macalester gave Humphrey a visiting professorship in political science, along with a house for him and his wife, Muriel, to use during his appointment.

In the fall of 1969, I made a new friend. The resident assistant (RA) on our floor was my age and a wonderful conversationalist—much more socially adept than I am, I thought. When I told her this at our forty-fifth reunion, she said, "Yes, I was popular, but you were powerful." Was I? She caught the flu sometime around November, and I brought her chicken noodle soup and saltine crackers. I felt quite flushed to dote on her, and one night I dreamed about bringing her gifts. All of this behavior should have amounted to another huge lesbo clue—one that I didn't see, but she did. She remembers that we talked about my feelings for her, but I don't recall it. I was so deep in the closet that I must have repressed the conversation.

By this time, I'd decided to major in history, and one of my teachers showed up in my RA's room some evenings. He was there for friendship, I assumed, because they sat with the door open, talking. He was young and untenured, with long hair, a moustache, and a nervousness that made him seem more approachable than my other teachers. He offered the contemporary, cutting-edge courses that I craved. The writers he chose—Black Elk, Malcolm X, Studs Terkel, and Vine Deloria Jr., among them—sang like trumpets beyond the mainstream walls.

One evening the three of us hashed over men's behavior toward women. I don't remember where our discussion started or where it was going exactly, but I remember that he asked if I'd ever heard of "The Redstockings Manifesto."

"Why?" I asked.

"You should check it out," he answered with a grin that left me curious. "Stop by my office and I'll give you a copy."

After a few days of procrastination, I stopped by his office, and my life changed.

"Women are an oppressed class," the Redstockings assert in plain, straightforward language. After the turn of the millennium, I assigned their manifesto in some of my women's and gender studies classes. My students as always had mixed feelings, but most of them could relate to it. I myself have read and reread it dozens of times, and I am still amazed by it. In those academic days, I learned that the Redstockings were mostly New Leftists in New York whose name alluded to the Bluestockings (intellectual women who preceded them) and to the Marxists who were red before neoconservatives appropriated their color. The Redstockings argue that men benefit from women's oppression through a set of unearned advantages called "male privilege," and that both women and men need to work to change the binary gender system that locks them into preordained roles. Before reading the manifesto, I'd had no language to understand female subordination, male supremacy, or the ways that the gender system pinned us into narrow, socially constructed versions of ourselves. I immediately recognized that I had felt the implications of those dynamics throughout my life.

When I was about seven or eight, I sat one evening with my father and a truck-driving buddy of his in one of the working-class bars near the railroad tracks in Minot. I don't know whether North Dakota allowed children in taverns or some friendly bartender was just indulging my dad, but it wasn't my first time in dim light and boozy-smelling air, listening to adult voices growing louder and fuzzier. At one point my dad's friend said, "I wonder what women talk about when we're not around."

"Men, I suppose," my dad said, laughing in a self-satisfied way that made his friend snicker too and hinted of things secret from me. I remember wondering how they could be so mistaken. I knew that women in the company of other women talked about children, friends, family, and their own projects. When they talked about men, it was often to complain about some gendered slight. We had no words for discrimination or sexual harassment then. Over time, I learned that lesbians often stand accused of hating men, but the bitterest anti-male complaints I've heard came from heterosexual women.

In the spring of 1970, I talked my adviser into letting me design an independent study course in feminist history. I had to take the course independently because no professor offered anything like it at Macalester at the time. As my feminist consciousness grew, so did my generation's angst over the war and the draft. The American massacre of villagers at My Lai shamed us and made some of us think that our parents' generation hadn't brought home the lessons of the Nuremberg trials.

Nobel Prize–winning writer Nadine Gordimer writes in her review of Simone de Beauvoir's autobiography, "If hell is seeing horrors done in one's name, then many of us have been down there with her. 'I'm French.' 'I'm German.' For me, a South African, 'I'm white.'" For me, I was white. I was American. And I was a woman on the way to discovering her lesbian identity. Like de Beauvoir, who never shook her alienation from the French government and her fellow citizens over their violent repression of the Algerian independence movement, I have never shaken my alienation from the power structures of my country and from my fellow citizens who refuse to see and solve the problems of patriarchy, racism, bullying, violence, and endless war. My friends and I did not want our soldiers to be forced to follow immoral orders. The young men we knew in college did not want to answer the draft call. We did not want to commit vast resources to war or let war crimes be committed in our names.

By the spring of 1970, some Mac students thought that our visiting political science professor, Hubert Humphrey, was using his teaching appointment to launch a run for his old Senate seat. A flyer from the Macalester Committee for Peace in Vietnam put the complaint this way: "Some people say Humphrey is a fine addition to the liberal reputation of Macalester. We say no; war crimes are committed by war criminals who add no prestige anywhere."

On April 14, Humphrey was scheduled to moderate a campus forum on environmental issues. A few students who called themselves Yippies invited the rest of us to join them in staging a war protest at the forum. I went to see what would happen—and probably to join in. I could be a fence sitter and still hadn't made up my mind when, at the last minute, the moderator announced that Humphrey was ill and wouldn't attend. The excuse sounded bogus, and one of the Yippies shouted that they were taking the demonstration down Summit Avenue to the Humphreys' house.

I marched along, hanging near the back of the crowd as we entered the Humphreys' driveway. One of the leaders knocked on the door, and Muriel answered. She stepped outside and told us that her husband wasn't home. I remember her courageous stance, head held high and hair gleaming like snow in the glow of her porch light. She gave tit for tat, arguing with the young men up front. I didn't remember Humphrey himself coming to the door, but when I looked online many years later at the campus newspaper account of the protest, I saw that he did come outside and invited the protesters in.

Browsing the *New Yorker* recently, I discovered that the investigative reporter Seymour Hersh met with Humphrey at Macalester that spring. Hersh had broken the My Lai story in America the previous fall and came to Macalester to speak against the war. In his *New Yorker* retrospective on the massacre, Hersh says that Humphrey asked to meet with him after Hersh's talk and told him, "I've no problem with you, Mr. Hersh. You were doing your job and you did it well. But as for those kids who march around saying, 'Hey, hey, L.B.J., how many kids did you kill today?' . . . I say, 'Fuck 'em, fuck 'em, fuck 'em.'" Humphrey's voice, Hersh recalls, "grew louder with every phrase."

Mac students barricaded Humphrey's office that spring, demanding he resign and give back his salary. Students also proposed that the whole Mac community, not just the board of trustees, should decide how to vote on the college's stock proxies. When the trustees turned down the students' proposal, I helped take over the business office. We sat in overnight to protest the proxy decision but also the bigger issue of corporations making money from the war.

At the end of April, Nixon announced that he'd expanded the war into Cambodia and Laos, and students around the country exploded in protest. When Ohio National Guardsmen shot into a crowd during an antiwar demonstration at Kent State University, we felt attacked too. They killed four of us and wounded nine! We had to do something!

So a lot of us poured onto Grand Avenue and blocked traffic. Our protest wasn't very well thought out. We mainly inconvenienced people on their way home from work, but the solidarity felt energizing. Students around the country called for a national strike, and thousands went to lobby in Washington. We saw pictures of New York University students who hung a bed sheet banner from a dorm window, painted with gigantic letters: "THEY CAN'T KILL US ALL." I hoped it was true, but I wondered.

On May 14, Mississippi police and reservists shot fourteen students at Jackson State University and killed two. So much protest spread over the violence and so much panic spread over the protests that Nixon appointed a President's Commission on Campus Unrest. I'd forgotten about this commission entirely until I discovered their report in a Web search on the Kent State shootings. Former Pennsylvania Governor William Scranton, a Republican, chaired it, but unlike Reagan and Hoover, who colluded to shame, blame, and target student activists, the Scranton

Commission members called on Nixon to use his "reconciling moral leadership" to stop the violence and build understanding. When I read their words nearly fifty years later, I felt our youthful idealism vindicated. The writers saw a new culture in the making by Americans with "high ideals and great fears," who believed in "the need for humanity equality and the sacredness of life." As they continued:

> They see their elders as entrapped by materialism and competition, and as prisoners of outdated social forms. They believe their own country has lost its sense of human purpose. They see the Indochina war as an onslaught by a technological giant upon the peasant people of a small, harmless, and backward nation. The war is seen as draining resources from the urgent needs of social and racial justice. They argue that we are the first nation with sufficient resources to create not only decent lives for some, but a decent society for all, and that we are failing to do so. They feel they must remake America in its own image.

In retrospect, I realize that I felt like a patriot in 1970, and I still do. Whatever happened to the idea of remaking America in its own image?

The Scranton Commission's report feels elegiac to me now. We have not managed to reroute resources from our war economy to address "the urgent needs of social and racial justice." Once again, we find ourselves at a crossroads, beset by violence and wondering whether we can gather the will to live together in peace and preserve even the American middle class while bombs explode, secrecy expands, and the wealth gap continues to grow.

4 A Room of My Own

In the fall of 1970, my take on the world changed to the root when I started my independent study course on feminist history. As I read Simone de Beauvoir, Kate Millett, Shulamith Firestone, Caroline Bird, and the writers collected in Robin Morgan's anthology *Sisterhood Is Powerful,* I began to see that I'd been participating all along in a system that was stacked against me—and against all women. Others have described their awakenings to feminist consciousness in metaphors I wouldn't even try to top: the world cracked open, I gave birth to myself, I saw through a different lens, and so on. In the shock of discovery, I raged, despaired, and decided that to have any hope I had to take action. Since I was a student, I used the tools at hand. I submitted a proposal to teach a class on feminism during the January interim term.

Interim term no longer exists at Macalester, but in the late '60s and early '70s, students and faculty were encouraged to take intellectual risks during an experimental January semester. So I found a faculty sponsor, wrote a class description, and submitted a proposal to teach a course I called "Is Anatomy Destiny?" I described it in the catalog as "a look at the woman problem, focusing on its modern aspects." I think my faculty sponsor suggested that wording. It sounded impressive and academic to me at the time, but in my sixties I wonder what "the woman problem" really meant. I see it now as code for a whole set of issues that feminists opened for discussion—topics not mentionable in most college catalogs, like sexism, menstruation, pregnancy, coerced and consensual sex, access to birth control and abortion, child custody rights, the social construction of gender, and many more. It seems to me now that "the woman problem" was really the patriarchy, misogyny, and sexism problem.

No one addressed topics like that in my other classes. In the reading lists, I remember only one book that focused on a woman at all, a study of the early twentieth-century evangelist Aimee Semple McPherson. Books written by women were even more rare on the lists (none, in other words). Only a few of us even thought about the possibility of books *for* women. The women-in-print movement was just beginning, and I knew of no women's studies classes—and no gender studies or queer studies, either.

Six students signed up for my class—not as many as I'd hoped, but enough for discussions that ran deep in many directions. Karen asked if she could sit in with us, and I agreed right away because I knew she would help keep us honest and searching. She had graduated the previous spring and was in a school psychology program at the University of Minnesota. We read Simone de Beauvoir and some newer women's liberation writing that I asked students to find and bring to class. We talked about our personal experiences, and I was taken aback by the devastating critiques the other students made of their relationships with men. They often felt unheard and powerless, especially during sex, which they thought centered on their boyfriends' orgasms, much as discussions about their future lives centered on their parents' expectations and their boyfriends' career goals. I realized that by not dating men I'd shielded myself from the most personal, intimate, and intense struggles over dominance and control.

Of course, I wasn't dating anyone at the time. I still didn't even know I was a lesbian, but that would not last long. We read Martha Shelley's "Notes of a Radical Lesbian" (in Robin Morgan's anthology), in which she calls lesbianism "one road to freedom—freedom

Louisa May Alcott Collective on Macalester College graduation day, 1971.
Left to right: Christine Wezeman Jenkins, Margaret Graham, Dianna Hunter,
and Janet Petri.

from oppression by men," and I remember sitting on a couch with Karen and talking about how much we liked the idea of feeling free from men's needs and demands. I handed out "The Redstockings Manifesto," and as I read it again I realized that the class itself was a manifestation of the Redstockings' call to action: "Our chief task at present is to develop class consciousness through sharing experience and publicly exposing the sexist foundation of all our institutions." The class was only a start, but at least we all left knowing that we were oppressed, that we participated in our own oppression, and that we had to understand how the system worked if we hoped to liberate ourselves. When the class ended, Karen and I continued our discussions in a CR (consciousness-raising) group. Sometimes we met at the professor's house that I sublet with Christine, Janet, and Margaret. Christine dubbed us "the Louisa May Alcott Collective" since there were four of us, like the writer and her sisters, and like Alcott's invented characters, the March sisters of *Little Women*.

Around that time, Karen discovered the Amazon Bookstore Cooperative in the Seward neighborhood of South Minneapolis,

and she started picking me up and driving me there in Richard's
VW bug. The bookstore, started by Julie Morse and Rosina Richter
in 1970, was located in a two-story house called the Brown House
that was also home to an antiwar collective. It was one of the first
two feminist bookstores to open in the United States during the
second wave of feminism. When Karen and I found our way there
in 1971, a serious-looking woman with long, tight braids jotted
down titles as we picked out feminist books, pamphlets, and tab-
loid newspapers with mastheads like *Off Our Backs* and *Ain't I a
Woman?* She let us take the publications on credit, and we hauled
them in cardboard boxes to Macalester and sold them from a card
table that we set up in the student union. Women from our CR
group and the Alcott House helped. We took no cut of the money.
Everything went back to the Amazons.

Sometimes more than one of us sat at the card table, browsing
through the merchandise and jawing with each other and anyone
else we could draw in. The display itself was provocative, with
many of the publications sporting images of feminist protests, lesbian embraces, and bold prints of icons like Sojourner Truth and
Emma Goldman. Still, most people managed to avert their eyes
on their way to get lunch at the grill. One day, a professor I knew
from my work study job in the English Department stopped and
took a hard look. He pointed at one of Virginia Woolf's novels
as he towered over me with one of those look-down-your-nose
expressions (or at least that's how it seemed to a North Dakota
girl with working-class insecurities). I think the novel was *To the
Lighthouse.* On the cover, a woman pulled the oars of a rowboat.

"You won't find that she's on YOUR side," he scowled.

"I won't?" I asked as if I didn't already know better. I'd learned
from my mother and grandmothers how to pretend passive ignorance in order to avoid conflict with someone who could make
trouble for you. Second-wave feminist literary criticism had barely been birthed, and Woolf's love affair with Vita Sackville-West
hadn't yet become widely known. Still, I'd managed to find my
way to "A Room of One's Own."

I wrote off the professor's ignorance to his gender and age, but when it came to the men of our own generation, especially the ones who styled themselves as cultural and social revolutionaries, I expected them to be open to our ideas. I was disappointed by more than one young man who, waving his long-haired flag of resistance to the war and mainstream culture, glowered as he passed, or even stopped to argue for what he saw as the "natural" complementary differences between the sexes. My friend Richard, on the other hand, saw himself as a new sort of man, gentle and somewhat sexually ambiguous. He supported us for a long time, even after he had to change his life to keep up with us.

Janet and Christine from the Louisa May Alcott House joined Karen and me in starting the consciousness-raising group. We met with anyone who showed up—usually four to eight women—and discussed a different topic each time. Taking to heart the women's liberation credo that "the personal is political," we talked about families, sexual relationships, our bodies, our hopes and fears, and so on. A woman I didn't know very well, Sadie Smith, came to our group and said that her father had always told her, "Never trust a man who doesn't carry a knife." Because of it, she said, she decided that a woman should be trustworthy and carry a knife too, so she always did. After that, I got a jackknife and carried it, and it made me feel safer. It came in handy too, especially later, after I got involved in the back-to-the-land movement and found my way to many different lesbian farms.

When two of our CR group members announced that they planned to marry their boyfriends, our conversations turned especially intense. For months they had shared how they lived with misgivings and contradictions, finding their lovers too often self-absorbed and not willing to grapple with male privilege. Some of us didn't see how we could solve those problems from within the institution of marriage, rooted as we saw it in male supremacy, female subordination, and a broad set of vows, practices, and laws that served to keep those dynamics in force. After the meeting the women who planned to be married told us they were quitting the

group, and one of our already married members told me with anguish in her voice, "All I want is to be with people, NOT in women's
heavy encounter groups."

For some reason, I thrived on heavy ideas. I kept looking for
others who did too, and Karen was one friend who always sat-
isfied my need for thoughtful conversation. Before the semester
ended, she told me that a coworker at the day care center where
she worked was a lesbian. The woman and her partner were out
and active in gay liberation, and Karen said that after talking with
them, she'd realized that she was a lesbian and that she was in love
with me. I felt my pulse pounding when she told me. The wonder
is that I didn't grab her and kiss her right then, but I wasn't ready.
I'd come to college at seventeen, cosseted, closeted, and clueless.
I'd missed the usual high school sexual experiments entirely and
hadn't done more than French kiss anyone. The next day, Richard
took me aside and said that he'd been in love with me all this time
too, and he wanted the three of us to be together. I didn't feel the
same way about him, and I guessed that he was grasping for a way
to hang on to Karen. I told him that I'd realized I was a lesbian too,
and after that I came out to the rest of my friends right away. Most
of them congratulated me as if I'd finally discovered something
that they'd known all along.

Karen left Richard and moved into the Emma Steffens commune where two of our friends lived. The commune was an inten-
tional community named in homage to Emma Goldman and Lin-
coln Steffens. When Karen invited me to spend the night with her
there, we made a date. The evening came, and I tried to act cool. I
got into bed with her and didn't say a thing about how scared I felt.
I didn't want to do something wrong that would embarrass me and
cost me my best friend. As it happened, she initiated. She stroked
my hair and asked, "Have you thought about what I asked?"

"I don't know," I lied. "I'm not sure I feel that way about you."

Did she know I was lying? (Later, I thought she must have
known because I had stripped off my clothes before climbing
into her bed.) Why didn't I just admit my fears to her? I'd like to

chalk it up to inexperience rather than some flaw in my character, though I suppose most of our shortcomings go back to both.
Karen and I stayed friends, but things changed between us. Love, I
learned, can endure many things, even not knowing its own name
or nature, but real love, the kind that nurtures both self and other,
requires honesty and courage when it counts.

Fortunately, we stayed friends. Karen's coworker and her partner invited us to their house for dinner. They were fun, young, and
stylish in a way that bridged hippie funk with a gender-bending
dyke chic that felt right to me. These two resonated like mythical
archetypes. Our First Dykes. They invited us to their apartment
in a red brick building near Loring Park, and after a little drinking
and smoking, they walked us up the block and down a short set
of stairs into the 19. That garden-level dive was my First Gay Bar.
We took turns buying beer by the pitcher, and I went away feeling that I'd entered a strange and longed-for space, both pleasur-
able and dangerous.

We met more young women at a bar called the Townhouse
in St. Paul's Midway district. More of us came out every week, it
seemed, and one of the slightly older lesbians dubbed us "the jeans
jacket gang" because of our clone-like outfits of bell-bottom jeans
and denim jackets. When the fast songs came on the jukebox, we
took the dance floor in a bluish mass, looking for love, community,
and physical release.

Meanwhile, Margaret moved out of Alcott House, and Richard moved in. He'd landed a job curating and driving an African
art van for the Minneapolis Institute of Art. He'd let his hair grow
into an Afro and groomed himself a King Tut–style beard, and
somehow he acquired a bright orange dashiki that he wore to work
with sandals. One morning, I watched him leave the house in that
outfit, get into his VW, and make a tight U-turn. A neighbor across
the street, a man I don't think any of us had met, hurried out and
chased after him, shaking a fist. I'm still not sure why. Making un-
seemly maneuvers in a middle-class neighborhood? Driving while
black and living with three white women?

Going through the world with Richard taught me something about the unearned advantages of my own white privilege, and we struggled over his male privilege. He didn't like cleaning house. Neither did we, but we'd long since decided to share chores and didn't plan to make an exception for him. Janet, Christine, and I had a lot to learn as cooks, but we looked for new recipes and tried them when our turns came. One of my recipes, "Quick Quiche," featured a crust made of crushed saltine crackers, which seemed gourmet compared to Richard's waffles from a mix that he served with maple-flavored syrup. When his turn to cook came, he would always—literally always—think a long time and then say, "How about waffles?"

And as if the waffle violation weren't enough, he also regularly forgot to put the toilet seat down. One day when it happened again, I painted on the underside of the ring, "UP AGAINST THE WALL, MALE CHAUVINIST PIG!" Later that day, he came down the stairs shouting, "Dianna, you've gone too far this time! Not all men are chauvinists!"

I probably answered that they most likely were if they could just look at themselves honestly enough. The whole house got into an uproar, and my housemates agreed that I'd gone too far. Their disapproval really made me question my own judgment, since I could usually count on them for support. In an alternate version of this story, Christine remembers putting "Smash Phallic Imperialism" stickers on the undersides of toilets. I think that came later, but I bow to the possibility that she could be right. As cognitive scientists, psychologists, and memoirists have processed our shared curiosity about memory these past few decades, one thing we've learned is that many factors influence how we store and retrieve our memories, including imagination, the context surrounding retrieval, and our psychological processing of past wounds and other feelings. Our memories become our personal revisionist histories, and yet we can search for shared threads, remnants of an objective past that can be checked against the memories of others and confirmed or corrected by whatever records we can find.

As I remember, I soon got back in sync with my Louisa May Alcott friends. We reserved the campus chapel and hosted my lesbian friends for a women's dance with recorded music. Karen was there with a new lover, Judith. She was friendly, clever, and good looking, with long bones, a slender build, and an expressive face that she used like a comedian's instrument when she felt like making people laugh. I liked her, yet when I spent time with her and Karen together, I couldn't help feeling that I'd blown a chance I should have handled. With no lover of my own in sight, I led with my head, as usual, and put myself through another round of independent study—this time on sex and my body.

I found *Women and Their Bodies: A Course,* the Boston Women's Health Collective's first edition of the book most of us remember from its second-edition title, *Our Bodies Ourselves.* In simple and accessible language, the writers explain that the vagina's "walls are ordinarily in contact; i.e. its space is potential, not actual." Hmmm. They illustrate and name the mons veneris, clitoris, clitoral hood, hymen, and labia major and minora. They say we should get to know our body parts and learn by touching them what feels right. I put myself to sleep many times in my room after taking their advice.

Somewhere in there, Richard and I drove up to North Branch to visit friends who had bought a small farm. A back-to-the-land movement was catching on, and these two weren't the first of our friends to move to the country. The woman was a friend from our CR group—one of the two we'd alienated by arguing against their marriages. I had to admit that she looked happy as she showed us their one-story farmhouse. I admired the work they'd done to modernize and spruce it up, especially the pine plank floors that they'd sanded and refinished so that they shined.

Still, I knew her life wasn't for me—not the heterosexual part of it, anyway. I'd been intrigued by stories about women's farm collectives in my feminist newspapers, and that was a direction I hoped to go if I could just find some like-minded women. On the drive home, Richard told me that he really wanted to move to the country too, so we asked our roommates if they'd like to join us. They asked what we planned to do about jobs, and we said we would find a place first and then look for jobs nearby. They told us to go ahead and check out how much a place in the country would cost. We found a place that we liked near Milaca, a sturdy, old schoolhouse, partially remodeled, on a few acres of land. The price was around $5,000, if I remember right. Richard and I signed a purchase agreement, but our roommates thought the plan was too risky. Without them, I wasn't interested. In the end, Richard called the realtor and told him we wouldn't be following through.

In the fall, he left us to live in the country with some of his musician friends. The rest of the roommates and I rented a turn-of-the-century apartment in Selby–Dale, just a few blocks from the Emma Steffens commune. The apartment had varnished woodwork, built-in cabinets, and leaded-glass windows, but the neighborhood was in the throes of urban renewal, with many similar, fine, old buildings being torn down all around us. My dog, Blitz, and I settled into a small room near the kitchen. I think it had been the maid's quarters. I had room for my twin-sized mattress on the floor, Blitz's bed, and a desk made from milk crates and a board. The only window looked into the back entrance, but I had a room of my own. I could continue my experiments in sexual pleasure, and I would have privacy to offer a lover, if I ever found one.

Janet and I took part-time jobs as teacher's aides at Webster School, an elementary school a few blocks from our apartment. As cool weather settled in, I walked to and from work, cutting a self-conscious figure in a black wool cape I bought at Goodwill. Living collectively in low-rent places, I didn't need much money to get by. Voluntary poverty and group living felt like the path to freedom.

In November, Karen and Judith introduced me to a woman named Marj. The four of us went to the Townhouse, and Marj and I talked and danced. She had long, dark hair and eyes that invited me to look deeper. We discovered that we had a lot in common, like folk music, guitar playing, and feminism. We danced to a couple of fast tunes and then tried a slow one. When we pulled each other close, I felt a shared eagerness. We kissed on the dance floor, and I saw Karen and Judith in the background, smiling and clapping their hands.

Our relationship started out sweet and comfortable, and it lasted that way for a few weeks. Before Christmas, I felt like something was missing, and I told Marj that I wasn't feeling the attraction anymore. I don't know for sure if that was accurate, or if I just craved broader experience. For the first time ever, I did not go home for Christmas. I wanted to be fully present in my burgeoning adult life, and I didn't know what I could say to my parents about it. By the end of the year, I had brought two more women to my room, including one named Ari, whom I met through a Minneapolis women's liberation group. My feelings about all of them ebbed and flowed mysteriously, in ways that weren't fair or rational. I recorded my confusion in my daybook at the end of 1971: "I feel like I'll never work out a solution to my feelings about Karen, Judy, Marj, and Ari."

Eros, I learned, can be a wandering dog.

5 Getting There

We needed a roommate in our apartment on Laurel Avenue, so my ex-lover, Marj, moved in. She soon started bringing home a woman named Summer and sometimes Summer's two-year-old son, Trent. Summer told us that she and her ex-partner in California had decided to have babies together and co-mother them before things fell apart, and Summer and Trent ended up in Minneapolis. I liked them both. Trent had long blond hair, an imp's body and sense of humor, and all the verve and energy my younger cousins had taught me to expect from a toddler. His mother presented as hard, strong, and butchy, but I loved the side of her that could turn soft and vulnerable. Like most of us, she could be sweet as molasses or caustic as tar.

I didn't see us as butches or femmes. My friends and I crossed and recrossed the lines between the male and female binaries we called "sexes" and not yet "genders." We claimed the right to define ourselves for ourselves, whether that meant lesbian feminists, dykes, androgynes, or something else. As my Alcott House friend Christine put it decades later, if the cultural rules weren't changing fast enough, we just kept on acting as if we had the right to be who we were. The same went for our relationships. We claimed them as ours to shape and manage, to hell with social customs and expectations. We changed the world by acting as if we had already changed it, but sometimes we stumbled because it was just so damn hard.

When Summer and Marj hung around in our living room, kissing and carrying on their courtship, I felt some envy because I wanted to find love, but to my surprise I didn't really feel jealous. Marj and I had managed to let go of each other cleanly, and I was at the beginning of what would turn out to be a longtime intermittent affair with Ari, the woman I'd met through a Minneapolis women's liberation group. My heart contradicted itself regularly. I was in love with her but afraid to let her know in case she wasn't in love with me. I wanted to be free to love whomever I chose, and I wanted to find the right woman and settle into some kind of marriage of mutual support and fidelity. When I felt tentative or not quite comfortable with a lover, I assumed we couldn't last and stayed on the lookout for the next best candidate for the long haul.

The next woman I met was not a lover but a fascinating companion and one of the people who helped me in my journey back to the land. On my way home from the bus stop near my Selby–Dale apartment, someone waved to me from the porch of the Emma Steffens commune. It was one of my college friends, standing there with another woman and gesturing for me to join them. When I mounted the steps, my friend flashed a broad, gap-toothed grin and said, "This is someone I think you need to know."

So K/T came into my life, and for a while I thought she might be the most interesting woman in the world. She presented herself to the world in black-rimmed glasses, an Army fatigue jacket, jeans, motorcycle boots, and a deadly serious demeanor. And then there were those slash-interrupted initials, which she used not just as a nickname but also a nom de plume. I had a feeling she would take me somewhere if I got to know her, but I soon found out that getting to know her would take some doing and some time. She liked to turn a card over here and there, but she kept the rest of her hand well guarded—at least from me.

She told me that she'd studied at New College in Florida with Robin Morgan, the editor of my beloved *Sisterhood Is Powerful—*

and also that the motorcycle sitting by the curb was hers. It was a small bike, more like a scooter, really, with a motor of maybe 100cc. Months later, after we shared some adventures, she told me the bike vibrated when she got it up to freeway speed. She said she rode it to New Orleans once, and afterwards she felt so sick from the shaking that she had to stay in bed for a day. This was a macho brag that she delivered with swagger and parallel columns of cigarette smoke blown through both nostrils. She smoked Marlboros, of course.

When the school year ended, I got my first chance to move to the country. Friends rented a farmhouse near Milaca and invited me to live there. I imagined we would garden and maybe hold meetings and make ourselves into one of those lesbian farm collectives I admired from the feminist tabloids. The dynamics weren't right, though. Two of the women were in love with each other, casting star-struck looks and sexual energy all around, and another of our housemates rarely came to the farm. Karen tells me that she and her new lover, Lena, were there too, and that Karen was sick. I can't account for why I'd forgotten that. I remember that Blitz and I entertained each other by exploring the woods, meadows, and banks of the Rum River. I relearned the awe of the natural world that I'd lost after grade school when I used to slip away to green spaces every chance I got. Every time I took my nail-biting, anxious, tomboy self to nature I came away restored.

At our rented farm, Ari visited me, and I took her to a swimming hole I'd found hidden in some brush. I told her it was a great place to skinny-dip, but I could tell that she felt unsure. I slipped off my clothes and entered the water, stroking the surface with slow, wide arcs. "It's great!" I teased. "Come on in!"

She looked over her shoulder. "I guess you're right," she said. "No one can see us."

I found Ari beautiful always, but when she took off her clothes and stood there naked with her brown hair shaken loose around her shoulders, I felt thunderstruck. She was going through a physical fitness phase, and her toned limbs gave her the grace of a heron entering the water. We brushed our bodies together and paddled around, and that night we sat outside watching the fireflies' pyrotechnic mating ritual before going inside to enact one of our own.

And then my roommates and I went to the city for what was supposed to be only a weekend, but at the end of a dinner that we shared with Judith, the two lovers had a spat. One of them bolted across a street in the Dinkytown neighborhood near the university and got hit by a car that broke both her legs. Shocked and wanting desperately to do something to help, we sat in the hospital waiting room for hours, until our friend's partner came and told us in the most wrenching way that she planned not to tell the hospital staff about their relationship for fear that her lover might not get good care if they knew she was a lesbian. She didn't want us to give away their secret, and she worried that our presence in the waiting room might do that. I had to admit she might be right, but I resented the hell out of having to worry about it. I felt the angst of internalized homophobia crashing in. I wanted to break some glass or smash my fist into something, but I restrained myself until a better time to lose control, maybe outside a bar after a half-dozen shots of Johnny Walker Red.

While we waited around in the city, wanting to help but not really finding good ways to do it, I read in the paper that heavy rains had hit the Milaca area. Floodwater took out culverts, and one of the washouts happened on our road. We weren't able to get home for a week. When we did, we found that someone had broken into our house and stolen all of our valuables, such as they were at that time. My radio, guitar, cassette recorder, and stereo were gone, and the mosquitoes had multiplied into biting clouds, thanks to the many new pools of water where they could reproduce. I was nearly broke and feeling defeated and unsafe, so I retreated to the city.

Judith invited me to join her in a basement apartment that Ari's ex-lover had vacated before handing the keys over to Judith. We were squatting. The electricity had been turned off, but she ran an extension cord to an outlet in the hallway to get some light. We decided to apartment-hunt together and found a restored upper duplex with leaded-glass windows and lots of sunlight gleaming on refinished hardwood floors. Come fall, I biked eight miles from Harriet and Twenty-fourth to my teacher's aide job at Webster School. Come winter, I hitchhiked until I had a close call with a driver who made sexual innuendos and reached for my breasts. After that, I took the bus. Judith had started a new relationship, and so had Karen. Ari and I kept trying to give each other what we needed, until one night she said, "I just get the feeling that you're not really into me."

I was so fundamentally insecure that I took her comment as a critique of my lovemaking and didn't say, "What? Are you kidding? I'm crazy about you!" We let each other go without any kind of closure, and I transferred my energy into creating a comic book about a lesbian superhero battling religious extremists who wanted to shut down the city by clogging its water system with Bibles. I went to work five days a week, and when I got home I walked Blitz. Most evenings I stayed in my room, writing and drawing, and thinking about the fact that my emotional withholding amounted to another kind of dishonesty that I needed to get beyond if I wanted to find and give real love someday. On weekends, I caroused with the jeans jacket gang at the Townhouse and tried not to smash anything.

And then one day, Karen picked me up from work in her lover's car. She told me that she was starting a Lesbian Resource Center (LRC), a place where lesbians could drop in, call for information, or just get together in a space that was our own, not dominated by straight people or gay men. "I applied for a grant and I got it," she said, letting loose that elfish grin that provided such an unassuming counterpoint to her ingenuity and courage.

Most of us had ideas, but we didn't know how to get the resources to make them happen. Before long, Karen had rented a rundown storefront four blocks from my Harriet Avenue apartment, at 710 South Twenty-second Street, just west of Lyndale.

She told me later that many landlords turned her down when they found out what she wanted to do in their buildings. The one who rented to her didn't care, she said, because he planned to sell the place. To get the word out about the LRC, some of us helped her post flyers in strategic places where we hoped that passersby wouldn't tear them down. Mostly, word spread through the lesbian grapevine.

Karen said that when she called the phone company to order service for the LRC, the woman who answered said, "A WHAT KIND of resource center?" She said she'd have to check with her supervisor to see if she could take such a listing, and when she came back on the line, she said that she could take the listing, but Karen would have to spell *lesbian* for her. Making that phone listing was a bold move toward visibility and self-assertion. As Barbara Gittings pointed out back then, most people saw us as mentally ill, illegal, and immoral. "Social anathema, even to you brave ones," *The Ladder* writer Gene Damon (pen name of Barbara Grier) called her lesbian self in *Sisterhood Is Powerful*. We had to fight on all fronts, against the homophobia of others as well as the internal kind that we inflicted on ourselves. In *The Women's Survival Catalog*, a feminist directory from 1973, Karen wrote in the LRC's entry, "We are now coming out completely, affirming that we are here and can no longer be ignored."

Many lesbians found their way to the LRC. I met businesswomen, teachers, and other professionals, as well as working-class women, unemployed women, military veterans, peace activists, mothers, divorcées, women still married to men, and many more varieties of lesbians, bisexuals, and women who were questioning their sexual identities. I also met an intersex person who struggled with us and with the broader culture over the idea that there could be only the gender dualities "men" and "women." As a self-involved young snip, I was drawn to the ones most like me—politically aware types who wanted to change the world.

Karen directed the LRC with charm, empathy, and a charisma that pulled many women into her orbit. Her funky bell-bottoms, bare feet, and secondhand shirts gave her a raggedy, adolescent, Tom Sawyer quality that didn't seem to square with her social competence. The resulting mental dissonance added to her appeal, I think.

She transformed the empty storefront by bringing in a desk, a bookcase, and enough books to set up a small library. Others brought easy chairs and a donated couch that sagged nearly to the floor. With interior house paint, I created a head-and-shoulders mural of two women kissing. I don't think it was particularly good. Karen told me later that someone had complained because she thought one of the women looked like a man. We lesbians could be hard on each other, almost never sparing a critique if we thought one was deserved. After long, contentious meetings, I rose from that saggy couch many times with a few grudges and an aching back.

We had some CR-style discussions. An Army veteran told about a witch hunt that her superiors conducted to out her and then stigmatize her with a dishonorable discharge. We talked a lot about coming out. Some confessed that they lived mostly closeted lives. Most of us were out to some people and not to others, in complicated and almost unmanageable versions of selective honesty meant to balance safety and freedom. Some had trouble using the word *lesbian* at first. I remembered how sibilant and sinful it had sounded to me in the beginning—and then I saw it as a source of power once I took it as my own to shape and define. Some of the young professional women seemed to have the world by the tail. One gave me a ride to the Townhouse and demonstrated on the I-35 ramp how fast her sporty new car could accelerate from zero to sixty. Her display excited me, but not so much that I envied what she had. I valued the free time I got from part-time work, even if it meant living in voluntary poverty. Sometimes, we just had fun at the LRC. We shot eight ball on the shabby pool table, flirted, argued, joked, and hashed out ideas.

Early in 1973, Jane announced that she was starting a journal. She set up a box for contributions and called a meeting to talk

about how the journal would operate. We decided on the name *So's Your Old Lady*. The work I'd put into my comic book prepared me to draw the cover art for the first issue, a brush-and-ink drawing of a woman lost in thought as she examines her own body. I contributed writing too—poems, essays, and fiction—and so did lots of others.

Many of us made clear in our creative work that we held society's institutions suspect. We longed to be loved, to be accepted by our families, and to be allowed to see ourselves as healthy, legal, and moral people, free from witch hunts, investigations, and physical assaults. We could hardly imagine the old social structures changing fast enough to include and support us in the ways we wanted. Same-sex marriage seemed like a pipe dream at best, and a wrong-headed replay of a flawed patriarchal institution at worst. We wanted to abandon the old social structures and support new ones, like the Amazon Bookstore and the LRC. Some of us could imagine shopping only at women's stores, eating only at women's restaurants, listening only to women's music, and reading only women's books. I still wanted to find some women to share a lesbian collective farm, and that would come in time. Getting there would turn out to be a process, a becoming, and the journey that lies at the heart of this story.

Barb Stone and Sara at the second location of the Amazon Bookstore on Cedar Avenue in Minneapolis in 1973

6 The First Lesbian Conference

I still had not come out to my parents when I walked into the LRC one day and Karen met me with an excited grin. She held up a copy of *Lesbian Tide,* open to a headline announcing, "1,000 Expected at Lesbian Conference."

I said, "Incredible!"

"Isn't it?" She looked proud of herself. She told me she'd already started organizing rides to take people from the LRC to the conference in Los Angeles. She asked if I'd like to sign up, and I said, "Of course!" None of us had ever heard of anything like this before because it hadn't happened—an open, nationwide gathering of out lesbians grappling with issues that mattered to us. The article said the conference program included keynote speeches by Kate Millett and Robin Morgan, exhibits and performances by lesbian artists and musicians, a dance on Saturday night, and "workshops dealing with everything from 'Fine Arts' and 'The Lesbian and Religion' to 'Radical Therapy' and 'Socialist Feminism.'"

At the time I knew nothing about the politics of West Coast lesbians. I would later learn that *Lesbian Tide*'s staff consisted of an upstart group of radical lesbian feminist change agents who had broken away from the Los Angeles chapter of the foundational lesbian organization Daughters of Bilitis. *Lesbian Tide* editor Jeanne Córdova was a core organizer of the conference. The magazine's

April cover featured a photo of Rita Mae Brown, one of the poets of our movement. Red capital letters, wrapped tightly around the photo, announced, "AN ARMY OF LOVERS SHALL NOT FAIL." I recognized the line from Brown's poem "Sappho's Reply."

Early in April our little Twin Cities unit of lovers and friends got together for a meeting to plan our trip to Los Angeles. There were at least thirteen of us. I remember that many by first name, even now. Looking back, I see that we were some of the younger, less closeted, and more politically active women who hung out at the LRC. Many, like me, worked part time, so we had the luxury of being able to drop everything and leave on short notice—even if we had to figure out how to have a great adventure with very little money.

That afternoon we soaked in a preview of California weather, a sunny, seventy-degree afternoon. The snow was gone, and our eyes feasted on green grass. We stood around in shirtsleeves outside until we started the meeting. We talked a while and decided that we would caravan in cars and camp along the way. Three or four women volunteered their vehicles, and the rest of us agreed to share the driving and expenses. We planned to bring snacks so that we could avoid spending money at restaurants.

The day before our takeoff the weather service warned of a snowstorm for southern Minnesota and Iowa, but we had already struggled to coordinate our many differing schedules and needs. We weren't about to let a storm warning force us into recalculating. The next morning, with Minneapolis getting only light snow, we set out, aiming to camp somewhere beyond Iowa that night. I carried a sleeping bag and backpack, and I tucked most of my spending money—roughly $50—into my sock, inside one of the boy-sized western boots I'd picked up cheap from Kaplan Brothers surplus store on Franklin Avenue. If everything went as I'd planned, the money would cover my expenses and my fabulous boots would catch many lesbians' attention.

The farther south we went, the heavier the snow. By the time we approached Albert Lea, where interstates I-90 and I-35 intersected, we had been pushing through drifts and blowing snow for nearly an hour. Our butchy-looking driver, high strung in the best of conditions, had fidgeted and furrowed her brow more and more as the snow deepened. When we fishtailed through a two-foot drift, she declared in a tone that warned against any second opinion, "We've got to stop."

She took the first Albert Lea exit, and we soon hooked up with the police somehow. Maybe we drove to the station, but the scene I replay in the sketchy theater of my memory is that the police called the Salvation Army for us, and the organization's local captain came right away to a room where we were waiting. After hearing us out, he said, "We've already put up all the people we can in hotels, but you can spend the night at our house if you like."

I remember looking at our driver in disbelief. How crazy was this—a baker's dozen of obvious young dykes, oozing political and sexual energy, in the home of the Salvation Army captain? We each assessed him as best we could right then and there, I suppose. I know I did because, after all, the situation seemed so potentially fraught. Could anyone represent traditional authoritarian social values in a more striking, iconic fashion than he did in his blue, military-style uniform? And could anyone represent the Dionysian, Sapphic threat to traditional Christian order more strikingly than we did in our men's clothes, uncoiffed hair, and butch chic disregard for bras, makeup, and other trappings of so-called femininity? Would we disgust him once we took off our hats and heavy coats and he could see how we were dressed and groomed? Would he feel obliged to try to convert us?

"My wife and I would be glad to have you," he said, and his mention of a wife made me warm to the idea. After all, we had no place else to go, and with a woman involved his offer seemed safer and less likely to lead to unpleasant complications. We accepted— provisionally—and soon were caravaning behind the captain as he led us through snowy streets.

I remember the house as neat and well kept, probably not one of the newer ranches or ramblers that would now be called "mid-century" or "atomic," but most likely an older, clapboard-sided, small-town Minnesota house, dating from the '20s or '30s. The captain's wife met us at a side door that opened into the basement, and I found them gracious and welcoming as they showed us the space—paneled walls, a carpeted floor on which to roll out sleeping bags, a couple of beds, a couch, and our own bathroom. I got the impression that we weren't the first strays they'd taken in, and we wouldn't be the last. And there was a pool table—just like at the LRC, only this get-together would be a sleepover!

We went to bed early so that we could get an early start, which we did the next morning, in darkness. Highway crews had cleared the freeway. We passed through surreal, square-sided snow tunnels near Mason City, Iowa, where the storm had hit the worst. Somewhere south of Des Moines we passed back into spring. We drove all day, changing drivers so that we didn't have to stop for rest until we got to Tucumcari, New Mexico. We pitched camp at a KOA there, in the shadow of Tucumcari Mountain, the town's five-thousand-foot namesake mesa.

There was something about that mesa from the first time I saw it, twenty miles or so out, on Route 66. It looked looming and solitary, with wide, sloping shoulders and a chimney top. When I revisited Tucumcari in my sixties, I noticed that the mesa's shape resembles a Mayan pyramid. Maybe the resemblance accounted, at some deep spiritual level, for the eerie attraction I felt for it at twenty-three. More likely, though, I think there was something much more worldly and psychologically compelling. I couldn't help but notice the mesa's resemblance to a breast.

We ate a picnic supper at the campsite, looking up at the mesa, and K/T asked, "Does anyone want to go for a walk?"

"I do," I said. To my surprise, no one else wanted to go, so the two of us set out. We didn't talk about how far we wanted to go or where we wanted to end up, but I think we both knew that we were headed toward the mesa. When we came to a pasture fence, K/T spread apart the wires by stepping on the lower two and lifting the top so that I could climb between them. It was the first time I had ever seen that old farmer's maneuver, and I returned the favor for her. When we got to the foot of the mesa, we saw a path and followed its spirals and switchbacks upward. The footing wasn't bad, until we came to a steep, rocky passage—not a trail so much as a climb—that led twenty feet or more up the chimney top. I would have quit there and called it a good hike and a fitting way to end an evening, except that K/T started climbing and reached back a hand to help me when we got to the riskier stretches.

From the top, we could see the brown desert, brushed in places with a purplish blue—a vetch of some kind, I think. The night was clear. The stars came out, more vivid than I'd ever seen. The moon was three-quarters full, and we watched the lights from ranches and towns blink on and off. There seemed to be enough light to move around safely, but when we tried to find the path we'd taken to the top, we could see only sheer drop-offs. What a difference perspective makes. On the way up, there'd seemed to be just the one clear way to go. Looking down, there seemed to be no good options.

I don't remember who said so first, but after a while we agreed that we would have to stay until morning. We'd worn light jackets, and the chill of night began to hit us. K/T said, "Let's hold each other." We found a large cleft in the rocks and sat down in it so that her front spooned my back. "This doesn't mean anything, you know," she said as she wrapped her arms around me.

"I know," I shivered, and I meant it. I would have been okay if we'd agreed that it meant something, too. I found many of my friends beautiful, including K/T with her dark hair and sharp, intelligent eyes. I never could predict the directions my erotic impulses might flow, but I was insecure enough to be easily turned aside, and we never got involved that way.

We never could find the path that we'd climbed up, either. At dawn, we started down the way we thought we'd come. We only realized later that it was another route altogether. Instead of the footpath we'd followed the evening before, we found ourselves on another side of the mesa, scrambling across a slope of loose rock. I slipped and struggled for balance in my cheap western boots, and when we got to the highway, we saw that we were so far from our campground that we couldn't even see it. We put out our thumbs to hitch a ride, and an RV rumbled to a stop on the shoulder.

The door popped open, and a gray-haired woman grinned from behind the wheel. She was maybe in her fifties, dressed in jeans and a short-sleeved shirt, with a butchy, close-cropped hairstyle. I thought she looked like a dyke (the highest compliment we could pay at the time), but who knows? She had three hippie hitchhikers seated at a table inside. We introduced ourselves and chatted. The driver told us the rig wasn't hers.

"I deliver them to their new owners," she said. "It's a fun job, but it can get pretty lonely. I like company."

When we told our story, she laughed with the others. She was still grinning when she dropped us off at the campground.

Karen spotted us first and said, "Boy, am I glad to see you!" She sounded annoyed as well as relieved when she told us she had to go call the sheriff's office right away because she'd reported us missing, and they'd said they would get a search together if we didn't show up soon.

My driver (the high-strung one in whose car I'd ridden from Minnesota) had been eager to get going, Karen said. She'd left and taken someone else in my place. So I happily switched to an even more simpatico group of traveling companions in the old blue station wagon Summer had donated to the LRC. I wrote the first draft of this memoir remembering that Summer was our driver, but she told me later that she was in Baja at the time and met us in Los Angeles. I think now that a trim, dark-haired woman was driving. This memory, too, could be imagined, but I know that Jane was with us, and two other women, both named Jan.

I tasted my first tamale from a roadside stand on the edge of Albuquerque. At an agricultural checkpoint at the California border, guards took a bag of apples from us. When we protested, they said we could eat them all right then, or we could leave them and go on. I wanted to eat them out of defiance and an urge not to waste, but my friends persuaded me it wasn't a good idea. Far-ther along, as we crossed through a long stretch of evergreens in what I think was the Angeles National Forest, our driver heard a noise that she didn't like. She steered into a pull-off to check it out, and we all got out of the car to stretch our legs in fresh, piney-smelling air.

The sweetness of the scene evaporated when I heard her cry from the driver's side, "Oh, my God! Look!"

The hubcap and two of the back wheel's lug bolts were missing—the nuts, too, but the most alarming part was those bolts.

"How could that happen?" I asked.

"Vibration, I guess," she said. "They must've sheared off."

While we talked things over, a man stopped to see if we need-ed help, and the Jan who was more of an acquaintance than our friend accepted his offer of a ride to LA. The rest of us stood there looking at the station wagon and trying to figure out what to do.

"Do you suppose we can even drive it?" I asked.

"I don't know," someone said. I remember a voice heavy with wondering whether we would be crazy to even think about it.

Someone thought we could possibly drill out the broken bolts and weld in new ones, or maybe replace the whole hub—if we could get one from a junkyard and if we had the right tools, which we didn't. We also didn't have enough money to hire a tow truck or get the car fixed at a regular garage. We decided to take the tire wrench and check the tightness of the remaining lug nuts. They seemed secure, so we checked all around the car and drove on. Our confidence increased with each mile.

We arrived at the UCLA campus early and frolicked with other women from the LRC on the grass outside the conference hall. I remember being drawn into a debate with a hippie woman who objected to our lesbian feminist vibe, saying in one of those mystic woo-woo voices, "It doesn't matter whether you're a man or a woman. We're all the same, you know?"

I did not know. My life experience told me otherwise. My memories of the conference itself are much more sketchy. What

I know for sure comes mostly from my research decades later. The dates were April 12–14, 1973. The recommended registration fee was two dollars. A boxed announcement for the conference in *Lesbian Tide* trumpeted, "Lesbian Expression: Our Art, Our Music, Our Poetry, Our Sexuality, Our Politics, Our Power."

My memories of the conference consist of weird and idiosyncratic scenes and impressions: looking out the window of a lesbian couple's house in the hills, where the conference committee had arranged free housing for us; a talk by Jill Johnston from which I recall just her swashbuckling appearance in what I remember as a cape, skinny-legged jeans, and tall boots; and a performance Jane was determined not to miss by M'lou, a folk singer and silversmith who called her jewelry business SisterSilver. She would later become Jane's lover, my adversary for a moment in lesbian back-to-the-land politics, and then my longtime friend. I also recall a reading by Kate Millett from her new book, *Flying,* and some interruption of Robin Morgan's keynote address that I didn't understand but later learned was a trans activists' demonstration, an early blow in their argument with radical feminists over who qualifies as a woman.

A women's band played at the end of the evening, and I spent a lot of time dancing with a friend named Barrett. She danced with energy and creativity, and I was covered with sweat when we noticed Millett arrive with a small entourage.

Barrett bumped my arm and said, "Let's go say hello."

"I don't know," I said. I had admired Millett's book *Sexual Politics* when I read it for my independent study class at Macalester. I didn't know she would one day be credited as the founding mother of feminist literary criticism, but I did know her as a women's liberation thinker who'd made the cover of *Time* magazine. She gave us a guarded look as we sidled up to her.

I stood there dumbstruck as Barrett said, with earnestness, "We just wanted to introduce ourselves. We're from St. Paul, too."

A long silence ensued.

"Like you," my friend added, to no reply.

I couldn't stand the dead air any longer and decided to jump in. "I enjoyed your poetry," I said.

Millett replied coolly, "It was prose."

And so it was. Barrett and I retreated quickly and slid back into the crowd. Even then, I felt embarrassed by the fact that we had acted like starstruck fans. Since then, I've developed even more suspicion of the shallow kind of fame ginned up through the American system of celebrity. "It doesn't permit fame in the sense of honor," Millett said in a *Lesbian Tide* interview a few months after the conference. "It only allows being a celebrity in the sense of notoriety. It's a very deadly affair."

After the conference we got back into Summer's wagon and drove it up Highway 1, the two-lane coastal road with sharp curves and rocky drop-offs, to San Francisco, where my friend Jan knew people who offered us a place to stay. As we drove, I settled into a peaceful denial of the danger we faced from the missing lug bolts, and later we drove the blue wagon safely all the way back to Minnesota.

The following summer, I used the conference to finally come out to Mom and Dad. I wrote them in April that I was going to attend a lesbian conference. I sent them postcards from the road, and when I got back, I wrote them about where I'd been. When I made my usual summer visit to Minot, I waited until my mother and I were sitting together at the kitchen table after dinner one evening, just the two of us, while Mom knitted under an overhead light. I mentioned the conference, and Mom took the opening, as I'd hoped. She asked, "How is it that you went to a lesbian conference?"

"Because I'm a lesbian," I said, keeping it short and blunt.

I should have done better, but how exactly? In fairness to my twenty-three-year-old self, I felt terrified about telling my mother this news. I didn't think I should have to articulate it. I thought she should have already figured it out. At forty-eight, she was a much more experienced grownup than I was, and I don't think she handled the situation any better than I did. She said nothing at first and went right on knitting. The sound of her needles, clicking and sliding, loomed like the beating of the telltale heart.

Finally she said, "Did I tell you that Uncle Elmer has decided not to retire this year, after all?" Elmer was her mother's half-brother who had exchanged V-mail with Mom during the war. When the war ended, he disappeared into drinking and wilderness, and she found him again decades later, living alone in a cabin, recovered, and working for the National Park Service in Glacier. He spoke in short, shy, barely articulate bursts and looked like the offspring of a Nordic farmer and some rangy woods spirit.

Mom said nothing more about my news, and I didn't bring it up again for a long time. After I got back to Minneapolis, she wrote, "Your father says he would like to get his hands on whoever did this to you."

When I shared his comment with Karen, she chirped, "Uh-oh!"

We both laughed because we knew the idea that lesbians get "that way" by someone doing something to us was an old misconception, and we knew it came from the stereotype of lesbians as predators. No one, of course, was more responsible for my lesbianism than I was, and now that I had seen the Lesbian Nation taking shape, I craved lesbian company and lesbian culture fiercely.

Since then, I've often wished that I could have come out to my parents earlier, in a more forthright, nuanced, and sensitive way. I know that our fears and silences were rooted in a sense of reality shaped by time, place, and culture. I also know we all did the best we could. When I pushed against the old reality, we struggled, but our love for each other did not give way. We grew.

7 Country Lesbian Manifesto

Jane collected work for *So's Your Old Lady* in a submissions box at the LRC, but I felt protective enough of my art to deliver it to her personally. For the cover of the second issue I handed her a brush-and-ink drawing of my hero Joan Baez. Joan had come out as bisexual and announced that she'd had a love affair with a woman. She was one of the first celebrities to come out, and her courage meant a lot to me. In the long run, some of my lesbian friends and lovers would come to see themselves as bisexual—or even heterosexual. At the time, though, we felt starved to see our lesbian selves represented in media. We celebrated every scrap of positive attention we got, since we were far more likely to see characters like us kill themselves in films (*The Children's Hour*) or be crushed to death by a tree (*The Fox*) or by a sculpture of a giant phallus (*Clockwork Orange*).

So's Your Old Lady felt liberating because we made it. It belonged to us. We poured our creative spirits into it, made ourselves visible through it, and shared our visions for transforming ourselves and our culture. When Jane put the newly printed second issue into my hands, I felt validated and proud. Besides the cover, she'd included an essay of mine, some of my poetry, and a comic strip featuring my fantasy alter ego, cowgirl Lily Dakota. Karen, Jane, and sixteen other writers also had work in the issue, along with visual artists and photographers. I signed with my first and last names, but not everyone who submitted work wanted it credited that way. The American Psychiatric Association hadn't yet declassified homosexuality as a mental disorder, and coming out was still fraught with all sorts of potential negative consequences. Some contributors used first names, initials, or pen names like Wigglesworth, LJ, and, of course, K/T.

I knew most of the contributors, but when I came across a piece called "A Country Lesbian Manifesto," I felt smacked in the heart. I'd read other articles in feminist tabloids about women's land collectives. They focused mostly on political reasons for living with women on the land, reasons like empowering ourselves; healing from the physical and psychological injuries inflicted on us by patriarchy; living in ways that didn't harm the environment; bonding with sisters; saying no to the war machine; and experimenting with romance and sex without ownership, male dominance, or routine female submission.

In a fresh way these two writers, Martha and Marea, spoofed and complicated the very idea of a manifesto. They called theirs a "good fart" and "dozen eggs," as well as a "collection of truisms" and "sisterhood." At the same time, their ideas felt plenty weighty as they explored connecting to the land, animals, and other lesbians as an antidote to sexual and economic oppression. They lightened their manifesto with word play:

> Sometimes I think that the duck's first egg of spring sprouting tomatoe [sic] plants and the pasture fencing have nothing to do with lesbian liberation. But we remember the motivation, the need to be self-sufficient and that means gettin' the Man off our backs wanting his rent and food money and gasoline and taxes and cunt. His Electric Society dues and I still see myself come whirling up as a lightbulb named Vi. Even tho we've dreamed and prayed and plotted for an Amazon Nation for years like you. We are going about it the best we can.

Marea (left) and Lena on Dick at Haidiya Farm

Martha and Marea dedicated their manifesto to Summer, and when I asked her about them, she said she would introduce me.

By early summer, I learned that she had moved to their farm, so I got a ride there with Lena, who also knew them. Their farm was located outside a little town called Gilman, Wisconsin, about 130 miles east and a bit north of Minneapolis. Close to their place we saw prosperous dairy farms with milk cows out to pasture. When we neared a T in the road, Lena gestured to the left and said, "There's Haidiya Farm."

I saw a mixed stand of hardwoods and evergreens surrounding a gray log house, horses, a weathered shed, a yard dotted with woodpiles, a pickup, two old sedans, and free-ranging chickens and ducks. Marea told me later that she named Haidiya Farm after the Arabic word for gift, and she spelled it as she did "in homage to a Saudi royal family." She and Martha were building an Arabian horse farm dream together. When we pulled into the yard, a curly-haired dog ran up and barked. Lena told me his name was Elderberry and he was friendly.

I let Blitz out, and while the dogs sniffed each other, a woman cantered up on a white horse and brought her to a skidding stop in front of us. She struck me as some kind of faerie, slightly built, fair skinned, and freckled, with hair the color of oat straw. Her mare looked muscled, athletic, and slightly dangerous. I thought I saw flashes of a slow-burning energy that could combust if not properly channeled by her rider, who seemed to be doing fine.

I was twenty-three, really into magical thinking, and under the sway of the idea that some mysterious force had led me to this place. Maybe I should blame eros, in the sense that I understand Audre Lorde to have made of it—the personification of our creative power and connection ("our language, our history, our dancing, our loving, our work, our lives"). I searched for nothing less than such connection, and at Haidiya Farm I thought I'd found it. Reimagining the scene now, I wouldn't be surprised if my tongue hung out about as far as Blitz's.

Marea and I introduced ourselves, and I asked, "What's your horse's name?"

"White Mare," she said, seeming relieved to have a reason to look at the mare's neck and tug affectionately on a tuft of mane. "Her other name is Valkyrie."

Of course it was.

Martha appeared from the back of the farmyard, fresh from

some project that I've since forgotten—digging in the garden most likely, or cutting wood, or hauling manure from the barn. She was a handsome woman, decked out in jeans, a plaid shirt, a rolled kerchief tied at the neck, and work boots with mud or something that looked like mud smeared on them. Her body had the kind of attenuated, muscular leanness that comes from hard, physical work. She gave a bear hug to Lena. I got a welcoming hello, and I thought I'd like to be Martha's friend and maybe work my way up to one of those bear hugs some day.

At her invitation, we carried our backpacks, sleeping bags, and groceries up the front steps and into the living room. Later, I used the back door and came through the enclosed porch past the steps that led to a cellar where a cold spring bubbled through the floor and proved useful for cooling perishables and beer.

Sara (front), Shirley (left), and Martha at Haidiya Farm about 1975

"When we looked at the place, the neighbors told us the house was built by a one-legged woman," Martha told us. "That made us feel like this was a good place for us."

It was amazing, I was learning, that when you looked for women's stories, you found them. When you looked for evidence of women's work, you found that, too. Invisibility really amounted to a failure of paying attention.

Inside the house, the gray log walls looked freshly chinked. Martha and Marea's bedroom lay to the left. Straight ahead, the living room flowed into the dining room, which the two of them had equipped with a rectangular table, a Hoosier cabinet, and a built-in cabinet and countertop that divided the dining room from the kitchen.

I'm sure we brought provisions. I don't remember exactly what, but I recall that Lena taught me by example never to go to Haidiya Farm empty-handed. I most likely brought homemade cookies or something from the new hippie food co-op on the West Bank—brown rice, beans, cheese, or whole wheat bread. I don't think I was a vegetarian at the time, but many of my friends were, and meat cost more than rice and beans. Some of us liked beer, and most of us liked to smoke weed. I budgeted my teacher aide wages so that I could afford both. Each time we showed up at Haidiya Farm, our socializing must have blown Martha's schedule.

She was one of the few women I knew with a full-time job. She worked for the U.S. Forest Service, doing physical labor Monday through Friday, and then she came home and did projects around the farm. I admired her. I felt pretty sure I couldn't do what she was doing. On Sunday morning, she fired up the woodstove to make coffee and fry eggs for us. She and Marea had fresh eggs from their chickens and ducks, and I hadn't tasted the rich, dark yolk of free-range eggs since the chicken farmers who peddled door to door quit coming to our neighborhood in Minot. I felt like a small part of a lost paradise had been restored.

8 The Trouble with Land

In 1972, the back-to-the-land dream was in the air for lefties and hippies as well as for lezzies—and especially for lefty hippie lezzies like me. Linda posted an announcement in *So's Your Old Lady* seeking women who wanted to work together to build a shelter in the country, and Jane put up notices at places like the LRC and the lesbian conference, inviting women to check out the land she'd bought near Aitkin. Later she told me the story of acquiring that land, which she and Linda called Rising Moon. The two of them sat under the full moon on the porch of a house they owned just outside the tiny town of Cushing, Minnesota, and they decided to buy 160 acres that had been offered to them for $3,500 through a friend of Linda's ex-husband. As they dreamed it, they imagined one nonnegotiable rule for their land: they wanted to open it to all women and only to women. Living only with women sounded good to me and to plenty of other lesbians at the time. We despaired of ever being able to change our misogynistic culture. Many of us saw separatism as a badly needed restorative step toward getting past our social conditioning and strengthening ourselves.

I responded to Linda's announcement, and she invited me to move in with her and her new lover, Tracy, in an old farmhouse outside of Cushing. I had no car, but Christine agreed to drive Blitz and me there. When the school year and my teacher's aide job ended, she drove us 120 miles northwest, past St. Cloud, to an old farmhouse and five acres of land on the highway just west of the National Guard training base, Camp Ripley. We arrived at dusk. No one responded to our knocks or our shouts, so we entered through the back door, down a couple of concrete steps into a garden-level room. There were no electric lights. We had to feel our way inside and let our eyes adjust a while before we could make out a cookstove, a kitchen table, some cupboards, and a hand-cranked Corona grinding mill.

After a while, Linda and Tracy appeared from upstairs, looking rumpled and cheerful. They offered us homemade muffins that had the consistency of hardtack when we bit into them. Many times in those days I needed to use extra torque in my bite because my friends and I were just learning the tricky art of leavening whole grain baked goods.

Blitz and I settled into the main floor bedroom with my books and supplies for writing and drawing. As I remember it, Linda and Tracy stayed upstairs most of the time, leaving Blitz and me to entertain each other. There was no phone for calling other friends, and, anyway, long-distance calls were a luxury. Sometimes Blitz slept while I played with lines on paper. Sometimes we walked into Cushing.

One of the townspeople we met was Frida, a friend of Linda, Tracy, and Jane's. She was in her seventies and spoke with a Swedish accent. I already knew that she held an almost mythic status as a role model for my friends. She lived alone, gardened, kept chickens, and made hay with a hand scythe and rake. She declined my help haying—wisely, though I didn't understand until later that scything was not as easy as she made it look with her smooth, round strokes. To lay the hay down evenly took skill, practice, and a good hand with a whetstone. The curved edge of the scythe blade had to be kept dangerously sharp, and the body mechanics had to be carried out just so, again and again, in a repetitive pattern while moving across terrain. In her youth Frida farmed with horses. Recently, Jane remembered lamenting to Frida that no one did that anymore. She said that Frida answered encouragingly, "You could do it!"

Not long before I arrived, Frida had sent her milk cow to live at a relative's farm because she didn't think she could keep up with shoveling the cow manure anymore. Tracy volunteered to clean the barn, and Frida brought her cow back home, which was lucky for me because she invited me for coffee and a buttery, homemade Swedish *kaka*. (For any multilingual smartasses out there, the word is not Spanish, but Swedish, for cake!) In my coffee cup, Frida's cream made magic, turning the coffee into a lustrous mocha. It inspired me to put cow toward the top of my shopping list of large animals that I hoped to have on my farm someday. A horse came first. That unrequited longing was left over from my childhood. Unfortunately, the small savings I'd managed on my teacher's aide salary were only enough to support Blitz and me for the summer.

With no job, no electricity, no modern conveniences, and no urban distractions, my hours stretched into weeks in the old farmhouse. Day-to-day life involved contemplation, mealtime conversations, and increased use of my body. We drew water from a hand pump, split and carried firewood for the cookstove, and walked to the post office in town for our mail. We ground our coffee and also our grains for flour and cereal in the shiny, silver-colored grinding mill that had come, like many of our back-to-the-land tools and supplies, from the co-op hardware store founded by New Left activists (like Linda's former husband) on the West Bank of the university.

I learned a new set of food preparation skills. For instance, wheat berries ground more reluctantly than corn, which in turn ground harder than barley or oats. When I made whole wheat flour, I had to stop and tighten the space between the grinding surfaces at least twice, running the cracked grain through again each time and cranking the handle with all my strength. The finer the flour, the lighter the muffins. The more torque used for grinding, the less required for biting. I loved learning such practical, physi-

cal things. I also liked the quiet. With no live, singing wires lead-
ing into the Cushing land and no electric motors, the only buzzing
sounds came from the plentiful pollinators and other insects.

I learned to adjust my hearing to a new, subtle level, except
when guns went off at Camp Ripley or when I listened to the Senate Watergate Committee hearings on my transistor radio. On nice
days, Blitz and I sat outside with the radio on. She was a mongrel
of the heart, built like a lab and colored black and white with a
stripe down her face. She lay on her side in the sun and napped
while I followed the political drama on the radio. I had hated
Nixon's dirty tricks, and I was glad to see him entangled in what
looked to be a mess of his own making.

I intended to stay with Linda and Tracy the whole summer,
but my emotions got in the way. I was still looking for love, and
I felt like I'd never find it without more lesbians in my life. So I
filled my backpack and led Blitz on a short rope to Highway 10,
where I put out my thumb. I'd never hitched with a dog before and
thought it might be hard, but the two of us actually caught rides
more quickly than I did alone. I arrived at my parents' front door
before supper. Dad had just gotten home from work and popped
the top of the evening's first beer when he came to unlock the
screen. He stuck his head outside and looked for a car.

"We hitchhiked," I told him.

"You crazy kid!" he said, half-admiringly.

When Blitz and I went back to Minneapolis, he and Mom
bought passage for us in a sleeping compartment on the train. The
ticket cost twice as much as a coach seat, but it was the only way
the railroad would let a dog travel, except in a shipping crate in
the baggage car. Luckily, I still had friends in the city, and there
was room for us to move back into the Harriet Avenue apartment.

Around July, Summer introduced me to a woman named Shirley, who had a daughter close to the same age as Trent. I don't
know why our paths hadn't crossed until then, because we knew
a lot of the same people. Shirley had dark hair and sharp eyes that
she used to interact with a kind of smoldering charm, and once I

got to know her, I realized that she also had an admirable social conscience. Jane told me that Shirley helped start the food co-op movement in Minneapolis by finding a bulk source of long-grained brown rice in Arkansas, where she'd grown up, and then making a trip down there to secure the connection. At the time, the co-op amounted to a few barrels of rice and beans on the porch of one of its founders' houses.

The next thing I knew, Shirley and her daughter, Sara, had moved to Haidiya Farm, and I didn't see them for a while. Shirley told me later that she and Summer had put up a tent in the pasture and planned to spend the summer there with the kids, until a thunderstorm blew the tent down on top of them. Shirley grabbed Sara. Summer grabbed Trent. As they ran for the house, they saw Martha in the doorway holding up a lantern to light their way. After that, they moved into the attic, a big, open space that Martha and Marea had insulated and covered with plastic sheeting. I visited a couple of times that summer, hitching rides with Lena.

I liked Lena and found her soft-spoken and kind, with soulful eyes and shaggy, dark hair that she pushed behind her ears when she felt nervous. We had writing in common, and the love of animals and country living. There was so much more to her, too, and to all of my friends. As I look back, I see that I didn't ask enough questions. As much as the women in our circle talked and shared, we shared strategically. We needed to shield ourselves from the pain that came with misunderstandings, rivalries, jealousies, betrayals, and lingering bad feelings left from our experiments with loving and collective living. And then there were traumatic pasts and the overarching angst of finding our way as lesbians in a heterosexist culture. We sometimes participated in heterosexism by hating or sabotaging ourselves.

I didn't see much of K/T for a while. She moved back to her hometown, worked at a turkey slaughterhouse, and smoked cigarettes to self-medicate (or so it seems to me). She wrote in *So's Your Old Lady* about keeping a tight grip on her Marlboros to help get through "queer's days," when her coworkers at the turkey plant pretended to be gay: "Ms. Marlboro, I think I just figured out why I like you so much. 'Cuz I just told you I was queer, and all ya' did was stay right there—staring at me with your same old expression, not moving an inch. Just like what I said didn't bother you at all."

Late that summer, K/T left her hometown for Minneapolis and moved into the Harriet Avenue apartment. One day, Lena stopped to get us and drove us out to K/T's family's farm in her orange Karmann Ghia. When we got there, K/T's mom invited us into the house for a cool drink. She reminded me of other moms I knew from the World War II generation—curled and combed hair, neat cotton blouse, weary eyes, and a gracious expression. We sat in the living room visiting while two or three of the littler kids flitted in and out. K/T had nine brothers and sisters, seven of them younger than she was, and I saw that Lena had a knack for talking to them. She'd already written and published a few

Women, children, and black-and-white animals at Haidiya Farm

children's books with her visual artist partner, Sally Miller, and I learned later that K/T's mother admired her very much for that.

K/T looked lost in thought through most of our visit. At one point, when the kids had almost thoroughly distracted Lena and me, I noticed K/T and her mother talking in tense whispers on the other side of the room. And then K/T got up and said in that forceful voice she sometimes used to mask self-doubt and steer things unequivocally the way she wanted, "Let's go outside." Lena and I got up and followed her out the door and past the barn. One of her brothers and a teenaged boy were unloading hay bales from a wagon onto a conveyor that lifted them into the haymow to be stored and then fed to the cattle over the winter. "That's Steve," K/T said, after the taller young man invited us in a joking way to join them, and she bantered back some equally tongue-in-cheek rebuff.

I don't remember feeling like K/T and I ever completely relaxed with each other that day—or ever, when I come right down to it—but some of the tension seemed to leave as she led us past the yard and into the pasture. We came to a barbed wire fence, and she used the nifty farmer's maneuver I'd seen at the foot of Mt. Tucumcari to help Lena and me pass between the strands. In the pasture I had to carefully choose where to place each step because the cattle had eaten the grass short and left big, wet puddles of manure in exchange. She led us along a path, and I saw a stream up ahead. As we got closer, I heard the sound of water rushing over rocks. Looking downstream, I saw that some of the cattle had waded in up to their knees, but she took us upstream, to a place where the water ran cool and clear over a rocky bottom.

It was the north fork of the Crow River, I found out from her oldest sister, Mary, when I talked to her forty years later over breakfast in a small café near Macalester. In the crazy way that life circles around, and (to borrow a phrase from Flannery O'Connor) we meet our selves coming and going, Mary teaches journalism classes now at Macalester, where I took journalism classes decades ago. Since the time we were with K/T at their parents' farm, she told me, the north fork of the Crow has been designated a wild and scenic river.

That day in 1973, I took off my socks and tennis shoes, rolled up my jeans, and waded in. The cool water flowed around my calves and made me feel so alive. It brought back that feeling of immanence I'd experienced as a girl—the deep knowing of my self at home with the earth and the water.

"I need to get back to the country," I said.

"It's beautiful," K/T replied with a skeptical note in her voice that made me know I should think again, even before she added, "It can be hard."

On the drive home, she told us that she was not getting along with her parents. She said they were having a hard time accepting her lesbianism, and her mom wanted to take her to be counseled by a local priest. K/T said she couldn't abide by the sexism and homophobia she found in the church teachings. She couldn't trust that a priest would be able to counsel her fairly. She also said that as a woman and the third child of ten she wouldn't be able to inherit the family's land. That grieved her. She loved the farm and wanted to hang on to it. As I understood her, she believed that Steve, the oldest son, would automatically get the farm and she would automatically get no part of it. This wasn't true, I found out later from Mary. At the time, though, I felt the stinging bitterness and injustice as K/T described them to me. I empathized with her sense of having been wronged. What I heard from her convinced me all the more that our only hope to set things right, to empower ourselves, and to have some chance for equality was to live on the land in a self-sufficient community with women.

In the fall, I responded to Jane's invitation to an equinox celebration at Rising Moon. I caught a ride there with someone (probably Lena again). I remember a couple of dozen women, a two-story farmhouse, an unpainted shed, the log walls of an old barn with no rafters or roof, and beautiful land full of possibility: hay meadows fringed with wild blackberries and hazelnuts; woods of oak, pine, and poplar; and pastures that sloped to the slender, winding thread of the Ripple River on its way to the Mississippi. I met visitors from the Twin Cities, Arkansas, New Mexico, and who knew where—mostly passers-through like me, who weren't sure whether they were staying or going. I remember a potluck dinner, a drinking party, and lots of exciting dyke energy. In the morning the house looked cluttered and dirty.

When most of us gathered in the kitchen around a table strewn with the remains of the previous night's partying, I remember a disagreement and bad feelings. Later, Martha told me that she saw it as a fight for control between the Minnesota and the Arkansas women. The Arkansans were hectoring Jane, asking how Rising Moon could be a collective when she owned the land privately. Actually, the ownership arrangement was more complicated than that. Kathy McConnell reported in *Gold Flower,* a Twin Cities women's newspaper, that Linda and Jane had put the land in the name of a third party to protect it from "sexist property laws which would have automatically put both husbands' names on the title." They both had been married and were going through the process of divorces and divisions of marital assets.

I remember Jane sitting at the kitchen table, holding her midsection, and saying ominously, "I just trust what I feel in my stomach, and when I look around here, it doesn't feel good." I remember feeling that many of us were drifting in one way or another in those days, trying to think and feel our way through patriarchy to the other side. We knew we wanted to make lives for ourselves that felt free and fulfilling but were not sure how we'd find the resources and inner strength to do it—or even whether we actually were crazy as charged and would crash to the ground like Icarus from the weight of our "abnormal psychology," which might have fooled us into thinking we had the outrageous right to reach for the sky.

My Haidiya Farm friend Martha, ever the pragmatist, said she just wanted everybody to get out of the house that Sunday so she could jack it up and fix a part of the foundation that had failed. She had brought a chainsaw and screw jacks from home, and the timbers were already there, along with plenty of women to lift them into place.

That fall, I caught rides with Lena to Haidiya Farm. She had bought Snow, a black-and-white paint gelding, from Martha and Marea and was boarding him with them. Summer had bought his mother, Lola, a brown mare with a frizzy mane and tail and a dorsal stripe that made people suspect she had mustang blood. I liked to feed and pet them and the other horses in the paddock. I felt drawn to their big nostrils, their fuzzy chins and noses, and the sweet, slightly acrid smell of horse sweat mixed with hay and manure. I liked everything about them. When I put myself to bed each night amid city sounds and smells, I dreamed of horses and powerful, outrageous women living on the land.

9 Suzanne Takes You Down

K/T and I shared the Harriet Avenue apartment with another roommate, Beth. Beth was warm, easygoing, and comfortable to hang out with, but as time went on I thought that my adventurous friend K/T grew more withdrawn and elusive.

One day in December, she said, "Why don't we make a list of the people we trust?" I thought she had an odd look on her face, and the project felt wrong. I should have made a case against it, but for some reason I sat down with her at the dining room table while winter light streamed through the leaded-glass windows, and I named names to add to the ones K/T had already put on the list. Saying that I trusted someone didn't feel wrong, but then there were the people left off the list. When she posted it on our dining room wall, I knew that I should have found a way to pull it down and explain why I wasn't comfortable with it, but I didn't.

A good friend came over and read the list, and I saw the look on her face when she didn't find her name there. The last time I'd seen her, I picked her up to go shopping for LPs at the Electric Fetus, and as I drove along Franklin Avenue, she told me that the people in all of the white cars around us were Scientologists keeping tabs on her. If she had said they were FBI agents, I might have been more likely to believe her, since I knew a little about the FBI's surveillance of activists and lesbians. About mental health and Scientology, I was mostly uninformed, but her thoughts didn't seem rational. So it was true that I didn't trust her, though I cared about her deeply. The bottom line to this story is that neither K/T nor I put this woman's name on the list, and I learned at a new level what I'd learned as a child—that leaving somebody out was an effective way to hurt her. And for what? Why did K/T want to create the damn list in the first place? In retrospect I've often wondered why I didn't pick up on what I soon came to see as a warning sign in K/T's behavior. An even bigger warning sign was yet to come.

Not long after the incident with the list, K/T came into the living room one afternoon and put a Neal Diamond album on the turntable. She lay on the floor in front of the stereo speakers and played his cover of Leonard Cohen's ballad "Suzanne" over and over again. This was odd behavior, the kind of thing one of my friends might do on acid, but I was pretty sure she wasn't on acid. Instead of feeling concerned, I felt annoyed and inconvenienced. I'd never cared for Neal Diamond's public presentation of himself or his music. I didn't know what she heard in it. I remember thinking how much I preferred Judy Collins's version of the song. At least in her smoldering contralto I could read in a lesbian story: "Suzanne takes you down to a place by the river / You can hear the boats go by / You can spend the night beside her / And you know that she's half-crazy / But that's why you want to be there." If K/T wanted to obsessively listen to "Suzanne," why couldn't she at least pick a version that I liked? That's what the self-involved twenty-four-year-old me was thinking that December afternoon as the sun sank early behind the duplexes and fourplexes of South Minneapolis.

So instead of asking questions or standing by to listen for K/T's take on whatever was going through her mind, I retreated to my room, my drawings, and Blitz's reliable, quiet company. Sometime after the evening went completely dark, K/T appeared in my doorway. She had on her heavy winter coat and I thought her face looked pale and distracted. She asked in a voice that sounded like it originated down some tangled neural pathway, "Do you have change for a twenty?"

"I don't think so," I said.

"Could you check?" she asked.

I got out my wallet and looked. "No, sorry."

She looked disappointed, so I asked why she needed the change.

"I'm going to shoot some pool," she said. I knew that she liked a pool hall on Lake Street. She'd never invited me to go there with her, and I didn't think I'd want to anyway, because she'd told me that the other pool players were men.

I asked her, "Can't you get change there?"

"I suppose," she said with what seemed like deep disappointment.

Why did she seem to regret so much that I couldn't give her change? She said not to worry about her afterward. She would probably get home late, as she planned to visit her aunt and uncle. They lived somewhere east of us, I thought, not far off Lake Street. I wondered why she didn't just plan on breaking the twenty at the pool hall in the first place, and then she left.

I was working on my lesbian superhero comic about Astrid, the caped dyke crusader who was trying to stop fundamentalists from shutting down the city.

A couple of hours later, Karen and I touched base. I thought she had called me, but recently I read her own account of that phone call, and she said that I called her, asking about K/T. When I told her how K/T had left the apartment, Karen said, "I'm a little worried about her. She left a note, and it sounds kind of like a suicide note."

"Oh my God," I said. "Maybe it is."

The missed clues came crashing back to me, and I shared them with Karen. Suddenly I wondered, was breaking the twenty so important to K/T because she didn't want to waste the change? Was the repeated listening to "Suzanne" truly obsessive—a symptom and a clue, not just an annoying way to behave? Karen asked for the phone number of K/T's aunt and uncle. I looked around and found it somehow.

"Do you want to call them?" Karen asked. "Or should I?"

"Why don't you?" I said, always happy to put off the emotionally difficult stuff if someone else would do it. When Karen got back to me, she said they were worried, too, because K/T had phoned them and asked for directions to the Lake Street Bridge. Karen and I knew the high, old, steel trestle that spanned the Mississippi between St. Paul and Minneapolis. We had crossed it often when we were driving to South Minneapolis, getting to know the women's liberation feminists at the Amazon Bookstore and making friends with lesbians.

Karen came in her lover's car and picked me up, and we trolled Lake Street. We stopped in front of the big glass windows of the pool hall, where we didn't see K/T. Karen parked and went in. When she came back, she said that they told her K/T had been there, but she'd left a while earlier. We drove slowly toward the river along Lake Street, keeping a sharp watch for her car coat and shoulders hunched against the cold. The single-digit cold snap was the first of the winter and not many people were out in the biting, windy night. We didn't see her, or anyone else, on the bridge.

When I looked at the steelwork and the thick, top railing that separated the walkway from the airspace above the river, I pictured K/T climbing onto that rail. I could imagine her mounting it with the same determination she had used to scramble ahead of me up the rocky path to the top of Mount Tucumcari. She was just that willful. Or was she really? Did I even know her that well, or just the image she projected? The idea that she might have already taken herself from the present tense into the past didn't seem possible to me. I could hardly imagine the force of will and self-negation that would allow a person to jump into that cold, dark river. For that matter, I couldn't really imagine dying. Death had always seemed like something I could put off to the future. I hadn't yet lost a friend to death by any means.

Karen took the turn that wound around to River Road on the St. Paul side of the bridge. She stopped and parked the car, and we got out and walked along the top of the steep bank. We hardly talked but went as far as we dared on some of the slippery footpaths that led closer to the edge of the bank. We steadied ourselves on tree trunks and looked thirty or more feet down to the surface of the river. We could only see black water dotted with ice floes. I kept looking at the floes as if I might see K/T on one of them. The wind bit our faces. I hadn't gotten used to full-blown winter yet, and in my hurry I hadn't chosen my warmest jacket. I could feel the cold seeping through the weave of the wool, but I didn't want to leave. We stood there a long while, staring at the river, looking for some clue to K/T's whereabouts, and shivering. We never saw anything down below but the snow-covered floes, floating like clouds in an inky, horrendous sky.

Finally Karen said, "I think she did it."

"I do too," I said, though I didn't understand.

"Let's go," Karen said, and I agreed. We couldn't do anything more at the river. I was glad to feel the car's heater kick in and steadily warm the front seat as we retraced our search, keeping a close watch for K/T all the way up Lake Street to Lyndale.

Later, Karen told me that the next day she and her lover went to the police station and asked to make a missing persons report. She said, "I could tell they didn't take us seriously. They saw us as ragtag lesbians." In our lesbian experience, there was always a double consciousness something like the sort that W. E. B. DuBois described black people experiencing: the double vision of seeing yourself through the oppressor's eyes as well as your own. It led to a lot of self-examination and opened the doors to shame and self-blame.

The police wouldn't let Karen file a report, but they took down information. A couple of weeks later, K/T's mom and brother arrived at the Harriet Avenue apartment with a truck and a trailer. They loaded up K/T's motorcycle and all of her other belongings—which amounted to a few boxes, a dresser, some hanging clothes, a rock tumbler and some polished agates—and they took her things back to the farm. I thought a palpable, sad awkwardness hung over our whole interaction. We treated each other cordially and cautiously, but I imagined they were judging me as a bad friend, an evil influence, a sick lesbian. I know that I was thinking about how K/T had felt hurt by what I thought was the family's disapproval of her lesbianism and their disinheriting her from the farm. We were being so careful not to hurt or upset each other that we said way too little and revealed almost nothing. I do recall her mother offering up a parting, positive thought, something along the lines of, "I hope she's just off on another of her adventures and we'll hear from her soon." I replied that I hoped so too, but I knew I was giving one of those diplomatic, dishonest replies. I agreed out of sensitivity and a desire not to heap any more pain or worry on her. I didn't believe we would ever see K/T again, and I blamed myself for not picking up on the messages she had sent. The way I saw it, she had disappeared on my watch. I hadn't done enough to take care of her. What kind of friend was that? I blamed patriarchy too, of course. I was still the undergrad feminist theorist. The church, the family system, sexism, and homophobia were to blame (and I still believe the institutions of patriarchy did play a part), but most of all, I took her disappearance as a personal failure. She haunted me, and in her haunting she provided the impetus I needed to get out of the city—to leave the LRC, *So's Your Old Lady,* the bar scene, and most of my friends. I needed to get on with doing what I wanted to do. I needed to get myself to a lesbian farm.

10 Family of Woman

K/T walked out of our apartment on a Tuesday. That week, my confusion over her and her fate would have preoccupied me entirely, except for my excitement that Family of Woman, a Chicago lesbian feminist band, was headlining a women's festival in South Minneapolis the following Friday. In memory I'd separated these two events much further in time. When I uncovered through research that they'd actually taken place just a few days apart, I realized that I needed to give my younger self a lot of credit for resilience.

The announcement that Jane put in *So's Your Old Lady* called the event "Season of the Witch: A Festival of, by, and for Women." The dance was part of a tour that the band called Circle of the Witch. Jane included a photo of Joan Capra, the band's lanky, dark-haired violinist, standing casually in a tank top and jeans, with her instrument cocked at an angle. Jane knew the band members, who also included percussionist Ella Szekeley and Linda Shear, who played piano and wrote the band's namesake song. The announcement promised workshops, supper, and local entertainment in addition to the Chicago musicians—all for a two-dollar donation. My friends and I had been buzzing.

Witches appealed to a lot of us. The women's liberation guerrilla theater coven, WITCH (for Women's International Terrorist

Conspiracy from Hell), outlandishly hexed Wall Street and the federal courthouse where the Chicago Seven defendants were being tried on riot and conspiracy charges stemming from the 1968 Democratic Convention protests. In a popular 1973 pamphlet "Witches, Midwives, and Nurses: A History of Women Healers," Barbara Ehrenreich and Dierdre English uncovered the history of witch hunts, torture, forced confessions, show trials, and executions that amounted to a holocaust against women who threatened men's power in the sexual, spiritual, and healing realms of medieval Europe. Our world really did crack open when we examined the history of men's dominance over women. We recoiled and needed an antidote. Music provided one.

We had rocked and slow danced at the Louisa May Alcott Collective's women's dance and also in the basement of a Dinkytown church after a women's conference that Jane and Linda put together in 1972. The music wasn't live, but taking a woman into my arms, moving rhythmically with her, smelling the scent of her shampoo, and feeling the soft touch of her hair against my cheek opened a new channel to sensory experience. Recorded tunes were not music that we could call our own, but dancing together had been a start toward discovering and reinforcing who we were.

We danced in the bars, too, but they were problematic places. Alcohol loosened our social anxiety and deadened the homophobic messages that we absorbed elsewhere, but it was an escape, not a solution, and the lyrics we heard in the bars weren't about us. They told the stories of heterosexual men who were trying to screw, screwing, or singing the blues about losing the right to screw women. The songs weren't for or about the gay men who shared the bars with us, either. Like us, they acted as if they were, but they did it in bigger gestures than we did. I took more than one accidental blow from a masculine arm, but when Aretha Franklin came on the jukebox, the jeans jacket gang circled up and claimed our space. We pointed our fingers like scolds as we acted out the lyrics of "Respect." When the beat slowed and the melody smoothed, as it did in Aretha's "Natural Woman," we held our dance partners close and fantasized about taking them home. The music we had wasn't perfect, but it was all we had, and we needed it.

That's what made women's music so important. We needed it, and the women making music needed an audience as they struggled against the usual sexism and misogyny. In 1973, I wrote in *So's Your Old Lady*:

> While Joan Baez, Judy Collins, and Joni Mitchell are famous enough and visible enough so that we can all hear their music and chart its growth, a number of women are playing good music for nickels and dimes. My friends and I have discovered some of these women through records we found at used record stories. It seems that promotional records that don't cut it at the radio stations get sold to these stores. And women don't often cut it at the radio stations.

Male singers, musicians, songwriters, technicians, producers, and distributors dominated the industry, just as men dominated the arts in general and most of the professions. We knew that the music industry belonged to the Man. That's why, when Family of Woman struck up their first chords, something stirred in us. Some corm of consciousness came out of hibernation and began putting out roots. We started dancing together in couples and in groups.

I was just getting warmed up, just feeling myself move into a consciousness of my own body, at home at last in a community of women, when someone yelled from the hallway, "There's a man trying to get in!"

Furious, I headed toward the entrance. I was not alone but part of an impromptu feminist posse that sprang into action, fists and shoulders clenched, determined to keep the intruder out. In those days, we harbored so much anger over the injustices we experienced. As the Radicalesbians put it in their manifesto, "A lesbian is the rage of all women condensed to the point of explosion."

What made this guy think he had the right to invade our one and only bit of self-created space? Couldn't he at least give us that? As I hurried toward the door, I heard other women's voices on the sidelines urging, "Stop! Calm down!" And then the woman who had alerted us to the intruder in the first place, said, "It's okay. He left."

When I turned to go back to the dance floor, I spotted an interesting woman sitting on a table in the hallway. I'd seen her before at the bars and the LRC, but I didn't know much about her except that her name was Molly. She had a lean build and long, sculpted cheekbones, which gave her face a striking, stony gravitas. I got the impression that she observed what was happening around her closely, but when I caught her looking, she eluded eye contact. She sat with her legs spread and swinging loosely. The style of her jeans and vest transited the range of gender-coded conventions we had grown up calling "masculine" and "feminine." All of these signs made me think that we might understand each other's signals very well.

I was brash enough to walk up and turn on the charm (whatever that meant at the time—a keen, charged attention, I guess). Hopefully, my onslaught was accompanied by some banter and self-deprecating humor. I wish I could say I remember what either of us said. In our sixties now, we've talked it over, and what survives for both of us, after forty-some years, is not specific words but the feeling that we were saying plenty about who we were and what we wanted from each other.

When the band struck up "Season of the Witch," the crowd came together. We danced in a circle, linked arms, and raised a kind of ecstatic energy together. I'm far from the first to point out that *witch* is a popular epithet, like *bitch, butch,* and *dyke,* used to single out an unruly woman and shame her in the hope of controlling her behavior. We did not intend to be controlled through shame and fear any longer. We didn't intend to live isolated, underground lives, separated from one another, and deprived of the healing power of our love.

As Linda Shear put it in the band's eponymous song:

Sisters, I can feel you
I can touch you
I can need you
I can kiss you
Now I can love you

Molly and I went home together that night—to whose apartment or to exactly what words and what acts I don't recall. She says that she doesn't remember exactly either. It seems that we enacted our love as soldiers sometimes say they enact war—in a fog of consciousness and memory.

11 Women, Horses, and Other Embodied Spirits

A month or so after K/T disappeared, I heard that Lena had moved to Rising Moon, and I think it was around this time that she renamed herself Lisyli. The name, she later told me, came to her through a friend's dream. Around Christmas, we got news from Rising Moon that the house had burned down. What happened, as I've heard in versions of the story told by different women over the years, is that the fire started on a twenty-below-zero night, either from candles in the children's bedroom upstairs or from sparks that slipped through cracks in the chinking between the bricks of the old chimney. One of the volunteers from the rural fire department told Lisyli later that young men from the area used to hunt the land and take potshots at the chimney. They didn't think it mattered because the house had sat empty for so long.

When the fire started, the women carried out their drums and musical instruments and whatever else they could grab. Maya started removing the animals. After a few trips back and forth, she realized that she was finding cats inside that she had already carried out, so she put them in the cab of a truck. That worked, and thanks to her only one cat died.

Fire department volunteers came, but the water in their tanks was frozen, or they couldn't get the truck up the driveway in the snow, depending on which version of the story you prefer. As the flames devoured the house, everyone stood around for a while, helplessly watching, and then the women got into a circle and started to drum and play their instruments. The Aitkin paper reported on the scene, and the Rising Moon women heard from a neighbor that one of the local preachers warned his congregation about witches in their midst.

Molly and I visited after the fire. Because of snow, we parked on the road and hiked in. When we got to the farmyard, Otter and Maya greeted us. They had made themselves a room in one of the corners of the old log barn, using straw bales and canvas tarps to add two walls and a roof. They had a cheap fishing shack stove for heat and slept in double sleeping bags under a pile of bedding to try to keep warm at night. The woman with the children had moved to an apartment in Aitkin. We all went there to warm up, and later we had lunch together at a café in town. On the way home, Molly and I talked about how much we admired Maya and Otter for sticking out the tough situation.

The week of the fire, Lisyli and Selenekore had been away. When they returned, they added plywood and insulation to an old shed on the property, using materials donated by a friend of Lisyli's and by Harvey, the next-door neighbor. At the time, Lisyli still boarded her paint horse, Snow, with Marea and Martha. When she took me along to visit them in January, Martha invited me to move to Haidiya Farm. She said that the house was too crowded to accommodate me, but she could offer me space in the toolshed. "It's not very big," she said, "but I think it would be warm enough if you put a heater in there."

I talked it over with Molly, and in the winter-spring cusp of 1974, I decided to make the move. When my mother heard about it, she gave me a feather tick mattress that had belonged to my Grandma Hunter. I left some record albums and the portfolio containing my comic book drawings with friends, and we loaded the rest of my things into the hatchback of Molly's Ford Bronco. Decades later, after I've inherited my parents' things and added them to my own lifetime accumulation, it's refreshing to remember that

I once owned so little. Besides the mattress, the things I carried to Haidiya Farm included my Grandma Hunter's reading lamp, the cornet I'd played since fourth grade, bedding, paper, pens, pencils, and books. Blitz came too, but not Molly.

She said she wasn't ready to leave the city, though she wanted to live in the country eventually. For whatever reasons, I felt like she was distancing herself from me, and I suppose thinking that brought out an emotional neediness in me that wasn't very attractive. When I talked to her about it later, she said that she was just not sure what she wanted to do, and she was in awe of Martha and Marea and me. I was in awe of her and the other women, too. Everyone seemed so much more competent than I. Others have told me they felt the same way, so it seems we all had each other fooled and impressed in ways that kept us from relaxing and really knowing each other's hearts.

From my point of view, I wasn't leaving Molly. I was leaving the city, the bar scene, and the lingering cloud left after K/T disappeared. I was after adventure, following my dream. Like the Fool in the tarot deck, I wanted to step off a cliff into pure, promising air. I wanted to act, to set things in motion, to let events cascade. The point was possibility. And hope.

I meant to move into the toolshed as soon as possible, but in the meantime I set up a sleeping space in the attic. I used the feather tick to make myself a bed on the floor, and I walled my small space off with blankets so that the Shirley–Summer family and I had some privacy from each other. I meant the arrangement to last only a week or so, but somehow I never quite got around to moving into that cold toolshed.

Blitz and I fell into a habit of getting out of bed when Trent and Sara started stirring. We slipped the domestic scene and walked outside ahead of the rest of the people, except for Martha, who usually beat us all out of the house on her way to work. In the city, I'd been staying up until the bars closed. At Haidiya Farm, I learned to like mornings, and I especially loved going out to pump water for the household and the animals. I liked the exercise, the bracing air, and the way the horses nickered when they saw me crossing the yard with buckets.

I learned that a full stroke on the long, iron handle of the pump brought up about a quart-and-a-half of water. At that rate, I needed ten or eleven strokes to fill a five-gallon bucket as high as I wanted, leaving space at the top to keep from slopping water as I carried. I liked to feel the effect of my work on my body: the flex, extension, and burn in my muscles. The work gave me something psychological, too—satisfaction from doing tasks that sustained us in ways I could plainly see.

I pumped.

I thought.

I felt.

I carried.

Descartes had it in the wrong order. I am; therefore, I think. I do; therefore, I am.

I smelled and observed the horses as they jostled one another for position and drank greedily, as if they were getting the last there would ever be of the water. I watched them raise their heads after drinking, lick their lips, and give me what looked like grateful grins. Some people call it anthropomorphizing to read human-like meaning into animals' expressions, but I've never believed we were all that different from each other. I didn't mind serving them in exchange for the ways that they served us.

One horse, an old gelding that Martha and Marea called Dick, interested me more than the others. *Gelding*, Martha and Marea taught me, was the word for a castrated male horse. A *hand* was how you measured a horse's height in increments of four inches. Dick stood about fifteen hands, measured to the top of his *withers* (that slope of flesh and bone where his neck met his back). The farm had its own vocabulary, and I was starting to learn it, thanks to my hosts and their book collection. A female horse is a *mare* if she's grown and a *filly* if she's young. A *colt* is a young male.

That spring of 1974, we had three geldings, two mares, and a filly wintering in a small, fenced area that we called "the paddock." They hung around on trampled hay and passed the hours with feigned fights and actual back biting, but mostly with eating, sleeping, and standing side by side, tail to the wind, helping each other conserve body heat. A purebred Arabian stallion, Sativa, lived in the barn. We could hear him squealing and snorting for the others, but he had to be kept separate to prevent his violent attempts to breed the mares and chase off the geldings.

I learned early on that a horse dealer gave Dick his name. If he hadn't, Dick would have earned it by dumping a lot of riders and by wrecking Martha and Marea's wagon when he ran it into the corner of their barn and sent Marea flying. For some reason, this irascible, old crank fascinated me. His red coat and golden mane and tail outshone the colors of all the winter-dampened coats around him, even though his muzzle and flanks were flecked with white. His withers looked sharp and boney. His right eye was not brown like his left eye but, instead, a cloudy blue.

"Why is that?" I asked Marea one day as we stood beside the paddock.

"He's blind in that eye," Marea explained.

"What happened?"

"I don't know," she said. "It happened before we got him."

"How old is he?" I asked.

She gave me a curious look that made me think she couldn't quite believe I had any interest in the old reprobate. "Seventeen or so, I think."

One winter day, early in my stay, the two of us decided to go for a ride.

"We usually put our visitors on Dick," she told me.

"That's fine with me," I replied. I'd wanted all my life to be a horsewoman. I loved the way horses looked, smelled, and communicated. When I'd begged Dad for one, he'd answered, "I guess you'll have to grow up and buy your own." People should always be more careful than that about what they tell their children.

Marea showed me how to hold the bit against Dick's teeth and slide my thumb and forefinger into the corners of his mouth so that he opened up and let the bit slip in. After that, she lifted the headpiece of the bridle, fit it around his ears, and carefully tucked it behind each ear, along with the forelock of his mane. The straps of the bridle had to be just the right length, neither too tight nor too loose, she told me. Dick had to feel comfortable in it, or he would fuss and throw his head.

Once she had everything arranged, she offered me a leg up. She squatted and made a basket of her hands. I put my foot in and launched myself into the saddle while she boosted me. "He likes to make right-hand turns into the ditch," she said as I picked up the reins. "Try not to let him."

I wasn't sure how to do that, but I was game to try. Marea vaulted onto White Mare's back and urged her into a brisk walk. Following, Dick and I got along fine at first. He was what farmers called a *heavy,* a riding horse–workhorse cross. His riding-horse half was supposed to have been Tennessee Walker, according to the horse dealer, and it might have been true, because he stretched into a long, smooth stride when Marea popped White Mare into a trot. When they started into a slow canter, though, Dick went into a bone-jarring trot, and I bounced off balance. The next thing I knew, he swung his head to the right. The left rein slipped through my fingers, and he took a hard right and plunged into the ditch, leaving me airborne behind the action. The snow and ditch grass softened my fall. I was up and brushing off my pants and jacket by the time Marea rode up.

"I see the old bastard got you off," she said.

The culprit stood a little ways off in the hayfield, looking at us with his good eye. It occurred to me then that there was a reason he always made right-hand turns when he dumped his riders, and the secret was that one sighted eye. It occurred to me, too, that if I could just hang on to that left rein and keep it short, he might not be able to make that hard right turn.

"You should get right back on him," Marea said.

"Okay," I said, trying to sound braver than I felt.

He let me walk right up to him and lead him back to the road. She dismounted and let out a smoky laugh. "I'll give you a leg up again. It's the least I can do."

When I was back onboard, I shortened the left rein and gripped it hard. A few hundred feet down the road, I felt him straining against it. I kept a death grip on that rein while also remembering to stay in balance. He broke stride, grunted his disapproval, and danced a few steps, but I stayed on and bumped him forward with my legs. He went on down the road then, and after a mile or so, he started feeling relaxed to me. I stayed mounted for the whole ride.

That evening after supper, all seven of us Haidiya Farm residents sat in the living room, talking and soaking in the warmth of the woodstove.

"I heard about what you did with Dick," Martha said. "I have to tell you I'm impressed."

She was impressed? She had worked in the woods for eight hours while I had gone horseback riding with her girlfriend and followed my bliss in many ways. I admired her fortitude, practicality, and earthy, muscular beauty more than she knew. She told me, "The old fart's managed to get everybody else off, you know."

"Yeah," Marea said. "His nickname is Lurk-in-the-Ditch. That's an old name for pennyroyal." They told me the story then that when they bought Dick, the horse dealer said he was nine years old and a well-trained carriage horse. Later, they learned about the old saying, "Beware of the nine-year-old horse."

When I asked what it meant, she explained that people claimed you could judge a horse's age by the length of its teeth and by the ways the teeth's chewing surfaces wore down with use. After a horse turned nine, people said, the chewing surfaces didn't change much, but the teeth showed other, much subtler changes. Martha and Marea asked another horse dealer to look at Dick's teeth, and he told them that he thought Dick was more like seventeen. Recently, I discovered online that horse experts don't think those wear patterns are really as reliable for indicating age as people used to believe. Genetics, diet, and chewing habits can affect them, too. So I guess we'll never know exactly how old Mr. Lurk-in-the-Ditch was in 1974.

12 Lurk-in-the-Ditch

Standing beside Marea outside the paddock where the horses lived, I watched them eat hungrily while she reached into her coat pocket and pulled out a bag of tobacco. Her hands shook with cold as she got out a rolling paper, folded it, filled it with loose brown leaves, and shaped a cigarette. Her wool coat sported mode-of-the-day patches, and the round, vintage vamps of her secondhand boots took her a step beyond the fashion-fringy work boots worn by the jeans jacket gang and many other young feminists around the Twin Cities. I couldn't help but notice how her pale skin stretched across the slender bones of her fingers, making her hands look delicate and vulnerable in the winter light. I felt like someone ought to help her warm them up. I had a powerful urge to be that someone, but I kept my mouth shut and my hands to myself.

Once the horses had finished their grain, they started a stylized ritual over the empty feed tubs. I'd seen them do it many times and had the impression that horses had been doing something like it for fifty million years or so, since their primordial ancestor Eohippus roamed the forest. Pretty soon, the big, half-bred workhorse Dick asserted his dominance by squealing, turning his butt, and flexing a meaty hind leg. The rest shook their heads and snorted disapproval, but no one challenged him.

"Grab the pans," Marea ordered with comic urgency, streaming smoke from her nostrils and looking exaggeratedly hassled for my entertainment.

Our life at Haidiya Farm felt highly entertaining at times, and like life at Cushing it conjured an era before indoor plumbing and the electrical grid. Mostly I liked that about it and often thought I should have been born to the early twentieth century instead of the frenzied, stressed-out, atomic second half of it. I've always sought quiet and solace in nature. Even as a little girl, I went alone to wild spaces: the woods along the river near my grandparents' home, a slough of grass and brush near our house, and the knobby prairie hills that rose around Minot from the river valley. I slipped away to those hills as often as I could. In spring, I found wild crocus and cactus amid patches of snow, and I learned that if you settled into a little depression, protected from the wind, you could stay warmed by the sun and watch the clouds shifting shapes while time melted toward oblivion.

At Haidiya Farm, I rediscovered the feral self I had nearly lost in the Twin Cities. In the evenings we sat around the woodstove in the living room, reading, talking, and smoking green and pungent homegrown weed. We shared books, and we all read. When we got excited about a writer like Mary Renault or Laura Ingalls Wilder, we binge-read collectively and talked about what we learned about farm skills, collective living experiments, classical history, feminism, spirituality, and writing. Marea told me how much she admired the activist philosophers Helen and Scott Nearing for living intentionally simple lives and sharing their Forest Farm gardens, produce, and buildings with like-minded others. She said they'd found that four hours of "bread labor" (gardening, gathering, construction, machinery maintenance, etc.) was enough to pay a person's way and keep the farm going. That sounded good to me. I thought we could do it too.

At times, we functioned like a study group, at other times like loving, supportive friends, or like a bickering collective of radical feminists whose lifeblood was criticism. Living with women on the land felt like it could be everything I'd hoped—an antidote to patriarchy, the war machine, wasteful consumption, and the destruction of the Earth.

One morning, when I came in the back door after chores, I smelled a nutty aroma mixed with wood smoke. I found Shirley at the stove, stirring grains in a cast-iron frying pan. She had cracked corn, barley, and wheat berries in the grinding mill and was roasting them. Afterward, she planned to add water and salt and let the cereal boil until it was soft. My appetite spiked while I smelled the porridge boiling. When we dished up, we added spoonsful of Martha and Marea's stiff, raw honey. It melted into the hot cereal like butter, and later, after Martha bought her little black cow, Beauty, we would add some of Beauty's milk or butter that we had made from her cream.

"My god, this is good," I said about the porridge.

"I know," Summer said, digging in.

Some days we had eggs from the Haidiya Farm hens, or bread that we baked from hand-ground flour. Martha sometimes made cream-top yogurt, letting Beauty's rich, whole milk ferment with yogurt starter in a gallon jar atop the warming oven of the cookstove. I remember seeing five or six inches of cream at the top of a gallon of yogurt. When we needed butter, Martha let the cream rise on fresh milk. We skimmed it off and took turns cranking the Dazey churn. The children, Sara and Trent, ate the same food we did, and we all thrived. I don't remember anyone complaining, though decades later Molly confided that when she visited us, she found the food "too grainy." Once, she said, she and a friend from college drove a half-hour or so to Ladysmith to get hamburgers.

I remember tears, illnesses, and temper flare-ups. These things happened with three-year-olds—and also with women in our twenties. Our periods synced up, hormones raged, and we had some rough times. Molly now reminds me that during that time she came for a visit once and found a note from us, telling her that we'd ridden our horses to the neighborhood bar and she ought to hop on Shirley's pony, Raffire, and join us. She tried. The excitable young gelding shied and dumped her at the bridge that crossed the Yellow River a quarter-mile or so down the road. She walked back to the house with an aching back and decided to churn some butter. She put milk in the churn instead of cream, so she cranked the handle for a long time and nothing congealed. When we got home, we laughed at her for not knowing better.

One afternoon, Marea and I went for a miles-long ride. The sun started setting as we looped around a snowy trail through a swamp. She cantered White Mare, and Dick kept us close on her heels. I felt the muscles of my legs start to ache and then turn to rubber, and he let out a string of groaning complaints. Near the road where we had found the trailhead, Marea turned around to see where we were. She said, with surprise in her voice, "Oh, you're right behind us!"

Yes, we were. Dick had grit and heart. Later, I read that the magical herb Lurk-in-the-Ditch (after which Marea had nicknamed him) is said to impart strength. Not long after our challenging ride—possibly even the next morning—Martha said to me, "We've been talking, and we figure that all the use you're putting Dick to is either going to kill him or get him into shape."

"Let's hope it gets him into shape," I told her while my thighs and butt sang a whiny little song of woe to me alone.

"If you're interested," she said, "we would sell him to you for seventy-five dollars."

"I'll do it," I said without a second thought. I was operating on modest savings, but my expenses had been small since I moved to Haidiya Farm. I could buy my share of groceries and Blitz's dog food, and I figured that I could afford to feed Dick, too. The next thing I knew, Martha and Marea were boarding another horse that they no longer owned themselves, and I was feeling my way into a stray attraction to a cranky old gelding. I hoped he would live a long time and carry me far.

13 Another Dance and a Funeral

One spring day at Haidiya Farm, Shirley and I came home from grocery shopping and found that Marea and Summer had given each other crew cuts. Using scissors, they had taken their hair down to a bristly half-inch, the most boyish of all haircuts—the kind the Army gave draftees to knock them down a few pegs, take away their individuality, and make them compliant. At first I was shocked, then envious. I saw that on a woman the signals reversed, and the crew cut became not masculine at all, but stark gender commentary. And brave!

I'd been wearing my hair long and straight since the late '60s, when hair became a hallmark of cultural revolution and outsider status. By 1974, when I saw what Marea and Summer had done, I was ready to reverse course. I begged, "Could you do it for me?"

Marea spent an hour or so clipping, snipping, and talking. Afterward, I was amazed by how many people mistook us for teenage boys, despite the fact that Summer and I had rounded bodies with (I would have thought) obvious breasts. I enjoyed the gender confusion. I thought it showed how stupid gender stereotyping was, but I didn't set out to be confused with a man. I wanted to feel freer and more empowered as a woman. Okay: I also wanted to mentally disturb anyone who chose to be shocked by a woman who colored outside the gender lines.

The next time I visited Molly in Minneapolis, I pulled off my stocking cap and said, "Look what I did!"

She ran her hands across my hair and said, "It feels so plush!"

Years later, she told me that she also wondered if I would be safe on the streets. My crew cut made me a potential target for lesbian-bashing homophobes, but the risk was worth it to me. Besides making a political statement, I learned how easy hair care could be when you hardly had any hair.

After my crew cut had grown out an inch or two, I visited my parents, and my mother and I went shopping in downtown Minot. In a department store we ran into the dentist who had filled all of my sugar-damaged molars and performed dental surgery on me when I was in junior high. He asked my mom, "Is this your fine young son?"

I thought, "Uh-oh, Mom's going to be embarrassed, and I'm in trouble now."

"That's my fine young daughter," she said with what sounded like pride, as he looked quizzically at me.

If Mom was embarrassed, she never told me. That doesn't mean she'd given up on cultivating my femininity. When any special event, like a family wedding, came along, I always prepared myself to hear her ask multiple times, "Don't you want to wear a dress?"

I honestly told her more than once that I didn't even own a dress anymore, but that didn't stop her from repeating the question. She passed her behavior off as teasing, but it felt like harassment to me. In the car on the day before we planned to drive to Bismarck for the wedding of one of my aunts, Dad drove us around town, running errands. Mom sat beside him and asked me again and again, "Are you sure you don't want to wear a dress?"

Finally, Dad interrupted and said, "Honey, if Dianna doesn't want to wear a dress, she doesn't have to wear a dress!"

For once I felt allied with Dad. Mom didn't bring it up again.

In March, Summer and I took our crew cuts hitchhiking. We had heard that Family of Woman planned to play a concert in

Madison. My college friend Christine was living there then, and she said we could stay with her. Someone gave us a ride to Highway 64, and we hitchhiked east from there. The first ride we got was with two cordial seventysomething women who couldn't have been nicer but were just going the mile or so into Gilman. Next, we climbed into a van with two guys. There were no seats in back, so we had to sit on the floor with a couple of snowmobiles. The driver pretended—or maybe he wasn't pretending—to try to hit a dog standing beside a mailbox. We got rocked off balance, and he barely missed the dog. Summer and I shot each other a wide-eyed look while the men laughed. After more swerving, inappropriate glee from them, and too much eye contact with us while checking for our reactions in the rearview mirror, the driver said, "Hey, you're not boys! You can raise your voices now!"

We hadn't been lowering our voices, but we laughed nervously at the thought of what our gender bending might mean to them. We definitely didn't want to get into it. Summer said, "You can let us out right here!"

I was relieved when they actually stopped on the spot and let us out. I'd had a few close calls and misadventures while hitchhiking, and this one felt as dangerous as any. We were lucky it ended as well as it did, though we were left standing in the middle of nowhere and had a hard time catching the next ride. By dark, we'd only made the hundred miles to Stevens Point, and a Wisconsin highway patrolman came along and warned us to get off the freeway and hitch from the top of the entrance. We found ourselves in the dark with few cars passing by.

While the cold of evening settled in, I realized that I'd made a classic March mistake. My wool jacket, so warm in the sun, wasn't nearly heavy enough, and Summer said she was freezing too, so we decided to walk to a tavern that we'd spotted from the highway patrol car. We hiked uphill to the bar, settled onto stools, and ordered beer. Before we finished, a young woman came over and introduced herself. She was blond and pretty and seemed to be with a guy, but she was fascinated with our story and invited us to spend the night at her house. "My mother won't mind," she said. "She loves company."

Somewhere in my reading on spirituality, I got the idea that guides appear when we need them, so perhaps I was overly trusting. This woman had come along so auspiciously that she seemed to fit the bill, so we went with her and were rewarded for our faith. She showed us to clean, warm beds in a finished basement, and in the morning we got breakfast and conversation with her mother, a heavyset woman who came across as one of those popular Girl Scout leaders or high school social studies teachers, unflappable and sardonic. She seemed to find us amusing—probably also refreshing and adventurous, I think, looking back. Not many women, then or now, dared to hitchhike across a state at all, let alone looking and acting like us.

After breakfast, our young host drove us down the freeway for about forty-five minutes, to a spot where she thought we'd be able to catch a ride. "I wish I could take you all the way to Madison," she said wistfully. "I love that town, but I've got other things to do today."

We made good time after that and found our way, walking the last little bit, to Christine's apartment in a neighborhood not far from the university. Peace signs and psychedelic posters hung in many windows. When Christine opened the door, she let us know that she was put out. "Everyone's been worried about you," she said. "Why didn't you call?"

We explained about the trouble hitchhiking. In our defense, long-distance calls were expensive at the time—a few dollars for a few minutes, but we knew we should have phoned.

"Your friends called from the farm," Christine said. "You'd better call them."

Summer said she'd do the talking, so I let her. From what I overheard, I gathered that something bad had happened. Afterward, she told me that K/T's body had been found. She said it had washed up near the Ford dam. That's a hydroelectric dam that the Ford Company built to power its plant on the St. Paul side of the

Mississippi, a few miles downstream from the Lake Street bridge.

"So she really did it," I said, letting go of my last tiny shred of hope.

"Yeah," Summer told me. "There's going be a funeral in her hometown, I guess. People are going from the LRC."

I knew that I'd be going too.

Poor K/T! It was hard not to go to absolutes when I thought about her. She blindsided us, and we failed her. She seemed so strong, and she misled me. She was supposed to be my friend, and I didn't know her at all. I had no idea how much she must have been struggling. Her serious demeanor and tough outward appearance must have masked a fierce vulnerability, like the Little Prince's rose who keeps four thorns against the world for protection. K/T's suicide made me wonder how attentive I'd been to my friends, and how careful I'd been with the affection they'd offered me. The answer seemed to be not nearly enough.

That evening in Madison, the three of us took a bus and then walked to the ballroom in the Wisconsin Union. Just as in Minneapolis, we found a large crowd of women waiting. I knew one of the band members and her girlfriend from a time when I visited Chicago with Jane and M'lou.

When the band played, some of the crowd danced. Some watched. On a fast tune, we grabbed hands and did a snake dance. When the band struck up a slow tune, the girlfriend of one of the band members grabbed me and steered me onto the dance floor, saying, "This will really give the band energy." She was vibrant, with a bad-girl/boy-girl affect, in a tank top and loose elastic-waist pants. She pulled me close, and when I caught a glimpse of her lover's expression, it occurred to me that I was being used to send a different message than I expected. It seems that I remained a pathetically slow learner when the subject was love.

Back at Haidiya Farm, Molly came for a visit, and I caught a ride back to Minneapolis with her. I made a plan to ride with Karen to K/T's funeral. She told me that the police had called her when they found K/T because of the report that Karen had tried to file. They asked her to identify K/T's personal effects. She said K/T had carried a notebook that was found in her pocket, and on one of the pages she'd written, "I wonder if I will regret it as I'm falling. Passed a church, and the door was locked. Figures." I remember hearing, whether from Karen or someone else, that she also had a rosary in her pocket and another note that said something like, "I'm going to meet the goddess." The idea of that rosary spooked me. I blamed the church for the sexism and homophobia the church fathers had fostered, from the witch trials to the contemporary teachings on sex and family that labeled homosexuality and contraception as elements in a culture of death. I couldn't exactly hold myself blameless in K/T's death, either. The whole thing felt like a waste and the biggest possible fuck-up by all concerned.

At the funeral, Karen and I sat in the church balcony with other dykes from the LRC. We talked about our worry that we might not be welcome. That old double consciousness made me prepare for the possibility of being judged or perhaps even publically criticized, but I knew that I had to be there for the memory of K/T and for my own healing and self-respect.

What I remember of the service is that K/T's brothers and sisters sang a song in her honor. They changed the gendered pronouns and paraphrased the lyrics of a Hollies song written by Bob Russell and Bobby Scott so that it became "She ain't heavy. She's our sister":

> So on we go
> Her welfare is of my concern
> No burden is she to bear
> We'll get there

Recently, when I sat with K/T's sister Mary over a Middle Eastern breakfast, I asked her about K/T's idea that she'd been disinherited from the farm by the law of primogeniture. Mary said, "That's bullshit! There's no law of primogeniture in this country!"

"I know," I said, "but what about in your family tradition? K/T seemed to think that she wouldn't be able to inherit the farm because it would go to her brother."

Mary said that her parents didn't even own the farm at the time. Her grandfather and great-uncle owned it. Her parents only bought it on a contract for deed after her great-uncle went into a nursing home. Later, some of the siblings went in together to buy forty acres and hold it in a family trust. K/T's brother and his wife farm the place now, raising and selling trees and vegetables and teaching market-gardening skills to local high school students.

When I asked her about the rosary that I'd heard was found in K/T's pocket, Mary thought a minute before she told me definitively, "It doesn't matter whether it was in her pocket. It was in her head." I had made a plan to meet with Lisyli later that same afternoon in St. Paul, and when I did, she told me that she believed K/T hadn't really intended to kill herself. She'd expected a physical resurrection.

Over the decades, I've come to realize how much I misunderstood the situation. For one thing, I thought that K/T's parents completely disapproved of her lesbianism, but when I talked to Mary, she told me that her parents liked Lena (Lisyli's earlier name) and wanted to encourage K/T's relationship with her. Since Lisyli was a few years older than K/T, a kind and caring person, and a successful writer of children's books, they'd hoped that her influence would steady K/T.

Mary told me that K/T's relationship with her mother had always been fraught. So many kids had come along so fast that it wasn't easy for her mother or for K/T. And something happened during K/T's first year at New College—maybe a bad trip, some assault or other trauma, or a biochemical imbalance—no one knew for sure, but K/T seemed to change. I wondered about sexual assault because so many times when one of my friends or lovers has struggled with mental health problems, I've learned that she was a survivor of assault or abuse. I haven't included those stories in my memoir because they're not mine to tell, but the experiences of my friends and family members have taught me that the effect of sexual assault on women's wellbeing is widespread and profound.

I'll probably always blame myself for missing K/T's warning signs, but I also realize that I might not have been able to do anything to help even if I had picked up on them. And I'm not really sure that the warning signs were as obvious at the time as they seemed when looking back on them. In the rearview mirror, the unforeseen can look inevitable, and we wonder afterward about our character and our actions: if I'd only paid closer attention, been more sensitive, asked better questions, done things differently. If only I'd had the skills and knowledge of a sixty-eight-year-old instead of a twenty-four-year-old that night in December 1973. Of course, that can never be.

At the time, my friends and I were all a bit quirky by mainstream standards. We were all fighting the idea that we were sick, immoral, and illegal. We were unsure of ourselves, all under stress. We could be too quick to judge each other sometimes, and also too quick to say that anything goes. Maybe K/T did expect resurrection, or maybe she was punishing us, or maybe she was just too tired in that moment to go on. As Lisyli told me forty-some years later, "She was a rescuer who needed rescuing herself." Fortunately for me, I had more strength and resilience than I knew. We can only live life forward, and that's what I did.

14 At the Speed of Hooves

On a day when spring teased our color-starved eyes by turning the branches of the pussy willows and dogwoods vibrant yellows and reds, Marea and I drove to a nearby town. From the road we spotted a good-looking yearling filly in a paddock full of horses. On the way home we noticed her trim, well-balanced build and her black coat with overtones of coppers and greys. I think we both pictured her in the Haidiya Farm pasture and thought about the nice foal we could get by breeding her to Sativa in another year.

We stopped and talked to the farmer, and he told us that we'd need to phone his daughter later if we wanted to buy the filly. I did call, and we negotiated a price. Martha and Marea had already added Roana, a gorgeous gray roan, to the herd of brood mares that they planned to breed to Sativa. The dream of building a horse ranch on a shoestring budget through vision and luck was Marea's most of all, I think, but I confess to also falling under the spell of glossy Arabian horse magazines with photos of horses offered for sale for tens of thousands of dollars. While we dreamed of five-figure horse prices, Martha made the land payments. She also took care of Beauty with great care and love. She shared the milk and cream but insisted on feeding and milking Beauty herself, even though I longed to learn about cattle and asked to help. She had the right, of course, but I always saw it as one of the subtle messages that we had begun to hear from her, alerting us that she wasn't happy with the crowding in her house and barnyard.

I wasn't sure how to respond and also hang on to my animals, my women's land dream, and my hope that Molly would decide to move to the country and live with me. I started thinking about how to make those things happen somewhere else. As either luck or my own manifestation of wishes would have it, one day in town Martha ran into a woman she knew named Maggie. Martha and Marea had worked on Maggie's dairy farm when they first moved to Wisconsin. Maggie's place wasn't far from Haidiya Farm—not by rural standards anyway—and Martha brought back the news that Maggie wanted to sell it. I don't remember the price, but it sounded reasonable at the time, so Summer, Shirley, and I went to take a look. We found more than enough pasture and hay land, a barn, a chicken coop, a two-story house, and a windmill attached to a pumpjack for watering the livestock. Plus there was an electric water pump for the house. This place was hooked up to the grid! I knew I wanted it, but we had no down payment. Before long, I came up with the idea of asking my parents to buy it. I hoped they would let us live there and buy it from them over time.

To my surprise, they liked my idea. They agreed that the price was reasonable and the land would make a good investment for their savings. They started picturing what they would do at the farm themselves. "What I would like," Mom wrote, "is a fairly small area, with many trees, a garden spot, chicken coop, shelter for a cow, electricity, a well, a fireplace. . . . All one needs to do is close the eyes, and it all unfolds." They called Maggie's realtor and sent a check for earnest money, but a few days later he called them back and said he was returning their check because Maggie had decided to sell to someone else. When Martha ran into Maggie again, she said, "Sorry about scuttling your friends, kid. I just didn't think it would work." Why not? We never knew for sure. Maybe she sold to a friend or neighbor, but I always suspected that she scuttled us because she didn't want people thinking she liked dykes.

Mom and Dad took the rejection in stride, and later Mom wrote that Dad told her, "Sometimes a person appreciates things more if they buy them themselves, anyway." I didn't like that much at the time but had to admit there was wisdom in it. Come spring, Molly moved in with us, and Martha helped Summer, Shirley, and me get jobs planting trees for the Forest Service. We earned $3.45 an hour—a fabulous sum, compared to the $1.60 minimum wage. We were each expected to plant five hundred evergreens a day across rough, recently logged terrain. The trees were seedlings, a little more than a foot long from root to crown. To plant them, we had to repeatedly swing heavy steel tools called grub hoes.

Our foreman was one of Martha's mentors—a cordial, middle-aged man. He showed us how to arrange a few dozen seedlings in a canvas bag so that we could reach in and grab one at a time without damaging the roots. "Never let the roots dry out," he said. "The trees will die if you do." Then he fastened the bag around his waist and instructed us how to plant while he demonstrated the steps. Swing the grub hoe overhead. Bring it down so that the blade cuts into the ground. Push the handle down to make a V-shaped opening as you're pulling a seedling from the bag. Slide the roots into the opening. Slip the grub hoe out and straighten yourself as you tap the hole closed with the blunt side of the hoe and take a step forward. Repeat 499 times, and you're finished with a day's work.

During breaks, the boss showed us how to forage for wild onions that some people call ramps, and we added them to our cheese sandwiches. I thought I'd grown used to physical work at Haidiya Farm, but after a full day of tree planting, I felt as if I'd abused all of my muscles. Every night we went to bed exhausted and got up sore. One morning we woke up to thunder and hoped we were going to get rained out from work. The storm passed, and we were so disappointed that we called the Forest Service anyway, to report that we weren't going in because of a storm. Summer did the talking, and I jiggled a sheet of tin in the background to sound like thunder. We knew our scheme was comic and lame, but somehow we got the day off and didn't get fired. We went back the next day feeling somewhat refreshed.

Not long after that, Shirley bought a muscular mare with a delicate face and a white blaze. She named her Cheyenne and soon learned that her mare could be flighty. She shied on the road and dumped Shirley on her head, and another time she threw Shirley and Sara. Shirley had Sara tied to her with a scarf around their waists, and as they fell, Shirley tried to shield her daughter. As a result, Shirley landed off balance and hurt her back in a way that still bothers her into her seventies.

That spring, Summer needed buckles for a set of old harnesses she was restoring, so we drove to the Amish harness maker's shop near Medford. A few Amish men had been talking together and went quiet when we walked in. I returned their cool, non-hostile curiosity with my eyes while the harness maker answered our questions and sold Summer what she needed. Frequently we passed Amish people in their horse-drawn buggies on the roads southwest of Medford and east of Gilman. I respected them for sticking to the old ways of farming, living in communities, and helping each other. I felt grateful to them too. Because they used horses and lived mostly off the grid, the local hardware stores stocked the kerosene lamps and other tools we needed.

One day Martha came back after spending time with the dairy farmer friend who had helped her find and buy Beauty, and she told us that he'd said something that surprised her. He'd said, "They took you, and I never had you!"

I still chuckle a little at his hopelessly misplaced sexual interest, and I also still bristle a little at the idea that the rest of us "took" Martha. When she repeated his comment, she brought us face to face with the issues we'd been avoiding. I thought I worked hard at Haidiya Farm, and I remember scrupulously paying my share of daily expenses. In the cold light of hindsight, though, I see that Martha was the only one contributing toward the cost and maintenance of the real estate. She told me later that she got angry when she heard me tell two visitors from the city that living in the country wasn't all that expensive. She subsidized us all, really, and I can see now that we didn't do enough to deal with the imbalance. I offered to help by doing more chores, but she said part of the problem was that she liked her chores and missed doing some of the ones that I had already taken on.

So my helping wasn't helping. I found myself in a double bind—doing too much and not doing nearly enough to support our life at Haidiya Farm. From my point of view, without some shared ownership, or at least some sense that we were building toward something we defined as shared, I felt more and more like we couldn't live together as a group. I don't blame Martha at all for feeling protective of her home or for not feeling compelled to open it to all women, as Jane had done at Rising Moon. Martha told me later that she thought she hadn't really been looking for a collective at all but, rather, a family. If *family* means unconditional and abiding love in relationships of mutual support, then I was looking for that too. But without some collective purpose and plan of action, I thought we shouldn't be surprised that one or another of us—maybe all of us—would end up feeling "taken."

So the rest of us talked and made plans. Shirley, Summer, and I decided that after tree planting we would move to Rising Moon. I hoped that Molly would move there with me, and she said that she might eventually, but she wanted to go back to the city and do some traveling from there first. She owned a canvas tipi and said I could put it up at Rising Moon and live in it for the summer, whatever happened with her.

Our plans fit our resources. I bought cedar tipi poles from a friend of Martha's, and Molly and I tied them to the roof rack of her Bronco and drove them the 240 miles to Rising Moon. Later she planned to take a driving trip to New Mexico while Shirley and I rode Dick and Cheyenne on county roads to Rising Moon. We planned to lead our young horses, Breeze and Raffire. Her collie, Niji, and my dog, Blitz, would walk alongside us. We would take the kittens we had adopted from Haidiya Farm's mama cats in our saddlebags, and Sara would stay with her dad until we got settled. Trent was already in Colorado, spending time with one of Summer's friends, but he was due home soon. Summer bought a '52 Chevy truck that she named Mabel, and she planned to come after us, bringing Trent, Shirley's things, and eventually her own mare, Lola.

Shirley and I used plat books, township maps published by counties, to chart our route. We planned to stay off paved roads as much as we could and make about twenty miles a day, camping at night in spots that we would locate as we went. We knew we'd need to find water for ourselves and the other animals, and grassy spots for the horses to graze, but we figured neither of those should be hard to find in the early summer when grasses spring up lush and green in Minnesota and Wisconsin. We planned to supplement the horses' grazing with grain that we would buy from farmers and feed stores along the way. There was one hitch: Sara's dad could only take her during the first two-thirds of our ride, so Shirley planned a place and time to meet him on the road, hand off Sara, and take her with us the rest of the way. They arranged their plan by letter and map.

The day we left, I sported a fresh crew cut, jeans, a plaid shirt, and a heavy-duty wide-brimmed men's hat that I'd picked up at some secondhand store. What I remember most vividly about riding behind Shirley is the elaborate Phoenix in flames embroidered across the back of her jeans jacket. She and Cheyenne looked splendid to me, and our first day went smoothly until we got to a highway bridge near Ladysmith. The horses didn't want to step onto the bridge's deck. Finally, after a lot of coaxing and nudging, Dick grunted and started across. Tied to his saddle, Breeze had no choice but to follow, and Shirley's horses came along to keep the herd together. The next day we arrived at a river with steep banks and concrete abutments where a bridge used to be. We saw a farmer in his yard and asked him, "What happened to the bridge?"

"That's been gone for years," he said.

"I guess we should have ordered newer plat books," Shirley quipped, and I laughed at the genius of our hindsight.

Dianna, Dick, Breeze, and kitten heading off to Rising Moon from Haidiya Farm

At the speed of hooves, we lost half a day backtracking and finding our way to a paved road with a bridge that actually did cross the river. Another day we found no water for the horses. We asked a young couple at a crossroads if they knew where we could find some. "There's a lake five miles down this road," they told us with the proud smiles of good Samaritans. They didn't realize that riding our horses there and back would shoot another half-day, and they would be thirsty again by the time we returned to the crossroads. Blitz saved the day by sniffing out a watery ditch obscured by brush. I used my hat as a pail to carry water to the horses, and we were on our way.

We met lots of people on the road. Most of them were open and cooperative, which surprised me because we looked like such obvious dykes. One woman knocking down beers with her strapping twentysomething son on the outdoor patio of a bar and grill, asked why we didn't have a man along. "Don't you need someone like him to protect you?" she asked, gesturing toward her son.

"But who would protect us from him?" I told her, paraphrasing a line I remembered from some Mae West movie I saw at Macalester.

The woman puffed out a smoker's croak that passed for a chuckle, and I saw in her eyes that she got my point: Man-as-Rescuer is a myth our culture keeps alive so that women won't start thinking we can get along without them.

I only felt in serious danger once on our cross-country ride, and even then we didn't need weapons, though the thought had crossed our minds that we could use some tools for defense. I remembered Sadie Smith's words from our consciousness-raising group: "Never trust a woman who doesn't carry a knife." I carried a hunting knife in a scabbard on my belt, and we packed a hatchet in our saddlebags for cutting up firewood. Most nights we settled into our bedrolls, tipped our saddles upright at our heads, and draped them with secondhand sheer curtain panels we'd sewn together to make mosquito netting. When it rained, we wrapped plastic sheeting around our bedrolls. Our dogs served as security guards, and our staked-out horses watched the perimeters, too. The horses' primary survival tactic was flight, and they snorted warnings to each other if they saw anything they might want to escape.

Camping like this we were able to tuck into small, grassy spaces and mostly go unnoticed. Sometimes we didn't cook at all, but when we did, we used a fire. For breakfast and lunch, we ate peanut butter, honey, and cheese, with bread or crackers and, sometimes, wild plantain and ramps. For dinner, we usually made pancakes from dried milk, water, and flour. For variety, we added sliced carrots and foraged greens.

In a resort town, we met a delicately built man with long, golden hair and a well-groomed moustache. He offered milk for our kittens, which he hurried into his house to get and then on his return set the saucer on the ground in front of them with a dramatic flourish. His house sat near a country store. As we stood in the shade of maples and pines, he told us that his lover was a doctor, and the people who ran the store and lived in the next-door house were his lover's parents. "We've been together twelve years," he said, "and it just keeps getting better and better. Every day is a honeymoon."

"Do they know about the two of you?" Shirley asked, gesturing toward the store.

"Oh, honey," he crooned. "If they don't, they'd have to be blind."

Of course, many people preferred to "be blind" in those days. My friends and I were in the thick of figuring out how to live a rural life that was visible and honest while also protecting ourselves as best we could from the homophobic blowback that sometimes came with visibility. We knew that the consequences of homophobia, then as now, could include discrimination, gay bashing, and murder. The wonder is that most of the time we felt safe.

The handoff of Sara went well, even without cell phones or GPS. We managed to arrive at the right crossroads ahead of the appointed time, and Sara's father managed to find us from the map that Shirley had mailed him. He spotted her red bandanna, which she'd tied to a willow as a prearranged sign that we were waiting in the clearing beyond. For the rest of the trip Shirley had Sara's things in her saddlebags, and her daughter rode behind her, attached by a scarf tied around their waists.

On a downhill slope near the bridge where we planned to cross the St. Croix River into Minnesota, two kids came along on bikes and asked what we were doing. One was a boy of about nine, the other a girl of about eleven. They rode off and then came back again to tell us that their mother and grandmother said we should spend the night at their place. They turned out to be a family of free spirits who kept a pet crow in the house and enjoyed the company of interesting strangers.

Twice on our trip landowners found us camped on their property and asked what we were doing. One decided it was fine that we stay. The other shouted angrily, "Get out of here! If I wanted someone camping here, I'd already have someone camping here!" He had a right to control access to his land. So we packed up and went on. We had stopped early that evening because Sara had been tired and cranky, and after hearing the landowner blast us, I felt tired and cranky, too. Most of the time, Sara was amazingly good-natured for a four-year-old on a cross-country horseback trip. I don't remember her complaining about anything except the mosquitoes. As we rode on that evening, a boy of around twelve came along on a bike in the fading twilight and told us that we could camp at his family's place, a little farther down the road.

"You better go ask your mom and dad," Shirley told him.

"My dad won't care," the boy answered.

She insisted, so he pedaled ahead and returned after a few minutes to say with a big grin, "He says it's fine." He seemed thrilled to be part of our entourage, shouting over his shoulder like a barker, "Come on! I'll show you where!"

When we rode on the next day, we thought our horses seemed a bit tired and sore-footed, and we were feeling bug-bitten, weary, and sore in the places that rubbed our saddles. We were about forty miles, or two days, short of Rising Moon on a county road west of Willow River, Minnesota, when I spotted a cattle truck parked in a farmyard. In the field beside the truck I saw a man and boy planting something with a hand-cranked seeder. The man sat at the front of a wagon with his legs dangling while he cranked and sent a cloud of seeds flying. The boy was pulling the rig with a tractor, in circles around the plowed and disked field.

"I wonder how much he'd charge to take us forty miles," I said. "It sure would be nice to get there in an hour instead of two days, wouldn't it?"

"Sure would," Shirley said, so we rode into the farmyard to inquire. A boy came from the house and told us to tie up our horses and come inside. In the kitchen we found a woman in a housedress, an older man in overalls, and more kids. The woman introduced herself as the farmer's wife and the man as her father-in-law. She kneaded bread dough at the cupboard beside the sink while he drank coffee at the table. Kids flitted in and out, grinning shyly and staring.

Mrs. B wanted to know our plans. We told her about free land, open to all women, our tipis, the Twin Pines store that marked our turn from the highway onto the township roads that led to Rising Moon, and the tiny town nearby where there was a bar called the Three Sisters and a convenience store run by four women.

"Is everything women there?" she asked incredulously.

"Seems like it, doesn't it?" I said. We didn't tell her that we had not been able to discern any family resemblance in the store-owners who claimed to be sisters. To us, they looked like two old-style butch-femme couples.

When we told her our idea about hiring her husband to drive us to Rising Moon, she said, "I don't think he can do it today. He's planting clover."

She sent a boy out to check.

He came back and reported, "Dad said he's got too much to do. He says maybe Schmidt can do it."

Mrs. B explained to us that Schmidt was a neighbor who hauled cattle for a living. She said she would call him. What we overheard didn't sound promising, but she told us after she hung up the phone, "He's busy, but his son can do it. He'll be right over."

Flies buzzed around her bread dough, thanks to the screen door flying open and shut with so many kids coming and going. The old man asked about our plans in what I took to be a slightly peevish tone: "What makes you think you're going to be able to live in tipis through the winter?"

"There's lots of empty farms around there," I answered him.

"We're thinking we might be able to rent one, or maybe caretake one for a while."

"They'll never rent to you," he said.

"Why not?" Shirley asked him in a voice that seemed to dare him to answer truthfully.

He shrugged it off. "I don't know. I just don't think so."

When the younger Schmidt arrived, we went outside to talk with him. He was a lanky, reticent, country boy with thick curls and glasses. "Where are we going exactly?" he wanted to know.

With the kids and the old man gathered around, I drew a map in the dirt using my hunting knife to scratch out lines that stood for roads and highways. Years later when I moved to a small farm on that same Willow River Road, a neighbor told me that he had already heard about me and our earlier passage through on horseback. "When you pulled out that knife," he said, "they thought it was kind of scary."

I had thought I was just using the knife as a tool that day, but apparently I'd been making a local legend. I don't know who felt intimidated, but young Schmidt felt secure enough to say he would take us to Rising Moon for fifty dollars. We accepted, and he helped us load our animals into the back of the truck, except for the kittens. We kept them in the cab with us. Schmidt made good time on the paved roads, until we got to the Twin Pines store, where we turned onto the hilly and curving gravel roads maintained by Glory Township. Schmidt slowed way down then and kept on crawling as he turned off the road onto the rutted driveway of Rising Moon. Branches of oak and pine scratched the sides of his truck until we burst into the broad daylight of a meadow, where we saw Otter squatting shirtless, milking a goat. Her sun-lightened brown hair fell in thick, full waves across her shoulders. Poor Schmidt didn't quite know what to do. Shirley rolled down her window and shouted, "We've got a man driving the truck!"

Otter's lover, Maya, came with a shirt that she draped over Otter's shoulders while Schmidt stopped the truck and recouped enough composure to help us unload the horses. We let the young ones run free and held Dick and Cheyenne's halter ropes while they grabbed a few mouthfuls of grass. We each counted out twenty-five dollars and handed the money to Schmidt. For fifty dollars in 1974, we could have bought a hundred gallons of gas, fifty bales of hay, or an acre of land some places in Aitkin County, but it was worth the price for us to arrive at Rising Moon and feel like we'd come home.

15 Rising Moon

That first night at Rising Moon we bedded down on bunks that Lisyli and some of the other women had built in the shed after the house burned. One of the neighbors told me later that the shed had been the summer kitchen of a family named Backa. Their names were still listed as the owners in the county plat book, which, besides the roads, showed the rivers, railways, lakes, and boundaries of land holdings in each township.

Our first night the leftover heat of the day pressed in on the shed. While laying out my bedding, I noticed that the windows were screened and decided that we could stand to catch a breeze. I fell asleep fast but soon woke to the stinging bites of mosquitoes. I pulled the sleeping bag over my head to fend them off, and as I tried to fall asleep again, I told myself I should have known that the walls and siding of the old shed would be riddled with chinks and cracks. I lay awake, listening to the drones of mosquitoes as they searched for openings in the covers. The sound itself was torture and seemed to increase the itching of my earlier bites, but I could only stand the heat so long before I had to unzip the sleeping bag, throw it off, and lay myself open to a new attack. I swatted until I was so tired that I had to cover myself again, and I repeated the routine through the night. In the morning I didn't exactly wake but just sort of rolled out of my bunk and staggered outside.

I'm sure I wasn't at my best around the breakfast fire where the other residents of Rising Moon gathered that first morning. We met a woman named Sierra who had come from Chicago with a dog she'd adopted from the streets and named Gorgon. Ancient Greeks depicted the Gorgons as female temple guardians with snakes for hair and gazes that turned men to stone. At this point I had nearly given up on men because they showed so little interest in taking responsibility for male privilege and sexism, but Gorgon seemed like an unfair moniker to hang on a dog, especially one whose life on the streets had left her avoiding eye contact and touch.

Besides Sierra and Gorgon, we newcomers shared the breakfast fire with Otter, Maya, Lisyli, Selenekore, and four dogs. I felt simpatico with all of them and hoped that we could get along and together give the slip to the whole patriarchal, militarized, racist, sexist, and materialistic society. I was prepared to do everything with women—to shop at women's stores, to read women's books, to eat food raised and prepared by women, to love women and raise children with women, and one day to hand off women's institutions like our collective farms to younger women. I knew we had a lot of work to do first.

At Haidiya Farm we had lived without electricity and indoor plumbing, but the conditions at Rising Moon ratcheted up the difficulty. Our friend Kathy McConnell called it "subsistence" the next September, when she wrote her reflection on Rising Moon for the Twin Cities women's paper *Gold Flower*. We did without a house, barn, fences, phone, furnace, electricity, power tools, and even some of the hand tools we needed. We borrowed them or improvised until we could afford them. We cooked over open fires, pumped water by hand, and staked our horses with ropes so they grazed the pastures in large circles, close enough to see each other and nicker back and forth, but far enough apart that they couldn't get tangled.

Martha arrived late one Friday night, bringing Shirley's tipi and remaining belongings from Haidiya Farm. She climbed down from the cab of her pickup in the dark and identified herself when we shouted to ask who it was. In the light of a kerosene lamp, she looked resplendent through weariness, as she so often did. She talked a bit like Sergeant Joe Friday, low key and worldly wise, as we caught up on each other's news. Our main topic was Summer, who as best we knew had gone west to be near Trent. That friend she'd sent him to stay with during tree planting had apparently taken him along on a burglary. They'd both been taken into custody, and a court had awarded custody of Trent to Summer's parents.

Shirley confessed that she'd begun to wonder whether Summer would ever join us. "I've got the feeling she's giving me the slow shake," she said. I didn't like seeing her doubtful and hurt. During our long ride from Wisconsin, I'd admired how she balanced our cross-country, back-to-the-land odyssey with keeping a four-year-old happy and staying upbeat herself.

Martha with Beauty's daughter, Grace, and Moonda (right) at Haidiya Farm

She set up their tipi, with help from me and probably others, in a meadow downhill from the summer kitchen. I remember helping her stand up a frame of tamarack poles that she had tied together about three feet from their tops. As we spread the bottoms apart at the base, the poles fanned out and made a cone shape with a twenty-foot diameter. Once the frame was in place, we unfolded the cream-colored canvas covering she had sewn and waterproofed. She arranged it on the ground around the base of the poles and tied the folded top to a pole she had saved for lifting the canvas. Then she hoisted the canvas and unfurled it. Once standing, her tipi made me think of the Sydney Opera House or, when the fire was lit inside, a gigantic Japanese lantern. It was a majestic, graceful, magical thing to encounter in a Minnesota meadow.

Lots of back-to-the-landers were experimenting with tipis at the time because they made inexpensive homes that were more time-tested and durable than tents. We knew we were borrowing a design perfected by indigenous, nomadic people like the Lakota and Dakota who migrated across my native state before the European trappers and settlers displaced them. I wasn't familiar with the concept of *cultural appropriation* yet, but even then I knew that we needed to remember whose shoulders we stood on and what the native people's dispossession from their land and ways of life had cost them. I thought that we needed to do more than remember, too. When disagreements over treaty rights, harvesting rights, and human rights flared, as they regularly did, we needed to speak and act as allies.

Soon after Shirley put up her tipi, Molly brought her tipi canvas from Minneapolis, and we set it up on my cedar poles in a meadow that felt private, separated from the main camp by a patch of wild blackberries and pussy willows. That night, we made a fire and experimented with setting the smoke flap, a part of the canvas covering that was left tied by one corner to the lifting pole so that it could be adjusted to catch a breeze and channel smoke. As the fire died, we fit ourselves together under my mosquito netting as we had done so many times in different beds, and I lobbied her to come and live with me. She said she still wasn't sure.

Shirley and Sara (on Cheyenne) at Rising Moon

Mosquitoes remained a big problem. The Ripple River valley curved around the feet of Rising Moon's hills. Its switchbacks, sloughs, and wetlands made a vast nursery for mosquito larvae and sent me searching for better netting. At an army surplus store I found a cloth half-sphere that resembled a parachute. I've never been sure it actually was a parachute because the fabric was porous enough to let air pass through, but it was shaped like one, with sections that came together at the center. I suspended it by strings from my tipi poles, and it made a beautiful canopy that covered two people comfortably.

Mosquitoes weren't the only bugs that plagued us. We were constantly checking our bodies and our animals for ticks, and during the day we swatted biting flies. We could usually thwart them by staying in the shade or, on a breezy day, on open, high ground. Our old hayfields had gone feral but still contained red and white clover, brome, timothy, and other domestic and wild grasses that gave us plenty of pasture for our horses and goats. We had trees for shade and firewood—oak, poplar, birch, and pine mostly, with tamarack and spruce in the lowlands.

To many onlookers, our lesbian-feminist back-to-the-land dream must have seemed strange and unrealistic, but we were far from the only ones who dreamed it. A decade later in her book *Lesbian Land,* Joyce Cheney anthologized more than two dozen stories from women involved in lesbian land projects in the United States, Canada, and Europe. Some of the separatist philosophies I encountered in it stretched even my imagination. She describes reaching out to groups such as the Francophone Dykes located outside of Montreal who, one of their friends told her later, rejected all parts of technology, including "the written word."

A woman who responded to Cheney's request for writing, Buckwheat Turner, describes the impulse behind A Woman's Place, in Athol, New York, in a way that strikes home for me. "Our original dream," she says, "was a women's utopia. We had a sense of wanting to move actively toward something rather than simply continuing to react to what society had designed for our consumption." At the women's farms where I lived, we were moving toward something, too, even though we never quite articulated our shared philosophies or goals.

Neither Shirley nor I can remember attending any meetings at Rising Moon, or participating in any organized discussions in which we made collective decisions about rules or plans. We talked around the fire circle daily and hashed out possibilities and ideas for what to do next. We reached decisions by consensus, with an ethic that, as I saw it, involved allowing everyone the most flexibility possible. No one took notes, and as far as I know no written records of our work exist besides this book and that retrospective that Kathy McConnell wrote for *Gold Flower.* When a friend shared a copy of her article with me decades later, lost memories of particular jobs and projects came flooding back.

She describes breaking ground for the Rising Moon garden by hand, painstakingly turning the sod with a shovel and a drum. She remembers one person digging while another beat a rhythm that somehow made the work easier. She writes of the toll our "simple" lifestyle took:

> Someone has read that living at a survival level this way takes three times more energy than living a "normal" gas, electricity, bathtub, four walls and a roof type life. Pump the water, haul the water, chop wood to heat it, *then* take a bath. Equal amounts of energy were spent initiating many Rising Moon visitors to the skills of the lifestyle.

Oh, yes, I'd almost forgotten about the visitors. Word traveled about Rising Moon, and women came from many places to camp with us and see what we had going on. All of them took energy. Some gave it back more than others.

An astrologer from Minneapolis visited that summer, and conversation turned to the Age of Aquarius, the spiritual awakening that many of us thought must be just about to dawn, ushered in at least partly by our work on the land. As I recall, the astrologer told us she had just returned from a gathering of colleagues, and most of them agreed that an age of love and understanding did indeed lie ahead, but she said we would first have to live through decades of fundamentalism and war. Her scenario seemed impossible. When the rest of us talked afterward, we didn't see how such a setback could occur. I can see now that we vastly underestimated the reactionary power of fear and misinformation.

Meanwhile, word about Rising Moon got around our Aitkin neighborhood, and some of our neighbors decided to check us out. A few came to shop at our food co-op, which Jane and the others had already started by the time Shirley and I arrived. Our inventory consisted of pinto beans and brown rice in two galvanized trashcans, plus a gallon of tamari sauce. We bought our bulk food from the new-wave co-op in Minneapolis that Linda's husband had helped start in 1971, and that Shirley helped grow by finding a source of brown rice in Arkansas. Like the other new-wave co-ops of the '70s, we stood on the shoulders of earlier farmers' cooperative grocery stores, feed stores, electric utilities, and gas stations. We had no interest in profiting from our neighbors. We sold to them at cost.

We also saw no sense in strictly enforcing the no-men rule against neighbors who came to shop at our co-op. There were few enough of them anyway—just the athletic Bryan who ate for good health, a hippie couple, the Zs, and an older couple who lived nearby, Mr. and Mrs. O. One afternoon I woke up from a nap in the summer kitchen to the sound of incoherent, disturbing moans and cries. A woman called repeatedly for her mother, and I heard her say, "There she is! I see her!" I heard other voices, too, of people attending to the woman. When I got outside, I learned that Mr. and Mrs. O had come to shop at our co-op, and Mrs. O had fallen down and stopped breathing. Otter had resuscitated her with CPR, and by the time I came on the scene, she was helping Mr. O get his wife into their car so that he could rush her to the hospital.

Mr. and Mrs. O had come from somewhere in the south (Texas, I think), where Mr. O's job had been located. He'd grown up around Aitkin, planned all along to retire there, and spoke without the drawl that I could hear in his wife's speech. She loved pinto beans and couldn't find them at either of the two grocery stores in town. After she recovered from whatever had caused her to collapse, the two of them came back often. They credited Otter for saving Mrs. O's life, and their gratitude spilled over into kindness toward all of us. Lisyli told me once that Mrs. O took her aside one day and whispered something meant, we think, as a friendly word to the wise. She warned about our neighbors: "They say you're prostitutes and worse."

We laughed off that "worse" part. We were something. That's for sure. As far as I was concerned, the ones who didn't know could keep right on guessing.

16 Making Hay

In early July, a slender, silver-haired man drove into the Rising Moon driveway in a Ford pickup. I could see a dog wagging on the seat beside him as our dogs improvised a welcoming dance around the truck. The man rolled down his window, and I walked over and offered an inquisitive "Hello?" I'd been headed toward the fire circle with a bowl of plump wild black raspberries that I'd picked near my tipi and intended to share with my friends for breakfast.

"I'm Stan Hestbeck, your neighbor over that way," the guy said, waving a hand toward the woods in the back of our land.

For some reason, we started calling him "Mr. Hestbeck" that morning, and afterward we always gave him the honorific title and never called him by his first name, unlike our next-door neighbor Harvey, who also became our friend and mentor in country ways. Harvey's land sat across the river from ours, and Mr. Hestbeck's farm bordered Elm Island Lake, about a mile from us cross-country, or a mile and a half on the Glory Township roads.

"Why don't you let your dog out?" I told him, since ours were bouncing off the doors of his pickup, and I didn't want them to scratch the paint any more than they already might have.

Mr. Hestbeck got out and let his dog scramble out behind him. I couldn't help but notice that the dog only had three legs and that

Mr. Hestbeck carried a plate of some kind of goodies covered in plastic wrap. "Here," he said, holding the plate out to me. "I just made these. They're bran muffins."

"Thank you," I said as I watched his dog bob and wrestle with our four-leggeds. I had to ask about the missing leg. Mr. Hestbeck gave a dismal frown. His thick silver hair and expressive eyebrows made his facial features look extremely pronounced as he explained, "My son-in-law did that with a sickle mower."

Or maybe he said his son did it. My memory of the exact culprit is sketchy and, anyway, not nearly as important as the idea he meant to convey that some upstart male had made the mistake. "He was in too much of a hurry," Mr. Hestbeck scowled, shaking his head. "I told him those sickle mowers are dangerous. They lay the grass down, and the dog sees the grass moving and thinks it's an animal."

I took his cautionary tale to heart, for whatever good it did me. His story foreshadowed one of the saddest and most traumatic events of my life. In the moment, though, Shirley joined us, and Mr. Hestbeck told us that he'd come to ask us to help him make hay. He said he lived alone. His wife had died a few years earlier, and their children had grown up and moved away. He wondered if we would help him in exchange for a share of the hay crop. We quickly agreed, since we'd been wondering how we would get enough hay to winter our animals.

Flush with excitement, I held out the bowl of black raspberries and said, "Would you like some?" I had meant that he should take a handful, as we would each do when we passed the bowl around our fire circle, but he understood the offer through a different lens. He took the bowl and said, "Thank you." When I thought about it, I understood the difference in perspective. There really weren't that many berries—just the amount you might offer a neighbor—enough to dress a few bowls of cereal or to make another batch of muffins. So it had been a pretty good trade, and Mr. Hestbeck became another of the men for whom we made an exception to the women-only rule. We talked and decided that for us the rule meant that only women and children would live on the land. More and more, we saw how we needed our neighbors, and how they sometimes needed us. Excluding them didn't make sense when faced with day-to-day life at a subsistence level. Besides, I had learned from my parents and grandparents and from Willa Cather and Laura Ingalls Wilder (and later from Wendell Berry) about the long tradition of neighbors helping each other, and I liked being part of that sort of community.

The first day we arrived for work at Mr. Hestbeck's farm, he proudly showed us his red gambrel-roofed barn, his milk cow, and his old-fashioned hay delivery system, a sling operated by ropes and pulleys that multiplied the force and changed the direction of the pull, so that he could lift a dozen bales into the hayloft at once with a rope tied to his tractor hitch. Inside the loft he directed us to stand safely aside, on bales he had already stacked around the outside walls, while he went outdoors to demonstrate. I watched in amazement as the sling of bales appeared in the doorway and traveled in along a track. When it arrived at a spot where he had set a tripping mechanism, the sling opened, and the bales fell into the mow, close to where he wanted them stacked. He soon appeared again and showed us how to fit the bales together like carefully overlapping bricks so that the stack wouldn't topple later. After that, he took us out to the hayfield to stand on the wagon behind his hay baler and stack forty-pound bales while he drove the rig around the field. The baler gobbled up the already cut and raked hay, shaped it into rectangular bundles, tied them, and delivered them to the edge of the wagon through a chute. We handled each bale three times before we were finished.

After that, Shirley and I, and sometimes Selenekore and Lisyli, spent many hot afternoons making hay with Mr. Hestbeck. Once, when I came to work alone, he sent me into the mow to stack bales. When he came to check on me, he exclaimed, "Hey! You've got it all stacked! I thought you'd need my help! You're doing great!"

I've always been a sucker for external validation, so his praise made my confidence soar. I was happy to do well and to find a new way to get exercise while earning something I needed. When we worked for him, he always fed us lunch or coffee with a home-baked treat, depending on the time of day, and while we ate he told us stories about our neighbors and what farming was like in the old days. Once, feeling in a rush to bale a field ahead of some rain, he worked alone and left the bales on the field, stacked in pairs on their ends to shed water. When the sun came out, he came and got us to help him pick them up. I lifted them by the strings and got them high enough that Shirley could reach them with a hay hook to pull them onto the wagon and stack them. When the stack got too high for me to reach, he showed me how to drive the tractor, and he threw the bales up to Shirley.

One of those days during haying, Sara's half-sister came to visit. While she was with us, Mr. Hestbeck came to ask if we could make hay. Since no one else was home at Rising Moon, we took the girls with us. Shirley told them to stay in the yard and play while we stacked bales. We were just coming out of the barn after one of the loads when a neighbor woman pulled into the driveway. She sat in her car, red-faced, and yelled, "Do you know where your kids are?" Before we could answer, she informed us that she'd seen a bear on the road a few days back, and the girls were so lit-tle. Did we know how dangerous it was for us to let them walk that road alone?

We didn't see the girls then, and I got scared. The neighbor said she'd picked them up on the road, and they had told her they were walking to the store. She'd asked where their mothers were, and they had told her they didn't know. In a righteous huff, she had delivered them to Rising Moon and left them near the fire cir-cle. As soon as Shirley heard this, she hurried home. She walked the land, calling for the girls, until finally she found them in Si-erra's tipi in the farthest-back meadow. They hadn't answered her because they were afraid she'd be mad. They'd found a box of fancy chocolates Sierra had stashed away, and they'd eaten all the candy. They had chocolate smeared on their faces and hands.

Most times working with Mr. Hestbeck went much more

smoothly, and less comically, than that. As we got to know each other better, he told us that we could use his phone and also that he would be willing to take messages for us, since we had no phone at Rising Moon. We made a few long-distance phone calls and settled with him for the charges. Using his phone was a big help because, until then, we had relied only on letters to keep up long-distance relationships and do our business. We had applied for a few jobs before that, but as soon as employers heard that we had no phone, they asked, "How are we supposed to get a hold of you, then?"

Lisyli and Selenekore soon got jobs cleaning at a motel in town, and another friend started working on the summer kitchen, fixing it up so that she could winter in it. One late-summer weekend Molly came to visit, and Lisyli stopped by our tipi to chat. She asked Molly about her plans, and Molly told her, "I don't know. I think I might want to do some traveling."

It was the first I'd heard of it and I felt hurt. Decades later, I asked Molly if she remembered that conversation the way I did. She answered, "Did I say that? What a little snot!"

I could be a little snot, too, at twenty-four. I'm sure I got angry about her plan to go traveling. A hot temper like my dad's has been one of my biggest shortcomings, but I could also be defensive and highly sensitive, like my mom. Looking back, many of my interactions with Molly seem fuzzy, but one thing seems clear: I hadn't learned to do my part toward creating the honest and lasting relationship I craved so desperately.

Whatever the reasons, we split up. After that, some of our friends found their way, one by one, to my tipi in the night. Some of those trysts went no further than hugs and mutual affirmations. Others went breathtakingly deep, to sensuous, mysterious places in cool night air, illuminated, literally and figuratively, by fire. I rushed ahead again like that Fool in the deck, stepping off cliffs and trusting some mystic power to lead me to love. It was a dangerous strategy, but as it turned out, the relationships that I nurtured at Rising Moon have lasted for the rest of my life, through varying degrees of friendship and fire. I found all of the women beautiful and still don't understand completely why I felt a stronger erotic tug toward one than toward another. I'm amazed that we loved each other as hopefully and generously as we did, since we had no template for loving each other at all. We'd grown up indoctrinated in the idea that men pursued and women surrendered—or demurred at risk of rape or of being labeled as frigid or lesbian. We not only had to learn to say yes and no to each other; we had to learn to pursue and initiate relationships, which involved a set of skills and risks that most of us didn't learn in high school. Sometimes we exhausted ourselves.

My parents came to visit that summer and sat around the fire with us, sharing meals and talking. Later Mom told me, "We expected to see a lot more activity. We thought you'd be busy doing things."

I felt guilty as charged, even though Mom was one of the world's hardest workers. Her parents had sent her to help out a dairy farm family at fourteen. After high school, she'd traveled the countryside around Minot, blood-testing chickens for an egg and meat packing company. During the war, she'd built bombers for Boeing in Seattle. For my whole life, she'd worked both for wages and at home. When I was in grade school, she took a midnight shift on a switchboard because it got her started with the railroad. She was always tired and always fighting it, downing coffee and carrying around a nervous, dogged energy that wouldn't let her relax. I never felt that I could keep up with her and at the same time hold my own anxiety in check. As Kathy pointed out in that article she wrote the next September for *Gold Flower,* we worked hard at Rising Moon, but all of our efforts just helped us get by from day to day. We could see what needed to be done for the long haul, but we didn't have the money or the energy to build a house or put up stout fences. I didn't know how to get from our hardscrabble reality to where I wanted us to be.

In the meantime, we made thrifty use of what money we had. We bought tools cheap at farm auctions, where we could sometimes find the old-fashioned kind that we needed. I found a harness that fit Dick. Most of the old harnesses we saw had been made to fit workhorse breeds like Clydesdales, Belgians, and Percherons. As a half-bred heavy, Dick was smaller. I took the dry old harness home, cleaned it, and brought it a good deal back toward life by soaking it in neatsfoot oil, an old-style leather softener made from the shinbones and feet of cattle. I replaced the missing brass rivets using a hammer and anvil, and I polished the buckles and decorations. Dick's new-old bridle had blinders that kept him from seeing what was coming behind him. He didn't panic when I put the collar on him, slipped the harness over his back, hooked the tugs of his harness to a rope tied around a log, and asked him to pull. Because of his disastrous wrecking of the Haidiya Farm wagon, I stayed cautiously behind the load, but when I asked, he stepped smartly and looked excited to have something to do. Soon we used him regularly to haul our firewood.

Dianna and Shirley on Dick at Rising Moon

I tried making a sulky for him out of a two-wheeled trailer that someone had left for junk in the yard at Rising Moon. I cut poplar poles and shaped them into shafts, but I couldn't get the curve in them that I needed. When I asked for Mr. Hestbeck's advice, he said, "Why don't you use that old lowboy sled you've got?"

I was clueless, and he explained that the heavy contraption of wood and iron I'd seen on the edge of our driveway, overgrown with grass and detritus, was actually a simple horse-drawn sled. By the next day, I had the lowboy dug free. I harnessed Dick and hitched him to it, and when I asked, he pulled it loose. When I saw that he didn't shy, I climbed onboard and stood upright on the lowboy. I drove him that way to Mr. Hestbeck's farm to say hello. On the way, an older man I didn't know passed us in a car and gave a broad grin and friendly wave.

When the cool of fall set in, Shirley and I rode Cheyenne and Dick to the vacant farm we'd noticed on a lake between Rising Moon and Mr. Hestbeck's farm. He told us that people named DeMar owned it, and the man's first name was Haven. He said they'd bought it from a family named Munson at an auction a few years earlier. The Munsons raised sheep and ran a campground on the lakeshore, and the farm they'd sold appeared to be just what we needed—a hundred acres of meadows and woods. Some of the pasture fences sagged, but they looked like they could be repaired. The house and barn looked straight and true. Someone had shot at swallows in the haymow, leaving a spray of BB-sized holes in the roof, but the insult appeared fairly recent. Rain hadn't rotted the roof beams or the floor. Two dried-up workhorse harnesses hung on spikes in the loft—most likely just as the Munsons had left them when they switched from a team to a tractor. The place felt like the past and also like our future.

"DeMar means 'of the sea,'" Shirley said, already dreaming ahead, like me. "So we should call this place 'Del Lago.'"

I loved the play on words, and we started looking for Haven DeMar. He was not in the phone book, and none of the people we asked claimed to know anything about him. Across the lake from Del Lago we could see a house owned by someone we did know. His name was Mel—a slight, soft-spoken man who lived and worked in the Twin Cities and had bought the old Wheatcraft farm for a country getaway. He only came in the summer, and we decided to ask if we could winter at his place while we continued our search for the elusive Mr. DeMar.

Besides housing, we had another problem. We needed more hay than we'd earned from Mr. Hestbeck. The hay crop hadn't been good that summer in Aitkin County, and scarcity had driven the price high. We thought we should cut Rising Moon's back mead-ow and put it up as loose hay. We asked Mr. Hestbeck to cut it, but he said our fields hadn't been worked in too long. There were too many rocks and other obstacles that could wreck his equipment. When we asked Harvey, our neighbor across the river, he said he didn't have time to do it himself, but he would loan us an old trac-tor and sickle mower and show us how to use them. I volunteered to drive the rig, since I'd had that little bit of tractor-driving expe-rience while picking up hay bales at Mr. Hestbeck's farm.

On a day in early October, Harvey drove his rig over. I think we always called him by his first name because he was so kind, open, and unassuming. He was handsome and solidly built, with dark hair and one eye that didn't always look in the same direction as the other. When Selenekore and I went with him into the field, he used a hand crank to start the old Minneapolis Moline tractor. He put substantial effort into it and warned us that if we turned the motor off before we were finished, we probably wouldn't be able to start it again.

"There's no brakes," he instructed as the Moline idled loudly. "Just stay in low gear and use the clutch to roll to a stop."

Selenekore took the dogs away for safety's sake, while I climbed up onto the high, steel seat. I made a round of the field while Harvey watched. He said, "You're doing fine," and left to dig his potatoes.

While I looked to see that I was cutting a neat spiral, lining up the next swath just beside the last one so that no grass went uncut,

Blitz appeared in my peripheral vision. She bounded toward me, on the side of the tractor without the mower. That seemed okay, and I didn't want to turn off the tractor and risk not being able to start it again. But then she saw the grass moving, and I saw her leap. Time slowed, and it seemed that I had to stretch much farther than my leg allowed to push in the clutch. I tried at the same time to punch in the power takeoff knob that Harvey had showed me would stop the mower blade, but when I got it all done and climbed down to the ground, I saw that Blitz was crawling on her belly. I'd cut off three of her legs, and her jaw hung by a thread. She must have reached down to defend herself when she felt the bite of the sickle.

I panicked. I didn't want to leave her there alone, but I felt that I needed to get help. I ran screaming for Selenekore. We had no operating car on the land that day, and I couldn't bring myself to kill Blitz or to let her suffer and die slowly. I asked Selenekore to help. She looked as appalled as I felt, but she did as I asked bravely, using tools that we had on hand. Afterward, Selenekore and one of our visitors, a dear friend, helped me bury Blitz between my tipi and the wild black raspberry bushes. I remained in a state of shock, grief, and guilt for days. As Gerda Lerner wrote about her husband's demise from a brain tumor in A Death of One's Own, "Nature is cruel, and dying is cruel, either by being too swift or too slow. The body has to be destroyed, and the will to live has to be destroyed and the two are not the same." I had watched my grandparents' deaths play out from a physical and emotional distance. I'd even been able to distance myself from K/T's death somewhat, since we didn't know for months what had actually happened to her, and Karen was the one who had to identify K/T's belongings. I didn't really know anything about death's cruelty, I learned, until I experienced it firsthand as the responsible party.

Ironically, we got little hay from that field. I questioned my own judgment on many counts, and I wrote my grief, shock, and self-reproach, complete with gory details, into letters to my parents and to Martha and Marea. I hadn't yet learned the importance of going inward to find the resources I needed to buck up my courage. I should have burned the letters instead of sending them, but I didn't. I tried to shake my horror and pain somehow by passing them along, and my correspondents let me know they didn't appreciate it.

In my forties, inspired by recently hearing a recording by Édith Piaf, I told Dad over dinner that regrets were useless, and I tried to live without them. "Do you?" He archly brought me back to Earth. "Blitz was my friend, you know."

I guess I expected to be shielded from life's terrors, to live without being touched by them. It was a young person's naïve expectation, and it came crashing down that October. Thirty-some years later I would teach women's studies classes at a public university and encounter Elizabeth Cady Stanton's warning that none of us can be protected from life's horrific events. "Women can't be shielded from harm," she told the assembled National American Women's Suffrage Association in her famous speech "Solitude of Self." "We experience life's darker events, too, and in those moments, every soul is on its own."

Regret has proved hard to shake, and yet I've rebounded. When I thought back on those days, I remembered feeling deeply depressed for weeks. And then Christine handed me a letter I had written her forty-some years earlier, while Shirley and I were raking that hay we'd cut in the back meadow. Not only was I more resilient than I knew, but our lives at Rising Moon were more nuanced than I could possibly remember. I began the story by mentioning a novel by Mary Renault:

> Today Shirley has been disturbed (and making me disturbed) because of *The Last of the Wine*. She wonders if it is honorable and good to be here in the north woods, living a "personal" life instead of a political life, helping the people who need help by changing the social structure. She wants a teacher as wise as Socrates. She's doubting the role of sexuality, thinking that the honorable way to

deal with that part of one's desires might be to dedicate it to the goddess, as Lysis, in *The Last of the Wine,* dedicated his to the gods.

We talked about all this stuff while making hay today. She would pitch a forkful of hay into Mabel and talk about how much more there must be to life than *this.* Then she'd get in the truck, back her up to the next little hay pile. We'd pitch more of the hay into the truck, and I'd say, "Yeah, but where's higher achievement going to leave you if you don't live a personal life as well?"

And then I'd climb up on top of the hay pile. She would come back and pitch and say that passion sometimes moves us to petty levels rather than heightened levels. And I would pitch and agree but add that I know I need a lover. And that's how we went on for an hour or so, until we had Mabel filled with mashed-down hay.

Then we drove out of the broad back field, toward the house. Kathy was sitting on the ground beside the addition she's putting on the cabin. She waved, and we waved back. Then she called my name, and I noticed something peculiar in the look on her face and in the way she sat, with her legs spread wide. We stopped and found that she had stepped on a nail shortly after we had left for the hayfield. It was still in a board, sticking about a half-inch into her foot. She hadn't been able to get it out herself, because of the difficulty of reaching the board to pull it straight away.

I pulled the nail out and washed her foot. Shirley went down to her tipi and brought back some medicinal, homemade dandelion wine. Then we all sat down and talked.

Shirley said, "To think that you've been sitting here all this time with a nail in your foot while Dianna and I argued philosophy." It did seem absurd.

Soon our philosophies and work at Rising Moon unraveled. Jane and her lover, M'lou, came to Rising Moon from Chicago, where they had been playing music, nurturing a lesbian-separatist philosophy, and studying martial arts at a dojo that mixed yoga and meditation with karate. Our athletic friend Bryan happened to be shopping at the co-op when they arrived. As I recall, they told us afterward that we'd have to follow the rule that the land was for women only, or we'd have to leave. Of course, we argued. We didn't agree with the rule, but we—or at least I—knew it was Jane's decision to make. We had no documents of ownership, no written agreements about residency or use. Jane owned the land, and we needed a house. We had planned to leave anyway, before winter set in, though we had expected to return the next spring.

In hindsight, I'm sure that their memories differ on some counts from mine, and I hold no grudge against any of my friends. As the stories in Joyce Cheney's book *Lesbian Land* attest, disputes were common at lesbian-feminist land collectives. How should power, resources, and ownership be distributed and shared? Should we keep animals? Eat meat? Use modern tools and technologies? What about substance use and abuse? And what about sex? There's no doubt that substance abuse and shifting sexual liaisons upset the balance at various women's lands. Some collectives tried to impose rules about abstinence or monogamy. We did not go there but continued to embrace the idea that, as Lisyli put it later, "we were free and did not own each other."

Otter and Maya had already moved to another old farm on a nearby lake. The rest of us moved to Mel's house. Sierra decided not to join us. Before she left Rising Moon, she said she didn't want to take her red dog, Gorgon, so I said I would adopt her. I saw her as a lost soul, a potential friend, and even a guardian, but never as that mythical beast that turned men to stone. I renamed her Eagle after Sierra left, because when she forgot her worries, she sat with her head held high and her gaze fixed far in the distance. I thought we both needed an eagle's farsightedness, and with it we might be able to help each other get back up off the ground.

17 Mel's Place (Dick Pulls Us Through)

I've often wondered what possessed Mel to say that we could winter at his house. He took a risk for us, even if I didn't think of it as much of a risk at the time. I had too much faith in human nature in those days, too much naïve trust, but I was young. He was not. Did he agree to let us caretake his place because we looked so fresh-faced and well meaning? Was he being a good neighbor? Did we remind him of someone he loved? Did he worry that if he didn't give us shelter, we might freeze to death and weigh on his conscience for the rest of his life? Whatever his reasons, he told us we could move into his house and spend the winter on his land, the whole kit and caboodle: four young dykes, one toddler girl, three dogs, five horses, a pony, cats whose number I can't account for now, and our assorted baggage, both psychological and physical.

Dick pulled my things to Mel's place on the lowboy sled. The rest we took by car. A snow had swept through in late October, but it hadn't muddied the ground too much when it melted, so we were able to drive a trail that skirted the lake through a neighbor's hayfield. The trail was what farmers call a *field road*—unimproved but good enough for farm machinery. As the snow deepened, we planned to park at Mr. Hestbeck's farm and walk to Mel's place, down the township road a quarter-mile and along a half-mile snowmobile trail through a swamp.

Dianna driving Dick on the snowmobile trail from Mel's place with Eagle in 1975

Inside Mel's house, we found a wood heating stove, electricity, a 1940s-era kitchen with knotty pine cupboards, a dining room, a living room, and four bedrooms upstairs that received very few BTUs from the stove. As I recall, Selenekore and Lisyli roomed together, and Shirley and Sara stayed in separate rooms. I took a room of my own with a window that looked out on the meadow and the fringe of woods that separated our place from Rising Moon, where our friend Kathy planned to spend the winter in the poorly heated and drafty shed she would describe in her *Gold Flower* article.

That fall, I answered a help-wanted ad for an Aitkin County Dairy Herd Improvement Association (DHIA) supervisor. I interviewed with four or five dairy farmers on the local DHIA board, and they hired me to do a part-time job that the farmers called "cow testing." The more highfalutin "supervisor" name came from the state DHIA, which was run by professional managers connected to the University of Minnesota. A computer at the St. Paul campus processed the data I recorded and shot production records and suggestions for changes in management practices back to my farmers.

To do the job I needed a car, so I asked Mom and Dad for a loan to buy a red Rambler sedan my friend Nancy had for sale. Dad wrote in the note that came with their check, "I hope you have good luck with it. You never know with used cars."

I was soon learning dairy farm vocabulary and traveling most of Aitkin County to visit farmers on my cow-testing route. DHIA testing was voluntary, and the farmers who participated paid for my services. I traveled to their farms, weighed each cows' milk at an evening milking and again at the following morning milking, took milk samples to be tested for butterfat content, and ear-tagged heifer calves (aka girl babies) so they could accurately be identified as they grew up, became cows, and entered the milking herd. I also recorded data in the farmers' record books, things like the amounts of grain and forage each cow ate, and the dates they calved, got bred, and went dry. A dry cow, I learned, was one that had tapered down her milk production and stopped milking entirely for a while until she calved again.

By the time I started the job, the weather had turned cold, and we needed to get up some kind of fence for our horses before the ground froze. With Mel's okay, we put in an electric fence. The fence charger looked like a round-edged steel case, the size of a shoebox, with terminals for hooking up a ground wire, a battery, and the fence wire. The electric fence looked fragile, but it packed a wallop. We attached the wire to insulators on light steel posts that were only a little bigger around than a pencil, small enough to push into the ground by hand. The horses could have pushed them over easily, except that every second or so, the charger sent a jolt of energy along the wire. Any animal touching it while standing on the ground got a shock. That went for human animals, too.

One evening early in my cow-testing career, I stood in the damp air of the Turnock brothers' milking parlor and told Franklin Turnock, the older, red-haired son of a longtime Aitkin County farming family, how I'd watched Shirley approach Cheyenne while carrying a metal pan full of oats. I started into the story: "She tried to hold it under the electric fence—"

"Who got zapped?" Franklin interrupted with gleeful expectancy. "Shirley or the mare?"

"Both," I said, and we belly-laughed with the kind of relief that comes from knowing that this time, at least, we had not been the ones who took the juice.

I stayed overnight with farmers who paid to be on what we called "official test." Farmers who opted to pay less could take their own samples, fill out their own forms, and be classified as "unofficial," but still have me pick up their milk samples and record sheets and take them to the butterfat-testing lab in Milaca. Some of the farmers were easy to get along with, others not. I found the Turnocks particularly exuberant and cordial. Chester and Lawrence, the original Turnock brothers, and Chester's wife, Evelyn, had built their farm and their Holstein herd from scratch.

The whole family helped with the cattle and the crops, and while they milked, at least when I was there, they passed the time with stories. This was true of many of the farmers on my route.

Sometimes I asked questions or told my own stories. Mostly, I listened and learned—and took in what amounted to a people's history of farming in northeastern Minnesota. I learned that as small boys Chester and Lawrence had picked wild berries on the way to town and traded them for groceries at the store. They were home alone when fire swept through and killed more than 450 people in the countryside between Moose Lake and Cloquet. They survived by running to a neighbor's farm and joining him and his family under wet blankets in the furrows of a plowed field. As the fire approached, Lawrence told me, the neighbor's house ignited. "Just whoosh!" he said. "That's how hot it was."

Farmers depended on nature's generosity and suffered from her cruelties. My own farming experiences stretched my heart in many directions. Before the snow got deep, Marea drove from Haidya Farm to visit. She and Martha had come to a place in their relationship where they needed space from each other. Marea seemed to be looking for whatever would come next, I thought, but that might have been a self-serving observation, since I had decided that while she visited I would tell her about my attraction to her. She arrived before dinner, smelling of wood smoke and patchouli and hungry from the long drive, and my insecurities kicked in. After dinner Shirley invited us up to her room, and we sat on her bed talking. I stayed passive and quiet until the time got late and Shirley teased Marea, "I guess it's about time to turn in. Who are you going to sleep with?"

"Me," I blurted. They both looked at me, and I added a qualifier addressed just to Marea, "I mean, if you want to."

She laughed at me and said that she did. We started a connection that to me felt tentative and tender that night, deeper than friendship and sublime at times for me, though I was never entirely sure what it meant to her. I could see that she struggled to piece the odd ends of her life back together. It may not have been fair or

Women and children from Rising Moon in Aitkin, Minnesota, in 1974

Lisyli modeling "don't eat" cookie dough at Mel's Place, Christmas 1974

wise to ask anything of her, but I yearned for her without realizing how much desire can cost.

Before Christmas, one of Shirley's friends brought her daughter to stay with us for a few days while she took a trip, supposedly "to the southwest." The woman wasn't one of our Lesbian Resource Center gang; she was a heterosexual friend who went back to Shirley's earlier life in Minneapolis. We met her and her daughter at a café. The girl was nearly the same age as Sara—four going on five, still shaped more like a bean than a sprout. She looked like she needed a nap, and her mother appeared completely frazzled. While we ate, she corrected her daughter for fussing, playing with her food, fidgeting in her seat, and more. She harped so that a woman in another booth turned and shot a disapproving look in our direction.

"I hate it when people do that," Shirley's friend said loudly enough for everyone in the place to hear. Her eyes burned like two manic suns churning their solar systems toward a black hole, and I cringed as she added for the stranger's benefit, "People should mind their own business!"

After lunch she left us to start her trip. Her daughter sniffled a little but held up like a champ as we walked down Main Street together and met a man in a Santa suit who stopped us to ask the girls what they wanted for Christmas. In the much more distant background, the Vietnam War still cast its long, divisive shadow, and Phyllis Schlafly was midway through her campaign to stop state legislatures from ratifying the Equal Rights Amendment. We walked with our heads held high in our thrift-store coats and insulated boots, with two little girls in tow, and I tried not to pay attention to the nagging voice of double consciousness that Shirley's friend had kicked off by drawing the attention of that stranger in the café. If the people we passed cared who we were and what we were about, we had to act as if we didn't care what they thought.

We drove the twelve miles from town and parked in Mr. Hestbeck's farmyard. From there, we walked the township road and the snowmobile trail through the swamp to Mel's place. When we got home, Shirley noticed that our guest's hair was dirty and matted, so she heated water on the stove and gave the girl a shampoo and rinse. The two of them and Sara sat beside the table, in the warmth of sunlight, while the girl's hair dried and Shirley brushed out the tangles.

The girl's mother was supposed to come back to get her before Christmas, but we hadn't heard from her by Christmas Eve. We cut evergreen boughs from the woods and hung them around the house. By Christmas Day, we still had no message from her. We gave each other gifts and included the girl—books, toys, drawings, homemade wooden buttons, and other useful, affordable things like socks, mittens, jackknives and horse gear. I made small deerskin pouches with leather drawstrings for everyone. The deerskin had come to me through a stroke of fate. A neighbor had been driving too fast down the middle of a hilly township road. He couldn't get over quickly enough as he crested one of the hills and met my Rambler. The dent from his sideswipe didn't affect how the Rambler functioned. The doors still worked, so I accepted his offer of tanned deerskin in exchange for not reporting the accident. The trade gave me material for my pouches, and I sold a few on consignment at the Amazon Bookstore.

On Christmas Day, Lisyli got out one of the children's books she'd written, *Cookie Art: The Don't Eat Cookie Book,* and made a batch of unsweetened "cookie dough" from the flour, salt, and water recipe in it. We let ourselves be kids with the girls, and we all sculpted horses, dogs, dinosaurs, and whatever whacked-out, silly, and beautiful things came to mind.

The next day Shirley called some friends and got a phone number for her missing friend's parents. She called them and afterward told us that the grandmother had asked her in a frantic-sounding voice, "You have our girl?"

She told Shirley that her friend had been arrested in some Mexican drug bust, and the grandparents hadn't known where their granddaughter was. As soon as Shirley gave them directions to Mel's place, the girl's grandfather and uncle set out from their home a couple of hours' drive to the west. Shirley gathered the girl's things, and we were just finishing lunch when the men crossed the snowy field road in their four-wheel-drive pickup and pounded on our door. They looked around uncomfortably, kept their distance, and turned down our invitation to sit and have something to eat. Shirley had just dampened a cloth to wash the girl's face when her grandfather scooped her into his arms and turned toward the door.

"I was just about to wipe her," Shirley said.

"That's okay," the grandfather said. "Don't bother."

Her uncle grabbed the girl's things, and they left. She still had jam on her face.

Not long after that Harvey, our neighbor, offered Shirley a job helping him run the township snowplow. It was an old road grader, fitted with a V-shaped blade in front and a rectangular wing blade on the side. Harvey was a thoughtful and peaceable man, an environmentalist by philosophy and temperament, a nurturing single father of two girls, a gearhead and shade tree mechanic par excellence, and a native-born steward of his family's land and his herd of Black Angus cattle. He kept generations of junked cars and farm machinery for parts, and it seemed to me that he could fix just about any machine.

Shirley said he told her that because of the way the snowplow's controls were designed, he could do a better job if he had help. Operating the wing blade was tricky. There was a timing to leaving the blade down long enough that you didn't dump snow across the entry to a driveway and also lifting it up soon enough that you didn't take out the mailbox. She jumped on his offer, and when it snowed more than a few inches, she dressed in her heaviest woolens and insulated boots and walked with snowshoes more than a mile across the fields, swamps, and river ice to Harvey's farm.

I had remembered that winter as a snowy one, but I'd forgotten what a huge storm hit on January 15, 1975. I wrote my friend Christine in Madison:

We're snowed in up to our armpits (literally, with some
drifts). Today Selenekore and I broke a trail for the horses
from here to the nearest road, a distance of about half a
mile. . . . Shirley has been gone since Friday. She works
with Harvey (our good neighbor) on the snowplow. . . .
They figured they would plow all night, but the snow got
to blowing so much that they couldn't plow at all. Then
they couldn't plow the next day for the same reason. The
first day they did plow, they got four miles in twelve hours.
They've been getting the snowplow stuck. Yesterday, they
had to dig, by hand and shovel, a hundred-foot-long path
in front of where they had put the plow into the ditch.

The next fall Kathy wrote in *Gold Flower* about that storm: "The
radio says it's the worst blizzard in 35 years. A Chicago radio station
calls it a 'snow hurricane.'" She tells how she struggled for three days
alone in the summer kitchen at Rising Moon to dig out her woodpile
and keep warm. When the storm ended, she put on her snowshoes
and trekked through the deep snow to our place. "As I trudged," she
writes, "National Guard planes flew overhead in search of stranded
survivors." At Mel's place we dug out our woodpiles from four-foot
snowdrifts and cut the logs into fire-sized pieces with the chainsaw
that our forest worker friend Martha had taught us to use. I wrote
Christine: "It's not hard, except that it *is* jarring. Hands get tired."

On more ordinary winter days, Dick and the lowboy sled
hauled hay, groceries, bags of feed, the luggage of our guests, and
other things too heavy to carry in and out on foot. If we didn't
have much to carry, we rode our horses. Mr. Hestbeck told us we
could keep them in the corral beside his barn while we were in
town. When deep snow fell, we broke the trail ourselves on foot,
because Harvey had warned us that struggling through deep snow
could lame a horse. He said his father had always sent the kids out
to break trail for the family's team.

That's how Selenekore and I ended up breaking trail after the
big storm. We took turns in the lead and were exhausted by the

time we'd traveled the half-mile snowmobile trail and returned. When we looked back on our path I thought it looked pathetically insignificant. I wasn't sure that Dick would be able to pull the low-boy sled through it. Before long, though, we heard snowmobilers. They ran the trail and packed the snow into a sidewalk-shaped track that Dick was able to travel just fine. We hated the snowmo-bilers' noise and exhaust, but their tracks made handy sidewalks.

As winter deepened, we received fewer visitors, though a few of our friends came from the city to spend time with us and enjoy the horses, snowshoeing, and the countryside. Meadow came often, shooting photographs and documenting our collective life.

In February, Shirley got the idea that the local radio station needed a women's music program. She talked to the station man-ager, and he told her there weren't enough female musicians to make it worthwhile. She told him he'd be surprised, so he asked her to cut him a demo tape. He said he'd consider letting her have a show if he liked what he heard. So we used my cassette recorder and LPs that we had, and we put together a tape that included commercially produced artists Linda Ronstadt, Joni Mitchell, Grace Slick, Joan Baez, Judy Collins, Aretha Franklin, and Bonnie Raitt, plus some of the women we'd found through the women's music movement, like Casse Culver, Alix Dobkin, and Meg Chris-tian. Shirley left her tape with the station manager. He didn't get back to her, so we waited a while, and then she phoned him. He told her he really didn't think it would work out. He couldn't say exactly why.

Lisyli and Selenekore were still working as housekeepers at an Aitkin motel. After the blizzard, something slipped out of place in one of Lisyli's elbows, and she could hardly use the arm. Going to the doctor would have meant spending money that was hard to come by, so she worked around her injury for a while. One day she went out to feed Snow and her pony, Llyprynod. Dick horned in and swung his big head, trying to out-alpha the other two horses, but he caught Lisyli's arm on his blind side. She felt a stab of pain and then relief. Old Lurk-in-the-Ditch had knocked something back into place for a change, and she was able to go back to work without pain.

Besides his accidental cure of Lisyli, Dick earned his keep hauling for us that winter. I loved driving him. I stood upright or squatted on the lowboy sled and felt like a circus performer flying along behind him. I had to mind my center of gravity and keep my body flexed to absorb the jerks and jolts of the snowpacked trail. As the snow deepened and the plow drift left at the end of our trail grew higher, I trained Dick to pick up speed as we approached. When he plunged down the other side and made his right-hand turn, the sled literally flew through the air. Somehow I always managed to stay on my feet, and the derring-do thrilled me.

Looking back, I see that I was lucky to have survived my horse-drawn acrobatics, let alone to have made it through unscathed, and I'm grateful. Unlike those who claim "the harder I work, the luckier I get," I've seen that there's plenty of luck to go around. Some of it's bad, and we can't always tell the bad stuff from the good until we get farther down the road.

Every day at Mel's I looked across the frozen lake toward the white house, the gambrel-roofed barn, and the pasture fences of Del Lago. The old farm looked like a palatial estate to me, and every day I visualized living there. Unfortunately, we still hadn't been able to find the elusive Mr. and Mrs. DeMar. They weren't in the listings for any of the nearby towns in our phone book. The plat book that the DHIA board gave me to find my way around Aitkin County was so old that it still listed Del Lago's owners as the Munsons. If I had been more sophisticated about real estate, I could have solved our mystery by making a trip to the court-house and asking someone at the county recorder's office to tell us who owned the land. At the time, though, I had no idea how such things worked.

And then Shirley came home from snowplowing one day and said that she'd asked Harvey about Haven DeMar. She said he'd grinned and told her, "It's Damar. Rhymes with hammer. It's Danish."

So we learned from Harvey that Haven Damar drove a mail truck between Aitkin and the Twin Cities, and he did custom butchering on other people's farms. His customers liked him because he spared their animals the stress of traveling to a slaughterhouse, and he was a fine marksman, quick, clean, and never cruel. Harvey said that Haven and his wife, Verna, also kept bees and extracted honey at their home place on the east side of the walleye-fishing lake Mille Lacs. He thought we ought to be able to find them in the Malmo listings of our Aitkin phone book, and sure enough we did. Harvey warned us that they were Swedish Baptists and might be a little conservative, but we knew we had to write the Damars, if only to find out what they'd say.

18 Del Lago

Shirley wrote to the mysterious Mr. and Mrs. DeMar who, as we had learned from Harvey, were actually the not-so-mysterious Damars. She used the address that we found in the phonebook. (It helped to look under "Da" instead of "De.") In a few days, we got a reply from Verna, written in a careful hand. She didn't shut down our caretaking idea immediately, as I'd feared she might. Instead, she said they would meet us at the farm across the lake from Mel's place. As we drove it in Mabel on our way to meet them, the driveway was about a quarter-mile long, running from the township road straight between two hayfields. I was struck once again by the beauty of the old farm—the green shoots amid the dry stubble of last year's grass, the red barn, the hilly pasture sloping to the lake, and the square white house where the Munson family had lived lives that depended on the various parts of their farm.

Haven and Verna appeared to be about my parents' age—early fifties, roughly. That seemed pretty old to me at the time, yet both of them looked fit and energetic, with pale, Nordic skin and light blond hair just beginning to go silver. Haven stood upright and most of the time looked confident and composed. He had a tendency to squint, which I took at first as a look of disapproval. My defensive young dyke self went on guard, but then I began to notice that he and Verna seemed to like us. She interacted in a kind way that made her feel approachable but not easy or too soft. As we talked, I heard them rue the scattershot holes that vandals had blasted in the roof of their barn, and I felt as outraged on their behalf as I had that day I came to the farm uninvited and climbed into the haymow. I'd already noticed the rows of red pine seedlings they had planted to ring the farmyard and make a windbreak for the future. As she showed them to us, Verna said, "You'll have to be careful. We've got a lot of work into them. We carried water by hand for the whole first year."

They told us that when they bought the farm they'd hoped to live on it in their retirement. Now Verna had developed "some health problems" (I knew the vagueness of that phrase signaled not to ask too many questions), and they hoped to hand the farm down to their son, though they weren't at all sure that he would come back from the southeast. They said he'd been stationed there in the military. He liked the warm weather, and if he did come back, he had plans for redoing the lakeshore and the house. I thought he was the luckiest man in the world to have a place like Del Lago waiting for him. All he had to do was say yes, but instead he said maybe. I didn't get it.

As it happened, we got lucky, too. The Damars agreed to let us stay on the farm in exchange for taking care of it, keeping vandals at bay with our presence, and paying our own utility bills. That included LP gas for the kitchen stove and electricity for the well, hot water heater, and lights. We were about to rejoin the second half of the twentieth century, even though we still planned to heat with wood, like many of our rural neighbors. Haven checked the chimney for chinks and obstructions. He showed us how to use a small mirror to look up the lining and see the whole interior. It seemed to me that the Damars liked their chances with us, and I intended not to disappoint them.

To prepare for bringing our horses to Del Lago, Shirley and I borrowed a fence stretcher from Mr. Hestbeck. One of his hayfields bordered Del Lago's back pasture, and he showed us how to use the fence stretcher's clamps and rope-operated pulleys to pull two ends of a broken wire together so we could repair it. Where we needed new posts, we dug holes with a shovel and post-hole digger and put them in. The pasture was beautiful and large enough for our needs—about thirty acres, I estimated, with plenty of grass and a section that bordered the lake. The horses could go down to the shore and drink whenever they wanted. We opened a new account with the electric co-op and paid our deposit so that we could get power, then we wrote the Damars and told them that we were ready to move in.

Verna wrote back that they would meet us at the farm to get the water pump going. For some reason I went by myself that day. Haven got out of his pickup and unloaded a few tools and a jug of water that he'd brought. He went down into the basement with wrenches and tried to prime the pump, but he gave up after a few tries. "The screen must be plugged," he said in a disappointed tone.

"Where's the screen?" I asked, feeling too curious to keep quiet, even at the risk of annoying him. The competing messages from my feminine upbringing and my feminist consciousness kicked in. The former said to keep quiet and out of his way, and the latter said to speak up and help if I could.

"The screen is at the bottom of the casing," Haven said patiently. His demeanor stayed even, and I was beginning to see him as a no-nonsense guy who was trying to get a job done and had the right to feel frustrated when things didn't go right. He sighed, "I guess I'm going to have to pull the pipe."

Verna and I followed him upstairs and watched him march silently to the pickup, get out a pointy-nosed shovel, and walk toward the house. He selected a spot roughly parallel to the place in the basement where the pump was located, and he started digging. The soil was sandy. He made good progress and soon exposed the galvanized pipe that led from the house. Using two big wrenches, he disconnected that horizontal pipe from the one that ran vertically into the well. He began to lift the vertical pipe, hand over hand, from the well casing.

After he had ten or twelve feet of galvanized pipe balanced

precariously over his head, he said, "I'm going to need some help here."

"Oh, Haven!" Verna chided. "I'm not a man!"

I wasn't sure how I was supposed to jump in after that without violating the male and female gender roles that Verna had just reinforced so passionately.

I said, "I'm not a man, either, but I think I can help."

"Okay," Haven responded gratefully. "Hold this while I get a new grip."

I held the pipe at about waist height. It wasn't easy, even though he did the heavier lifting, hoisting five or six feet of pipe at a time. After each hoist, I needed to square myself and readjust my stance so that I could balance and hold the increased weight above my head. Thankfully, the well was shallow. We soon had the whole pipe clear of the casing and lying on the ground.

What Haven did next surprised me. He got a hunting rifle from the cab of his truck. He said there was a metal screen at the bottom of the casing, and if he shot into the well, the water's density would stop the bullet, but the reverberations from it should shake loose the rust and residue from the screen. He aimed and fired. The air smelled of smoke and sulphur. He fired again, and said, "Well, I hope that did it."

After he put the rifle away, we lifted the pipe and reversed what we'd done before. He reconnected the pipes, went back down the basement, primed the pump, and started it. This time we heard gurgling water and air, and then the water flowed. For decades, I've wondered if the water in that well really did have enough mass to stop a bullet or if he had actually shot two holes in the screen. Recently, a quick Internet search told me that a few feet of water can indeed stop a high-powered bullet, so either it's an Internet myth or Haven's plan worked.

We had plenty of water as long as we lived at Del Lago, and after Haven started the hot water heater, I was able to wash my hair under a faucet for the first time in more than a year. It felt wonderful, and ever since, my idea of utopia has included hot running water. In April, we didn't have a television and were spared the video images of would-be refugees grabbing for the landing gear of helicopters evacuating the U.S. embassy in Saigon.

Around this time, Shirley saw a handwritten ad on a bulletin board at one of the Minneapolis co-ops. Someone wanted to sell two part-bred Arabian mares near a town way up north called Gheen. We wrote the woman, and she invited us to come and take a look. When we got there, I thought she seemed like our kind of horse-crazy woman. She was lanky and blond in jeans and a hippie-style tunic, and she talked of horse dreams and plans to live in a tipi in Missouri. Shirley fell in love with Miaheyyun, a ten-year-old stout gray mare. I liked Taja, a spirited six-year-old that our new friend called the Red One. Shirley worked out a trade that involved her tipi poles for Miaheyyun, and I paid $225 cash for Taja. After that, the woman and I corresponded for years, and she shared with me that after selling the mares she'd had nightmares of panicked, running horses. She wrote how glad she was that Taja had found her way to someone who appreciated her fire.

Shortly after she delivered Taja and Miaheyyun to us, we rode them to Mr. Hestbeck's farm. He came outside, looked them over, and went on a long while about Taja's coat, conformation, and energy. Then he said of Miaheyyun, "Why, she's just an old gray mare!"

Shirley took offense, and I did, too, for Shirley's pride and for the sake of her honest and gentle mare. Inwardly, though, I congratulated myself for choosing a horse that could carry me into the future. Dick was still healthy, but I had ambitions of raising part-bred Arabians and selling some of them to earn income on the farm. A gelding was not breeding stock, and I now had a gorgeous new mare that could produce foals. The Red One's coat looked a lot like Dick's rusty orange sorrel, but age had dulled his luster, while she had the iridescent sheen of youth. On the downside she could be flighty. If she saw a bag or a branch, she leapt sideways, but she had no meanness in her. She never took advantage or tried to dump me after she got me off balance, as Dick had done in his Lurk-in-the-Ditch days. She always gave me time to rearrange myself, and I came to trust her without doubt.

We trotted the township roads regularly with Eagle at our side, and after a few months Harvey told me about someone he knew who wanted to give away a part-bred, black Lab puppy. I went and looked. She was twelve weeks old. Her breath no longer smelled like milk, but she gave generous kisses and felt like an old friend. I named her Onyx. She grew fast and ran along on our rides when she got older.

Shirley and I settled into an uneven friendship that spawned warm and philosophical conversations at times and at other times devolved into fights that stubbed out whatever was left of the intermittent, sparky, friends-as-lovers type of moments that had arced between us in the past. We butted heads over where to put the garden, how to design stalls and a goat-milking stand in the

Molly at Del Lago in 1976

barn, and anything that involved decision making and control. At least, that's how I saw it, and I imagined she felt the same way about me. When I had the money and could get away, I went to Minneapolis, where my friends and I visited the bars, the LRC, the newly opened Women's Coffeehouse, and the Amazon Bookstore. I continued to earn a little pocket money there, selling my leather goods on consignment.

Women from the Cities visited us often, especially Molly, Nancy, and Kathy, our friends from Rising Moon and Minneapolis. I felt especially warm toward Nancy, since she had visited me in my tipi, and we discovered a comfortable connection that we kept on exploring without committing to anything long-term or monogamous at first. She was a cute, blond, butchy girl, younger than I, sweet, and game for work or play. I continued my long-distance relationship with Marea, too, by letters, poems, drawings, and phone calls. She and Martha had separated. Martha had taken a different lover who would eventually become her legal spouse, and from a distance I felt that Marea's life had become chaotic. She took a job as a waitress at a small-town truck stop. We made plans to meet there and drive together to an Arabian horse show in Madison, where two horse trainers she admired, a husband and wife, were scheduled to give a clinic on training problem horses.

Christine still lived in Madison, and she said we could pitch our tent in the yard outside her house. In our private space, we made love, and once again I fell under the sway of old primordial Eros. In the morning Christine made us eggs, and we caught up on news and said our good-byes before she left for work and we packed up and headed for the horse show. From reading Marea's Arabian horse magazines, I should have known what to expect, but I wasn't really prepared for the flashy display of wealth and privilege: the new trucks and multi-horse trailers, the pricey horse flesh, and the grooming, polishing, and costuming of both horses and handlers. The expensive gear for sale in the hallways around the arena made me start to question whether my horse dreams could really be practical on my low income, though fully realizing this second part turned out to require a lot more thinking and a drawn-out period of trial and error.

The trainers who gave the workshop, John and Sally O'Hare, amazed me with their practical know-how. First Sally, then John demonstrated how to press a leg against a horse's flank, shift your weight in the saddle, give a quick swat of the quirt, and adjust a grip on the reins so that a horse bumped gently against its bit, collected its body, and felt compelled to comply with the rider's cues. What they demonstrated was control, and I might have objected to it on some moral grounds, except that I could see that their kind of control was rooted in calm will and clear communication, not in anger, supremacy, or brute force as we saw in some of the books by self-styled "cowboys" who advised people to "break" horses by hog-tying them and other harsh methods. The O'Hares taught me that human psychology lay at the root of most horses' problems. I saw that if I wanted to train horses, I had to be willing and able to exert my will in a calm and confident way. I also needed to understand horses, but I thought I had a pretty good beginner's grip on that.

"I'd swear sometimes that horses are psychic," said Sally O'Hare. "Sometimes you get the feeling they're reading your mind."

Marea and I exchanged glances then, and I felt an electrical charge spark between us. I thought that we had just heard a deep, mutually held truth confirmed, and the look was as much about our simpatico spirits as it was about our shared understanding of horses. But the weekend was soon over. Marea was back to her waitressing job, and I was back at Del Lago.

Before long, Shirley announced that she, Sara, and Molly were moving to an old farm they'd rented in the woods between Duluth and Two Harbors. I wasn't sure if Shirley and Molly had become lovers, but I thought I'd picked up cues that they had. Shirley and I argued over every detail of their leaving, and in the end we were glad to be rid of each other for a while. The world hadn't stopped turning over for me, though. Marea wrote that she planned to go to farrier's school in Oregon to learn the trade of trimming horses' hooves and shoeing them. I felt abandoned in so many directions that it was all I could do to try and keep up a courageous front. Molly said forty years later: "You stayed so calm. You were determined to do what you wanted."

Did I? Was I? Inwardly, I didn't feel calm at all. My idea of utopia had been a women's collective farm. I'd never imagined spending a winter alone at Del Lago. By this time I had four horses and a flock of chickens. In addition to Dick, Taja, and Breeze, I'd bought Lola's filly, Lhasa, from Martha and Marea. So much could go wrong with the animals, the woodstove, my old car, the weather, and just about any variable I imagined! I thought about selling all of them and moving back to the city, but then I got a second job as an activities aide at an Aitkin nursing home. I used some of the money I earned there to buy leatherworking tools and heavy cowhides for making belts and horse gear, hoping there'd be more profit in selling them than in pouches. I cut my firewood by hand with what we called a Swede saw, foraging windfall trees along the sides of the roads.

One day Breeze came up from the pasture with a dozen porcupine quills in her snout. I tried to pull them with pliers, but she threw her head so violently that I was afraid she would smack me and do some serious damage. I didn't think I had the money to pay a vet, so I called our patient and helpful neighbor Harvey. He came and helped me tie her head in the crotch of a double-trunked elm growing near the house. She couldn't thrash around then without breaking her neck, and we were able to pull out the quills with locking pliers.

To celebrate, I invited Harvey and his family for a supper of chicken and dumplings. We sat around my table and filled our bellies with comfort food while he recounted stories of former neighbors and Glory Township in the 1940s and '50s. "There were families on every forty- and eighty-acre place when I was growing up," he told me. "We had footpaths beat between them from visiting back and forth. Everyone knew everyone."

"What happened to them all?" I asked him.

"Eisenhower," he said. "And his damned price cuts."

Of course, he knew the politics of farming were even more complicated than that, but he also taught me that in farming as well as in feminism the political was personal. What had happened, he explained, was that the Eisenhower administration ditched Franklin Roosevelt's New Deal farm price supports for a flexible program that let prices fall low enough that most farmers could no longer afford to make a living on the marginally productive land around us. The empty farms that provided cheap homes when we came along were there when we needed them because so many farm families had given up and left. I started to realize that while we thought we were doing something new, we were really just living out the latest chapter in the long story of dispossessed people yearning to go back to the land.

That fall Harvey asked for my help. He planned to build a two-story house for his family on the hill overlooking the river, not far from the trailer house where he lived with his mother and two daughters. The girls were about ten and twelve at the time.

Jane haying with Minnie and Pearl at Rising Moon in the late 1970s

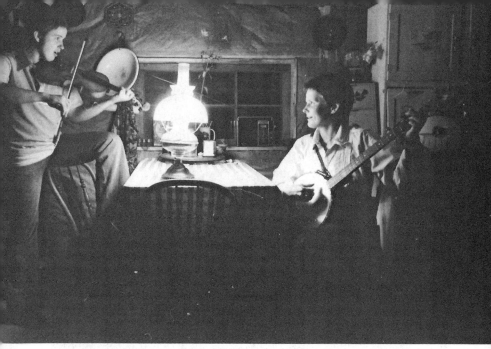

Jane (left) and M'lou play music by lamplight in the house they built at Rising Moon

They all needed more space, and he was anxious to complete his dream house. He had been selecting trees, cutting them, and letting the logs dry for the past couple of years. Not long before, he had sent the logs to a sawmill down near Malmo. Now the sawyer had called and told him it was time to saw. Harvey said he needed someone to help him load the lumber as it came from the mill.

When we got to the sawyer's house, his wife invited us in for coffee. The wiry white-haired sawyer spoke with a Finnish accent. He poured his coffee from his cup into his saucer before drinking it—a custom from the old country, he said. When we went to work, he and his son ran the logs through the mill. The blades whined and buzzed, and the smell of hot pine and oak filled the air. Harvey loaded the freshly cut lumber onto a flatbed truck, and I threw the lighter slab wood that came from the bark edges of the logs into the bed of his pickup. I came home weary but glad to have been of some service to Harvey for a change, after he had done so much for me.

That fall the Damars invited me to their farm, and when they sent directions, I was surprised to see that I regularly passed just a mile or so from them on my cow-testing route. Haven showed me their bee boxes and honey-extracting equipment while Verna set a table for us in the house. She served us homemade whole-wheat bread and homegrown honey. She said the health problem she'd been diagnosed with was an autoimmune disease, and people had told her that raw honey from her local area might help reduce her body's tendency to inflame. At the time I had little need of reducing inflammation (though that would change), but I appreciated both the home cooking and the company.

Once the snows started, I could barely keep up with my firewood needs. I looked for fallen dead trees and branches on the edges of woods near roads. I got permission from landowners, cut the wood by hand with my Swede saw, carried it across ditches, and hauled it home in my Rambler. One day, Jane and M'lou came by and said that they wanted to buy me a chainsaw. We'd visited back and forth since they'd moved to Rising Moon. They had built themselves a home over the foundation of the old log barn. They farmed there with a cow and a team of horses.

I harbored no anger against them, just some regret over the loss of the collective dream of Rising Moon. I admired how hard they worked. Jane told me recently that they lived at Rising Moon five years without incurring any utility bills or payments of any kind. Back in 1976, she told me they had a new project. She said they had created a fund to make small gifts to help women's dreams come true. That's why, she said, they had decided to buy me the chainsaw. After getting past my surprise, I accepted and found a small Swedish-made saw that fit my ability. Suddenly, I could cut a week's supply of wood in the time it had taken me earlier to cut a one-day supply. One of my DHIA farmers offered me all I could use of some tops and branches that had already aged after he'd logged a stand of oak, and a bunch of my friends came up for a weekend and helped me cut and haul the wood.

When Christmas Eve came, Harvey invited me to spend it

with his family, so I made a wreath of balsam, looped it over my saddle horn, and rode Taja three miles or so on the roundabout township roads to their house. Besides the wreath, I gave them some cookies that I'd baked. Harvey's oldest daughter gave me two of her original pastel drawings of horses. One she identified as an Arabian mare named Flaia, the daughter of Raffles, a renowned progenitor of Arabian horses in America. In the border she drew around the other drawing she wrote, "Lossa." Forty and more years later, I see that what she gave me was the gift of timeless-ness: a turquoise sky, an Earth of emerald grass, and an elegant, long-necked version of my Lhasa, still young and resplendent in her russet coat and unruly coal-black mane.

19 Thundering Ice, Talking Spirits

That solitary winter at Del Lago I had plenty to do—the so-called men's work of the farm as well as the women's work. I fed animals, exercised horses, shoveled snow by hand, cut and split wood, washed my clothes at a laundromat in town, bought and cooked my own food, took care of the house and barn, and showed up on a regular schedule for my cow-testing duties and my new part-time activities aide job. In the evenings, I wrote letters, played guitar, listened to music, read, and watched TV. The old house had an antenna on the roof, and with it I was able to get two channels on an old portable black-and-white set that my parents gave me. When night came, exhaustion usually made a good pillow (to paraphrase Laura Ingalls Wilder), but some nights I lay awake, feeling abandoned and full of self-reproach. You can't be a utopian without being a perfectionist, and my mistakes haunted me. I wondered whether I really had what it took to become the farmer, friend, and lover I wanted so much to be.

Some nights I heard the lake ice crack like thunder as it expanded in the subfreezing temperatures. One day I realized that I had left my supply of calves' ear tags across the lake, in the cellar under Mel's house. I needed those tags for my cow-testing job, but there was no way I could drive over there to retrieve them. The snow lay too deep across the field road. To walk around the lakeshore on snowshoes would take hours, I figured, with time added for falling through the crust, tiring from the effort, and slowing down. On the lake I could see patches of nearly clear ice where wind had scoured the surface, so I decided that's where I needed to cross. The ice had set for weeks in extreme cold, and I felt certain it would support me—almost certain, that is, except that throughout my life I've always retained at least a little bit of doubt. There could have been a spring, or some other current under the ice, weakening it.

With no one at home to watch out for me, or even to notice if I went missing, I prepared as if my life depended on it. I found a long pole to carry, and I put a few six-inch nails in my pockets. My plan was to keep a tight grip on the pole so that if I did fall through, the pole would reach across the hole I fell through and keep me from slipping entirely under. Then I would use the nails as spikes, driving them into the ice with my hands and using them to pull myself out. It all seemed reasonable, except I had heard that in such cold a person's clothes would freeze solid almost as soon as she emerged from the water. I decided that if I had to, I could strip and run for home, and the effort might warm me enough to keep going.

So I had a plan. If I remembered right, Mel's house had an old-fashioned external cellar door that hooked from the outside. I decided to trust my memory on that particular point, and I set off across the ice on a clear, cold afternoon. Despite all the mental drama, everything went as planned. I got there safely, unlocked the cellar without any trouble, found the ear tags where I thought I'd left them, refastened the cellar door, and as far as I know, Mel never knew I had been there.

A couple of weeks later I heard a car pull into the driveway late one Saturday night, and when I went to the window I saw a man I didn't recognize emerging from a pickup. I watched him walk purposefully toward the house, and everything about the situation felt wrong. Onyx and Eagle flew into the entryway, barking and carrying on like fierce protectors. When he banged on the door, I looked around for some defensive weapon other than claws and fangs, but I found nothing close at hand.

"Who is it?" I asked through the door, feeling my pulse pounding from my temples to my solar plexus.

He told me his name, and I knew that he was a neighbor I'd met once, the husband of the woman who had picked up Sara and her half-sister on the road near Mr. Hestbeck's farm.

"What do you want?" I asked through the closed door.

"It's so cold," he said. "I thought maybe we could get warmed up together."

I never locked my door, but I threw the bolt then and was glad to hear it latch with a clunk.

"Are you locking me out?" he asked with what sounded like genuine befuddlement.

Mrs. O's story about the neighbors who had pegged us as "prostitutes or worse" came to mind, and I tried to think of what to do next. After what seemed like a long time but probably amounted to no more than a few seconds, I said, "Why don't you go home and come back to visit in the daytime with your wife?"

I hoped that mentioning *daytime* and *wife* might break through the fog of his misperception. I had no idea whether it was the right thing to say, but it worked. I heard his footfalls down the steps. His starter motor engaged the engine, and the sound of his car grew gradually fainter until I saw his headlights through the porch window as he headed down the long driveway. The fear hit me hardest then. He left me shaking. Would he come back? Would he take no for an answer a second time, or might he bring some tools to force his way in? I put a hammer and axe in the entryway, just in case, and spent some fitful hours on the couch longing for the company of people who knew me and cared about me. I never did change out of my clothes that night. I listened for his car engine and questioned my decision to stay alone at Del Lago. He hadn't touched me physically. In that I knew I'd been lucky, but he had pierced my solitude and made it feel like isolation.

The next day I felt calmer, but when the sky darkened in the late afternoon I felt apprehensive again. After that night and several more passed without a return visit, I started to feel upheld by an inner courage that let me believe and trust that I could still be okay alone. I still had support from a long-distance network of family and friends. I had a phone at Del Lago, and I let myself splurge on long-distance calls for a while. Mostly I relied on letters exchanged with my mother, Martha, and Marea. Marea disappointed me by writing about exploits with her male farrier school classmates. I would have waited for her, but she didn't seem to want me. I knew I couldn't expect her to change, and she was not the only woman I found attractive. I thought there must be someone I could love who would love me mutually.

Soon Nancy visited from Minneapolis, and we rekindled the romance we'd started in my tipi at Rising Moon. She was a few years younger than I, and I found her earnest, hardworking, and very attractive—both pretty and handsome. She was a Nordic boy/girl with short blond hair and luminous blue eyes. When we fit our bodies together, she felt comfortable and safe. She knew how to fix things that most women left up to men to fix, and she wanted to live in the country. Eventually, we decided that she should move in with me at Del Lago. She came in the early summer, with a pickup truck and a collection of tools.

I quit my nursing home job, and Nancy and I both took jobs as gas station attendants for a horseman who managed the Fasgas station in Aitkin. We could wear our everyday clothes, and he accepted us as we were. There were few professional boundaries to navigate—only the expectations that we would provide good service and the till would balance at the end of the day. Gas stations were all full service then. We actually pumped the gas, selling two dollars' worth at a time, or five, ten, or a fill—whatever the customer wanted. We also cleaned the windshields and asked the customers if they wanted us to check the oil and the air in the tires.

In a local advertiser I saw an ad for stallion services, and since Lhasa, Breeze, and Taja were all of breeding age, I drove to a farm near Ogilvie to check out the stud. A heterosexual couple around my age owned him; Marl and Fred raised and trained part-bred Arabians. They returned my visit, and when they saw Breeze they were smitten. She looked sound and beautiful at two, with a strong, square build and a black coat graying across the back and haunches. They wanted to buy her and breed her to their stallion, and I decided to let her go. She was a slower learner than Lhasa, and I thought that two mares, Lhasa and Taja, would be enough for me.

Marl asked if I knew of a gentle, well-trained older horse for a friend of theirs, an adult woman who was just learning to ride. I thought right away of Dick. Since I had bought Taja, I'd ridden him less and less, so I told Marl about him—both his good points and his Lurk-in-the-Ditch ones. She asked to ride him, so I saddled him and gave her a leg up. When she rocked back in the seat, held him gently with the bit, and pressed her legs together, he backed up just as I'd trained him to do.

"I'm impressed," she said, not to me but to him. "Let's see what else you know." She moved him sideways in one direction and then the other in a maneuver called a side pass. Next she took him down the driveway, came back in a fast, smooth Tennessee Walker gait, and said, "I'm sure she'll want him. I'll talk to her."

Soon I helped load one old friend and then another into Marl and Fred's two-horse trailer. As I watched my horses' rumps disappear down the driveway, I felt sad but mostly resolved. I knew I'd done right by them while I had them, and I'd placed them with people who could care for them. Afterward, I had more money to buy feed for Lhasa and Taja.

Nancy and I planted a garden at the top of the hill. The sandy soil dug easily, and rainwater drained from it fast. As summer went on, the rains stopped and a drought set in. I picked up some garden hose at a farm auction and felt glad to have running water so that I didn't have to carry buckets up from the lake for the garden. Our hot-weather tomatoes and eggplant thrived, but not our cold-hardy chard or lettuce. By August, wildfires were breaking out all over northern Minnesota. I watched a towering column of smoke rise over the woods to the north of us one day and set out in the Rambler to find the fire. I followed the ominous cloud for a long time but gave up five miles from home when the fire didn't look any closer than it had looked when I started. Wherever it was, it must have been huge.

We heard that the DNR was hiring firefighters, so we went to the station on the edge of Aitkin and applied. The ranger put us on a peat fire crew with a muscular young man and an older guy who looked like he could have been Olive Oil's male doppelgänger. The older man told us what to do. He led the way to the fire in a pickup with the young man beside him, and we followed in the Rambler. We could smell the fire from miles away, musty and organic, like a smoldering combo of dung and rotten wood.

Our crew chief drove past the smoke and pulled over beside a small lake, where he directed the young man to lift a pump out of the truck and set it on the shore. He told all three of us to start stringing fire hose from the pump to the peat bog. The hoses came in fifty-foot lengths, with connecting ends about four inches in diameter. We strung out probably four to five hundred feet of hose before we reached the fire, and then the older guy put a splitter on the end and added two more hoses, each with a two-foot-long nozzle on its discharge end. He took the young man back with him and got the water pumping from the lake. For the rest of the day Nancy and I moved around the fire with our hoses, sticking the nozzles into the burning peat, and standing by while water poured in.

"Peat fires run deep," the crew chief told us. "Sometimes you think you've got 'em, and they flame back up. You've got to flood 'em out."

Firefighting left Nancy and me exhausted. We came home smudged and stinking of smoke, but at least we stank together. We cleaned ourselves with sponge baths, washed our hair under the kitchen faucet, and I felt grateful for our hot, running water and paychecks.

The letters from Marea kept coming, with stories of boy-friends, shoeing horses, and partying with other farriers-to-be. I didn't hide how I felt about Marea from Nancy. I told her that I loved Marea but she wanted to be with men. I could tell from Nancy's face that she felt warned, but she wanted to be with me. She could be a little rough around some of her edges and didn't always pay attention to the same details I did, but she was real and soulful and capable, and I wanted to be with her. We exchanged rings. We couldn't have a legal marriage, but we had a marriage of mutual agreement. When she bought a few acres of land up near Duluth, she put my name on the title.

Winter snows ended our firefighting work, and as winter deepened Nancy started talking about how much she wanted a baby. I had never wanted to have sex with a man, get pregnant, or give birth, but I loved kids, and I'd always kept open the possibility of adopting a child someday. I decided that if Nancy wanted to have a baby, I could raise a child with her. She made an arrangement with one of our male friends, and after their date night we waited to see if she was pregnant. As it turned out, our baby didn't materialize. If a baby had been coming, I might have done things differently, but before we could try again, the thaw started. One night I woke from a dream that I was in the woods and branches were snapping all around me. I realized that someone was knocking at the door, and as I tried to disentangle myself from our bedding, I remembered that I'd read in one of Carlos Castaneda's books that his shaman told him dreams of breaking branches mean spirits are present.

I hurried to the door. "Who is it?" I demanded gruffly.

I heard the rain spilling off the roof in a gush, and a smoky, tentative voice said, "It's Marea."

"Who is it?" Nancy yelled from the bedroom.

"Marea," I answered.

"Oh, shit!" Nancy said.

Marea's soaked hair was plastered against her head. She shook the water from it and said, "My car just died in your driveway."

I saw the old green sedan shedding rain by the barn—a rounded, steel-bodied, early-1950s model something. The next day,
after Harvey checked it out, he delivered the official post mor-
tem. The car was indeed dead. The motor had run dry and seized.
Even a shade tree mechanic as talented as he was could not revive
it unless Marea wanted to spring for a new motor. So the three
of us coexisted for a few days. We put her in one of the upstairs
bedrooms, and I don't remember what got said or done. I don't
remember fighting with Nancy, but I do remember finding ways
to spend time with Marea whenever I could. I don't think Marea
intended to break us up or even to get together with me. I was in
love with her and wanted to be with her, but at the same time I
felt bound by my promises to Nancy. We had just enough time to
make a tangle of it all before I drove Marea to Wisconsin and came
back to the big mess I'd made of my formerly peaceful relationship with Nancy.

Throughout my life, I've thought of that rainy night, especially
two decades later, when I left Cedar, my partner of nearly ten
years, to be with the woman I have stayed with more than twenty-
two years now and married, legally, in Canada before we could do
it here. When my mother heard that I was leaving Cedar, she said,
"You're not very loyal, are you?"

I understood from the context that she meant *faithful*. I felt
upbraided, brought up on a serious charge. My mother and father didn't always get along. The sticking points between them
sharpened as they aged, but as far as I could tell they were loyal
and true to their vows. Most times, I could see that they enjoyed
each other's company. There was something solid and comfort-
ing in knowing that they would stay together, but there was also
something disturbing in the ways they acted out their frustrations
through picky little fights, pointed withdrawals, and sighs of despair. What about loyalty to the self? Was it wrong to want a solid
relationship without the anguish? That's what I'd been hoping
to arrive at with Nancy, and we might have got there, except for
the hazy territory between erotic desire and domestic life. In the

aftermath of the prophetic dream, when I heard Marea's voice through the kitchen door and felt my body respond with a rush of blood and hormones, I knew that everything I'd planned with Nancy had just gone up for grabs.

And then came the two big coincidences, or fated events, depending on how you choose to interpret such phenomena. Not long after I got back from Wisconsin, I went to buy dog food at Ziske's Feed Store in Aitkin, and I saw a familiar-looking woman with long dark hair. She was dressed in jeans, a casual jacket, and work boots, and she turned out to be Sadie Smith, the woman from our consciousness-raising group at Louisa May Alcott House who never trusted a woman without a knife. "Are you living at a place called Rising Moon?" she asked.

"Not anymore," I said, "but I used to. Why?"

"Oh, people always think I'm from Rising Moon," she laughed. "They say it's because of my work boots."

Sadie told me that she and her husband owned a farm in the southeastern part of Aitkin County, on the Willow River road. As she talked, I realized that Shirley and I had traveled past their place in the cattle truck on our way to Rising Moon. The Smiths had a son and a daughter, aged about five and three, and they all planned to move to a farm that his parents owned in Indiana. They were leaving in the next few weeks, and she wondered if I knew of anyone who might want to rent their Aitkin County farm. She said it had a house, a barn, and eighty acres of forest and pastures.

I wrote to Marea right away to ask if she would be interested in bringing her horses and living there with me. She replied that she would. Encouraged by that, I went to visit the Smiths and check out their place. At this same time I heard through the dairy grapevine that the Carlton County DHIA board was looking for a new cow tester. They had more farmers on test than Aitkin County did, so the job paid more, and I could keep both jobs because the Smiths' farm was located near the county line. I applied for the new job and got it, and I rented the Smiths' farm. Marea wrote that she loved me and thought about me often.

As I packed my things and tried to make a peaceful transition from Nancy and Del Lago, I felt ashamed as well as hopeful. Following my heart had made me heartless, and I had trouble coming to grips with the paradox. I understood from my own experience why Nancy felt angry and hurt. Even as we bickered and I prepared to leave, I grieved the home I had found in her and in the old farm. I comforted myself with the idea that I'd been honest with Nancy all along about my attraction for Marea. Nancy had always known, as I did, that we had the freedom to change and move on, and that this had been one possible way that our relationship could end. That didn't make it easy.

At one point, she asked me bitterly, "What if she leaves you for some prick? Will it be worth it then?"

"I know it could happen," I said. "I only know I'm in love with her, and I have to try."

I didn't mind Nancy invoking the *prick* word because of any sensitivity toward men's feelings. In the long history of patriarchy, I knew that men had used all sorts of vulgarities comparing women to animals and verbally reducing us to our sexual parts. I figured they could withstand whatever slings and arrows some dyke hurled in the heat of angst. I did mind how angry she was with me. I knew I was guilty of faithlessness, but the way I saw it I was also innocent because circumstances had aligned in such a way that some sort of magic had to be at work behind the scenes. The signs seemed to indicate that everything was unfolding just the way the universe intended.

20 Ravenna's Refuge

When I told my dairy farmer clients that I planned to move across the county, one of them offered to haul my horses with his pickup and trailer. Jack Hardy was a horse-and-cow-man who seemed well named because of his resemblance to the Jack of Spades— slim, dark haired, and sharp featured. We made the move on the same day that the Smiths planned to set out for Indiana. As we approached my future home, Jack looked over the swampy meadows and low-lying woods and wondered, "Why would you want to move here?"

I didn't feel like explaining. I knew that the land wouldn't have begun to feed a Holstein dairy herd like Jack's, but at least the farm offered pasture for our horses and a chance to earn hay on shares by working with the neighbors. Yes, the land was low lying, wet, and not nearly as lush as the pastures and hayfields of Del Lago, but I didn't want to admit any doubts. Neither did the Smiths, it seemed, as they said good-bye to Pliny Township for Indiana. We traded last-minute notes, too full of excitement and kinetic energy to give any hint of second thoughts or possible regrets. I gave them the rent money. They gave me the keys and a list of instructions that included their new address so that I could send them rent and an update on how things were going each month.

Meanwhile, Marea wooed me long distance, in aqua-colored

ink and flowing cursive. In her letters she called the Smiths' place *Pliny* because it was located in the township that may or may not have been named for the Roman philosopher and naturalist Pliny the Elder. I liked the idea that it was, just as from the start I had loved the ways she played with words and the uncanny connections she made in writing. In this letter she lifted the mundane toward metaphysics (one of those leaps she was so good at making that made me fall so hard for her). She said that she liked sending me the rent money for Pliny because "it gives me a sense of saving grace, if you know what I mean."

I thought I did. In my mind the home that we needed had been provided by some cosmic grace. Call it luck, synchronicity, or magic, it felt clear to me that our partnership had been blessed. The evidence could be found in the series of events that brought us to Pliny—her car dying at Del Lago, the branches breaking in my dreams, my chance meeting with Sadie at the feed store, and my sudden opportunity to take on the Carlton County cow-testing job. Never mind that she'd written about dates with another man she'd met at her waitressing job. All that would end when she was with me. I felt sure of that.

The day I moved into the Smiths' house, the pastures of Pliny lay under snow, but I could make out the contours of meadows interspersed with brush. The tin-sided barn looked perfect for our chickens and horses. I found the house funky-good—two bedrooms with built-in wooden bunk beds that Sadie's husband had made, two single beds in the kids' room and two double beds in the parents' room. There was also wood heat, an outhouse, and electricity—about what I was used to as far as modern conveniences went, with one big improvement: in the basement there was a shower plumbed over a sump hole with a pump in it that kicked on and off while I showered. Standing on a slatted wood pallet above the sump, I worried a little about electrocution, but the pump was a submersible type, made to operate in water. Since I'd lived without a shower for four years, the benefits seemed to outweigh the danger.

Marea arrived with the first batch of her belongings and her gray tabby cat, Daphne, in a 1960s-model International panel truck she'd christened Lady Rig. We unloaded her stuff. She caught up on sleep. We made love. We got a beer at a nearby bar and gas station called Dad's Corner and met the friendly owner who also tended bar, sold groceries, and pumped gas. She told us that the *Dad* in Dad's Corner referred to an earlier owner, but she wouldn't change the name because she believed it would be bad for business. We drove around a long while exploring our new neighborhood. I could see from the plat book that the state and county owned much of the land around us. That usually happened when landowners fell on hard times and couldn't pay their taxes. We found a railway crossing sign that let us know there was once a town called Solana a mile or so to the east of us, where we saw only railroad tracks and trees. On a Sunday, Marea got back into Lady Rig and returned to her waitressing job and her horses. When I received her next letter, I smiled at her salutation: "Dearest Dianna and Daphne in Solana Quadrangle."

The best news was that she had given notice at the truck stop, and soon her horsewoman friend Linda would haul Marea's White Mare and two yearling colts to Pliny. For the time being the ground remained frozen, which meant good conditions for driving the Smiths' old tractor into the woods. They left us a 1940 orange Allis Chalmers and a homemade trailer, along with directions for locating the dry tops of poplar trees they had cut and left in the woods a year earlier. When I wasn't cow testing, taking care of animals, or making belts and wallets, I hauled home branches that I cut into stove-sized pieces in the yard. Poplar goes by many names, including aspen and in northeastern Minnesota popple. It cuts easily because it's not as dense as other hardwoods. It also burns fast.

"Do you know what people say about popple?" Chester Turnock teased me one evening in the milking parlor after I'd told him about my firewood project. "It warms you three times—once when you cut it, once when you burn it, and once when you haul out the ashes."

I teased back, "So I've noticed!"

I couldn't really work up much resentment over handling ashes that I found so useful. I dumped some down the outhouse holes for neutralizing the night soil. I carried some in a pail in my pickup to spread for traction in case I got stuck on ice. The rest I dumped into the compost pile to add alkalinity and potassium to our collection of horse manure, waste hay, and kitchen scraps. The acrid smell reminded me that spring was coming.

One afternoon while I still lived alone at Pliny, our neighbors to the east stopped by to introduce themselves. A tall and lanky hippie couple, they resembled each other a bit. Rod worked for the DNR and drove a half-ton Ford pickup that looked new to me, and Rochelle said that she had a horse and would like to go riding. I said yes with excitement and tried not to envy that new truck. My twelve-year-old GMC, the ride that replaced my Rambler, was having intermittent starter trouble—a frustrating problem and one I didn't know how to fix myself. When my talk with Rod and Rochelle turned to living off the grid, they asked if I'd met our neighbor Alice Mudrow. Rochelle said there was a good chance I'd already seen her on the road. She was in her seventies, lived without electricity on her family's farm, kept chickens, heated with wood, and drove a '40s sedan back and forth to church on Sundays. "You'll know her when you see her. You can just barely see her eyes and forehead above the dash when she drives by," said Rochelle.

"Oh, I've seen her, then," I said, remembering the curious-looking driver and iron boat of a car that floated by while I stood in the yard one Sunday morning.

"Why don't we ride our horses over to her place?" Rochelle suggested. So one sunny day not long after our conversation, I saddled Taja and rode east with Eagle and Onyx. Rochelle mounted her brown mare when we got to her house, and we rode together for another mile or so to Alice's driveway, a rutted and overgrown track that snaked through a regrowth forest of hardwoods and evergreens. Alice stood in the yard and greeted us with the shy surprise of someone unexpectedly transported out of solitude. I knew the feeling. She was small, hunched in the shoulders, and dressed in slacks, a wool jacket cinched at the waist with a leather belt, and a babushka holding gray hair in place.

Once she got past the shock of finding two mounted women in her driveway, she seemed delighted and proud to show us around. She'd been born here, she told us. Her buildings included an outhouse, a coop filled with mixed-breed chickens, an apple orchard, and sheds in various stages of falling down. She talked about the blacksmith shop as if work still went on in it, and when I looked I saw rusting iron machinery under a collapsed roof and walls. I had little experiential knowledge then of the way time speeds up on us as we age, but I understood that the past was very much alive in her. In the old days, she told us, traveling salesmen had come by the farm selling all sorts of things, including flour and sugar by the hundred-pound sack. The train took people from town to town, and the whole place almost burned in one of the massive fires that swept through in 1918, but it was spared when the wind shifted.

As we rode away, she called after us, "Come again!" I shouted back that I would. I admired her for living independently in a place she loved, despite the fact that her relatives wanted to move her to a house in a nearby town. That house even had a chicken coop, she said, but she was not ready to leave the land. I wanted to get to know her and learn what I could from her experience and intrepid stubbornness.

Near the end of March, Linda and Marea arrived with the horses. White Mare and the two yearlings squealed from the trailer while Lhasa and Taja thundered along the paddock fence, whinnying and bucking from excitement and wariness, despite their heavy pregnant bellies. White Mare was due to foal any day, and Lhasa and Taja were due in a month. After the foals arrived, we would have eight horses, plus the kid that would soon be born to the milk goat Marea brought.

After we unloaded her animals and put her horses in with mine, we watched them prance and cavort until they settled down.

Marea with goat and kid at Pliny in 1977

I hurried then and served some kind of lunch so that Linda could get back on the road. She had a long drive ahead of her and wanted to sleep at home that night. When Marea and I were alone, she told me the story of her first paying farrier job. She'd answered a call to cut a pony mare's hooves just before leaving Wisconsin. She drove to the job in Lady Rig, with her anvil and other tools in the back.

The pony's people had let her hooves grow so long that they curved like skis. Then because he knew that curved toes didn't look right, the husband trimmed the excess with a hacksaw, parallel to the pony's leg. Marea called the man Father Farmer. She described with disgust how he had left the mare's hooves looking like pegs. Properly trimmed hooves should look like wedges, I knew, thanks to Marea and the books I'd read on horse care. Thinking about the pony mare's peg feet gave me a chill, but Marea said the mare was lucky. Her hooves had been so long that when Father Farmer sawed off the tips, he'd removed only dead tissue. He'd left her legs out of balance, but at least he hadn't cut into the blood-filled layers inside the hard shells of her hooves. While Marea worked, she said, Father Farmer stood by the whole time, glowering and making critical comments. "He didn't mean to put me down personally," she said. "It was just the idea that I could be better than he was at doing anything at all."

I thought she was being way too considerate.

"It's different when you watch me work," Marea said. "I can tell that you expect me to be capable."

Dang right, I expected her to be capable, and I wanted her to thrive! The part of her story that really got me was that under Father Farmer's gaze she felt so nervous that she cut her hand and then passed the blood off with a joke about finally getting her hoof knife sharp. I started thinking how I would have liked the pony mare to give Father Farmer a kick in an anatomically sensitive region, but of course such a blow would have only reverberated badly for the pony, just as thinking about it reflected badly on me. As it was, Marea told me, the pony gave her a nose kiss to thank her for the trimming job. The man's wife thanked her, too, by taking her into the house and restoring her with coffee, a donut, some antiseptic, a bandage, and a muffin recipe.

We needed a farrier in Aitkin County, and I thought that helping Marea find customers might be good for everyone. The next time I cow-tested at the Hardy farm, I told Jack and his brother about her. They owned registered quarter horses, and they'd complained about how much they had to pay to get a farrier to drive all the way from St. Cloud to trim and shoe their horses. When I told them about Marea, I saw in their expressions that they had doubts. Fair or not, I assumed their doubts were sexist ones, like Father Farmer's, but before I could judge them too harshly, the younger brother said, "I guess we could give her a chance."

When I went home and told Marea about this opportunity,

she agreed to do it, but I thought I detected some doubt. A few days later we arrived at the Hardy farm. The brothers didn't like that she had no portable forge. She could fit factory-made shoes by cold-hammering them into shape—a reasonable but not perfect way to fit shoes to the shape of the horse's hooves. The Hardys were exacting people and preferred hot shoeing, a process in which the farrier heats the shoe in a forge and shapes the iron while it's red hot. Reluctantly, they agreed to the cold shoeing and brought out a quarter horse gelding. He got skittish while Marea was shoeing him. He danced, caught a horseshoe nail in her leather apron, and dragged her a few feet before the boys got him back under control. Marea stayed on her feet, but we all got scared. I noticed her hands shaking while she finished nailing on the shoes. On the way home she lit a cigarette and took deep drags from it without much talking. I wasn't sure that I'd done the right thing by arranging that job for her.

A week or so later I was back in the Turnock brothers' milking parlor, trading stories. When Franklin heard that Marea was a farrier, he was curious to know more. I told him that she really needed a portable forge to make the kind of custom-forged shoes she had learned to make in farrier school. He thought a minute and said, "We've got an old portable forge laying around here somewhere. Why don't you take it for a while?"

"You're not using it?"

He shook his head.

When I returned to draw the morning milk samples, he had the forge and its hand-cranked blower lying on the ground outside the barn. He directed me to back up next to them, and he lifted them into the bed of my pickup. "No hurry to get them back," he said. "We haven't used them in years."

I went home excited, but when I showed the forge to Marea, she seemed to have mixed feelings. I didn't get it. I thought she'd be thrilled. Had something changed that day at the Hardy farm? Did I rush her into taking that trimming job? Did I overstep my bounds again by bringing home the forge? I didn't know for sure what had happened, but something seemed off. In fact, something seemed off between us overall, and neither talking nor lovemaking ever got us to the heart of it.

And then life became complicated within our growing web of friends, neighbors, and work connections. In the next few weeks our mares foaled—a filly for Lhasa and colts for White Mare and Taja. Marea took a part-time job waitressing and tending bar for Bev, the woman who owned and ran Dad's Corner. I was cow testing still, and I kicked up the gear on my leather business, making belts, wallets, and horse gear that I planned to sell at summer art fairs and the Michigan Womyn's Music Festival. While the other foals thrived, Taja's colt *scoured* (a farmer's term for diarrhea in suckling animals), and even though we trailered him to a veterinary clinic, he got dehydrated and died. Taja ran the pasture fence line and screamed for him for days.

I also continued to cow-test. Alice, my solitary friend in Solana, told me how much she missed the fresh milk she used to get from her own milk cow, so I started bringing her milk that I bought from my dairy farmer clients. Some of them would sell it fresh from their bulk milk tanks to buyers who brought their own jars. Alice supplied me with antique green two-quart canning jars, and when I exchanged a full one for one of her empties, she smiled with relish and told me, "That gives me pep!" I knew what she meant. Fresh milk, fresh garden vegetables, and our own eggs were some of the main reasons I still lived in the country and hadn't bolted for town like some of my back-to-the-land friends.

I kept in touch with Nancy, who wasn't alone for long. A woman named Blue came from Oregon with two friends, and they moved into Del Lago while Nancy and Molly went firefighting for the summer on a traveling hotshot crew. Blue stewarded Del Lago for years after that. Many women shared the journey, and I lost track of her housemates and visitors. One hot afternoon at work on the firefighting crew, Nancy and Molly told me, the men were playing horseshoes at the headquarters building. The men took off their shirts, so Nancy and Molly did, too. Their coworkers got nervous, but the game went on, and then a stream of administrators passed by in uniforms on their way to or from some meeting. Pretty soon the rule came down from management that the firefighters all had to keep their shirts on.

Our Pliny neighborhood was short on feminists but long on hippie back-to-the-landers, and Marea and I made friends. A potter owned an eighty-acre parcel of grass and woods next door to us. Her brother had built her a simple wooden house, a potting shed, and a kiln on the land, and I wanted to meet her. I watched for her for weeks on my horseback rides before I spotted her in the yard and stopped to introduce myself. She looked to be about my age, with sky-blue eyes and collar-length brown hair. I found her quick-witted and droll, and one day I saw her tossing pots like baseballs, smashing them into a pile of shards. I rode in, and she told me that she had just opened her kiln to unload it after a firing. She said she wouldn't sell a piece that she considered imperfect, and she got some cathartic satisfaction from smashing her mistakes. I had to think about that ethic a long time, and I still haven't learned to let go of all of my mistakes.

We met more hippies at a Fourth of July party in Arthyde, a mostly depopulated logging town a few miles northeast of us. We got to know a strapping young blond man who lived in a log cabin he built himself, and a couple who were farm-to-table pioneers growing snow peas that the husband peddled to Asian restaurants in the Twin Cities. The party hosts lived in a stone house located next to the Arthyde railroad crossing. They told us that a lumber baron had built their house during the get-rich-quick days when timber companies logged the virgin white pine forest to oblivion. Sinclair Lewis visited, they said, and he wrote his impressions of the house, the lumberman, and his wife into the novel *Cass Timberlane*.

After the Fourth of July, we started working for the neighbor who used to own our place and the potter's. He needed help making hay, and we agreed to do it for a share of the crop. Our neighbor and his wife raised a big family in our little house before they sold it, but the kids had all grown and left the farm.

Around that time, Marea got an idea for a new project—mentoring women who wanted to learn about horses and country living. She called it Ravenna's Refuge. I remembered that she had described Lilith-Ravenna in a letter, and from her description I understood her to mean a dual goddess, who much like the Greeks's Persephone shows us death as an indispensable aspect of life and the shadow side of the world we inhabit. In my own research, I've managed to find little about a goddess Ravenna, but Marea read more widely in spirituality than I did. She also channeled directly from her muses sometimes. The one thing I know for sure about her Ravenna is that Marea didn't mention the goddess in her flyer. She drew a raven on the front, like the ones we saw flying over our Pliny home. Inside she described country activities that might entice guests. She mailed the flyers to feminist bookstores and lesbian centers. Before long, paying visitors from Chicago and Minneapolis called, and we soon hosted a college professor and her lover, a firefighter and her lover, and a group of three young women from Chicago who had never been on a farm. We taught horseback riding lessons and gardening skills and felt so simpatico with one couple that Marea didn't want to take money from them. We discussed it, and they insisted we take the money. Our fee was low, and they had enjoyed their stay.

Marea and I disagreed a fair amount, it seemed, and we never quite clarified or resolved much. We let our differences dead-end into drinking, smoking homegrown grass, or going to our separate spaces. In August a friend of hers dropped in from Wisconsin. I had met this woman, Theia, at Haidiya Farm, and I thought she could be quite insightful but also annoying and strange. She had been married when I met her and living with her husband and a couple of kids, but by August she was on her own. Sometimes she didn't seem entirely present and at other times hyperalert. She said she was on her way to Oregon in the old car she had spray-painted, graffiti-style, with drawings and phrases like "El Primo

Indian Car," which might have passed as an insider's joke in the right context, but she was no insider. She was pale and wan, with piercing eyes and the overconfident air that goes with believing you speak from your own particular, idiosyncratic version of divine authority. She also saw flying saucers regularly. One day as I stood on the road with her, she said, "There goes a cigar-shaped one."

"Where?" I asked.

"Right there above the treetops." She pointed. "Can't you see it?"

I looked, but I only saw trees and sky.

"It's right there," she said disappointedly, as if some failure of belief kept me from seeing.

Actually, if there had been a UFO, I didn't want to miss it. Marea and some of my other Wisconsin friends had told me they saw flying saucers, and I'd read that so many people reported sightings in parts of Wisconsin in the mid-1970s that psychologists were speculating about some kind of shared psychosis. I preferred to believe that people actually did see UFOs. Since this was the time in my life for magical thinking, I was practically calling the UFOs to me. I was begging to get a glimpse, but no matter how many times I looked all I saw were trees and sky.

A few days later Marea told me that she was leaving for the West Coast with Theia. She didn't know how long she'd be gone. I could tell from their body language that they'd either become lovers or soon would. I was in shock. I could hardly believe that Marea would go with Theia and leave me to take care of a pregnant Daphne, a goat, and seven horses. When I tried to talk to her, there was always Theia in the middle of the conversation.

"I can't stand the way you look at me," Marea said.

"How is that?" I asked.

"With such scrutiny."

Before I could respond, Theia interjected: "Scrutiny is what the sculptor carves with."

I felt vindicated in a way that didn't help the situation at all, and minutes later Theia whipsawed and asked, "Do you really know what it is to love someone, Dianna? Have you ever really loved anyone?" Her accusatory, Cassandra-like air overwhelmed me. I only knew that I wasn't feeling loved at that moment, and I doubted myself deeply.

When they left, my grandmother's feather tick went missing. A week or so later I found a fifty-dollar bill in a canister where I kept conchos for my leatherwork. I assumed the money was supposed to compensate me for the theft and abandonment, but it only made me feel more violated. Three weeks later I got a letter from Theia, describing how they drove straight through, in forty hours, from Pliny to Ashland, Oregon. Her tone was officious. She told me that she and Marea had stopped communicating, and Marea wanted to hitchhike alone to the ocean. Theia convinced her that they needed to talk it over with Theia's Oregon friends, so the four of them had a confab and decided that Marea could go. Eight days later she showed up with some twenty-six-year-old Leo, Theia wrote, and both of them left again before Theia woke up the next morning.

The next day I found a letter from Marea in the mailbox. Standing on the edge of the road, I ripped open the envelope and read:

> M___ and I spent the night in the national forest high on
> the mountains to the south of Ashland, me singing and
> laughing with the planets and stars around my head,
> in my head, below, above, through. The sun rose in the
> morning—it was incredible. Then we went to the ocean
> via the Applegate and Jacksonville and Selma and salm-
> on dinner in Port Orford and sunset in New Mexico
> and many friends along each step and a swim in Patrick
> Creek and we drove back here late in the night. I could
> fill volumes with the above story. M___ and I are getting
> married on the equinox. We filed our application at the
> Salem Courthouse yesterday and got our bloodtests done
> and bought some brown rice and a pineapple. Expect the
> unexpected.

Literally moments later, as I walked back toward the house, my parents pulled up beside me on the road in their Datsun sedan. I'd been expecting their visit, but I hadn't been expecting Marea's letter. And there I was, caught with the evidence of my emotional situation, my poor judgment, my inability to expect the unexpected, my failure in love. Tears streamed down my face, and the letter felt like poison in my hand.

"What's wrong with your eyes?" Dad asked.

For God's sake! Did I have to tell him I was crying? I tried to explain without too much sarcasm shaping my voice, "I just got a letter from Marea. She got married! To a man!"

"I don't see what's wrong with that," Dad puffed in his awkward way.

"Well, she just met him, two weeks ago," I said. "Doesn't that seem a little sudden?"

He shrugged. "Sounds normal to me."

Dianna and her father, Everett Hunter, at Pliny in 1978

I struggled to process that from his point of view the problem was my lesbianism and not my broken heart. I couldn't believe he didn't have the instinct to comfort me, and I decided to handle my hurt feelings by exiting the scene temporarily. I told them, "Make yourselves at home. I need to go water the horses." My escape didn't come off as planned, though.

"I'll come with you," Mom said. In the barn, she sat on a hay bale while I drew buckets of water from a tap and delivered them to the animals. She looked around, and I could tell she was happy to be there in the presence of old wood and hay and animals, even though right then she'd set herself up for a hard parenting task. After a moment, she asked, "Do you think you'll ever find a boy and settle down and have children?"

"I don't think so." I was working my way into the sentence, searching for a way to let her down easy. "I mean, I would never say *never,* because people change, but I can't really see it. I like kids, but I'm just not attracted to men."

She looked so sad but kept her voice cheerful. "When people ask us when you're going to settle down and raise a family, we just tell them you haven't met the right boy yet." There was that familiar psychological strategy, denial, again, and I saw that it was their way of trying to protect me from the judgment of their friends and family, and possibly a way to protect them from it, too, and to defer their disappointment in me. Coming out, I saw, hadn't ended yet, and it looked like it might be a long and patchy process.

In October, after letters and phone calls from me that alternated between pleading and demanding, Marea returned for her animals, and we went for one last horseback ride together. We took the trail we'd discovered that ran parallel to the county road, through recently logged wildland overgrown with new shoots of poplar. We didn't get far before Taja squealed and struck out with both hind feet at White Mare. I heard a yip, and when I looked back at Marea, she was rubbing her shin. Her face was a storm of rage and pain. She got down from her mare and tried the leg. "No broken bones," she said as though I'd planned the whole thing. "You and your damn familiars!"

Not long after Marea had left for Oregon with her animals, I got a postcard from Theia asking if her winter stuff was still at my place. She said to send it to her care of the board of regents, University of Alaska, Fairbanks. Thankfully, I had nothing that belonged to her and no reason to respond. I hoped to never see her again.

Alone again, I did what I could to try to keep from falling into despair and depression. As usual, I kept busy, and just before Halloween I hosted a party for Outstate Lesbians United, a group of dykes who lived in the country north of the Twin Cities and got together monthly for social events. I started going to meetings and agreed to serve as secretary.

Despite my added activities, doubts kept slipping in. I was twenty-eight years old, grieving the marriage I had hoped to have with Marea. As I turned things over in my solitude, I could see that I had no choice but to give her the same freedom I had expected Nancy to give me. I had to let Marea love whom she chose, whether it was Theia, some twenty-six-year-old Leo, or anyone else.

As for me, I was still looking for love and afraid that I might never find it. What if Theia was one of those spiritual messengers, like the trolls and wizened old ladies in the folk stories? What if her questions amounted to a supernatural aid that I needed to understand before I could move on? Then again, what if all that mystical stuff was bunk? Even then, I thought, her accusation stood. What if I had never loved anyone? What if I didn't have a clue how to love?

21 Dancing Leads to This

Late in the fall, Blue invited me to a square dance in the barn loft at Del Lago. As I drove the sandy driveway toward the barn, I felt a tug of mourning for my old life. The lake still smelled of weeds and fish, and in the barn I caught a whiff of the dry dung left by Taja and my other horses. My nostalgia soon changed to excitement, though, once I got into the company of the other lesbians who had come for the party. As Alix Dobkin put it in her "Amazon ABC" lyrics, "D you're so Dykey / E, how you Excite me / How F-ortunate a Female Faculty." Women I already knew greeted me with hugs and kisses, and I met a few new women, too, with smiles and pleasant talk.

A mutual friend introduced me to Ellen, and I was struck right away by her sense of humor, sparkling eyes, and supple figure. She had decked herself out in a cowgirl skirt, western blouse, and boots. I found her willingness to make herself the center of attention both brave and charming. We chatted on and off, and partway through the evening I asked her to dance. A woman from the Cities barked instructions. We linked arms and coupled and twirled and decoupled and made a tunnel with other dancers and looped around through. I had never been any good at folk dancing when our gym teachers made us do it, but on this particular evening I laughed, managed to make mistakes with self-effacing grace, and shook off introspection for a while.

After the music ended, a bunch of us got ready to bed down in the loft, and I asked Ellen if I could put my sleeping bag near hers. She cast her gaze sideways, dropped her eyelids, and said yes. We spent the night side by side but apart, in the company of friends, and talked each other to sleep while watching the stars through the open hay door. In the morning we exchanged phone numbers and mailing addresses, and later we planned a face-to-face date for New Year's Eve. I drove down and met her at the South Minneapolis apartment she shared with Kathy, my old friend from the LRC and Rising Moon. We made a shy, sweet start to a romantic relationship that we carried on long distance, through letters, phone calls, and visits that winter and into the spring of 1978.

One night in March, while I was alone at Pliny, I heard the frenzied howling of brush wolves in the woods behind the barn. The next day I snowshoed into the spruce bog with Onyx and Eagle and discovered the remains of a yearling whitetail buck. I've always feared violent homicidal death more than any other kind, and I hoped that he had starved or frozen to death before the brush wolves got him. Their tracks lay all around what was left of him—his head with its pronghorns and his tongue hanging out, his torso with the rib cage partly chewed and the interior emptied, a hard ball of twigs that must have been the contents of his stomach. I have never done much journaling, but I wrote a few pages after coming onto this grisly scene. Because of the journal, I know that I went into the house afterward, turned on the radio, and heard Judy Collins singing Leonard Cohen's "Joan of Arc": "Myself I long for love and light / But must it come so cruel, and oh so bright?" Myself I needed an antidote to nature's cruelty. I longed for Ellen's company and our unique, intermittent love trysts, so warm and passionate.

My wayward poet Marea and I still exchanged letters between Pliny and Oregon, but I hadn't shaken the pain and self-doubt left in her wake. I had closed down her Ravenna's Refuge project after she left because I didn't want to carry it on alone, but a woman named Shary contacted me after seeing a flyer. She seemed agreeable and genuinely interested in adding to what she already knew about country living, so I invited her to bring her horse and live at Pliny for a while—not for profit or as a potential lover but as company and an apprentice of sorts, though that went both ways. She turned out to be a friend and a peer, and when she asked about contacts with women who lived farther north, I gave her Shirley's number. By this time Shirley had bought some land from our old friend Jane, and Shirley helped Shary locate a piece of land not far from her own. Shary started an organic farm, and she still makes her living growing berries.

Ellen and I kept up our long-distance relationship for the first couple of years we were together. I wanted stay on the farm, and she wanted to finish some college courses and earn the credits she needed for a bachelor's degree in communications. She had started college right out of high school but took a break to work for a while. She had a part-time job for a video production company when I met her, and once she was back to school she felt frustrated by trying to balance school, work, and her relationship with me. She procrastinated on her schoolwork and wished things were different between us. We planned to live together after she finished school, and she had already moved boxes of her things to Pliny, when she wrote in a moment of doubt:

> Will you come and live with me? I hate the thought of moving all our stuff and leaving your little scene, but I can't stand this anymore! It drives me nuts. It seems like if I just had you sleeping next to me at night some of this horrible studying wouldn't be so bad, and if I didn't spend so much time missing you I would get more done. Right now I just want to scream.

I met her frustration with stubbornness. I didn't feel like I could move. My "little scene" involved thousand-pound animals that wouldn't fit the zoning codes in the Twin Cities. And as it was, my income barely covered the bills when I paid the Smiths only fifty dollars a month for rent at Pliny. I didn't see how we could afford a farm in the suburbs, and after all I'd been through, I wasn't about to abandon my animals or give up my goal of making a living from the land.

That particular crisis between us passed, as our flare-ups of impatience and temper always seemed to do. I think we recognized how to accept those particular flaws in one another and recognize that we both sometimes exacerbated them. We settled into our own kind of normalcy that ran the gamut from great sweetness to turbulence and volcanic passion. On New Year's Eve, 1979, she invited me to a lesbian prom organized by the Women's Coffeehouse in Minneapolis. She wore a full-length burgundy velvet dress, and I wore pants, a wool vest, a man's dress shirt, and a fedora. Looking at the photo of us, I see a chubby-cheeked, smashing young couple. This was my first prom, and she gave me a pendant that she had hired our silversmith friend M'lou to make: a sterling oval engraved on the back with the date of our first anniversary and on the face with a portrait of a wedgy-headed mare who looked like Taja. I saw it as a token of our solid relationship. We sometimes struggled over getting what we needed from our long-distance arrangement, but most of the time we supported each other and gave each other room to grow.

I read Willa Cather's novels that winter and into the spring of 1980. In April after I had finished *Lucy Gayheart,* I stopped to talk one cold, squally day to my potter neighbor. She knew the story and its dismal plot in which the main characters are dragged down by mediocrity, repressed love, lies, silences, patriarchal conventions, and twists of fate. We talked about how life seemed too often reduced to mediocrity, including our own efforts toward excellence. "The miracle is that genius appears and flowers from time to time," I wrote in another of those sporadic journal entries that spring before my thirtieth birthday.

When Ellen needed a project for a photography class, she

went with me on my cow-testing route and snapped photos of the Hardy boys and their dad as they milked. The Hardys had the newest, cleanest dairy barn on my route, and they seemed proud to show it off. They also seemed to enjoy Ellen. Her good looks opened doors, and her personality got her invited inside. I loved bringing her into the farm community as my partner—not that I introduced her to all of them in such an explicit way. I didn't think we needed to come out to everyone. It was enough to be together and go through life meeting whatever support or resistance we did in the heterosexist world. As *Dyke Shorts* comics creator Mary Wings put it in the '70s, "The incredible people we must be to become and stay lesbians creates amazing stories of *bravery* and *subterfuge* getting our strokes!!!"

I came out strategically to some but hid in plain sight from others by not saying explicitly that I was a lesbian. One of the Aitkin County DHIA board members who hired me in 1974 owned land that bordered Rising Moon, and because of that and the way that stories traveled in the rural community, I assumed that most people knew my sexual identity. Country people talked and learned

Dianna (left) and Ellen at a lesbian prom organized by the Minneapolis Women's Coffeehouse in 1979

almost whatever they wanted to know about each other. This is one of the reasons that longtime activist Del Martin advised conflicted young lesbians who wrote her from rural places to move to a big city. I heard her say this in Minneapolis when she gave a talk as part of a tour promoting *Lesbian/Woman,* the groundbreaking 1972 book she cowrote with her partner, Phyllis Lyon.

Being out had felt easier to me when I lived in Minneapolis and my neighbors didn't know me. I felt no such safe reserve while living alone or with just one other woman in the country, so I worked out a way of not being explicitly out to the people I didn't trust. I talked to them about my life and my companions and let them make of it what they would, remembering the words of that husband of the gay doctor in Wisconsin who told Shirley and me on our horseback ride, "If they don't know, they must be blind." As far as I was concerned, people could choose to be blind, or they could choose to see. I came out to the ones who saw.

Two of those were Bob and Margaret Roseberg. Bob had been one of the Aitkin County DHIA board members who interviewed me when I first applied for the cow-testing job. Tall and blond, with a droopy moustache and a nearly ever-present grin, he was a socially gifted, good-natured man. His wife, Margaret, worked changeable nursing shifts at the hospital in a town thirty miles from their farm. She had boyishly short hair and an incisive and clever manner. I liked to talk to her, though I often felt I blabbed too much. She practiced the wise art of withholding as well as disclosing.

When she heard that Ellen and I planned to spend Christmas together at Pliny that year, instead of traveling to Minot or Madison, where Ellen's parents lived, Margaret invited us to spend Christmas Eve with them and their families. On this particular Christmas, their first son was learning to walk, and they set up a portable gate to keep him from wandering out of the living room. When Ellen went to the kitchen to refill a glass of wine, she cleared the gate in a single smooth motion, and Margaret's mother said to Bob's, "Isn't it nice to be young? Don't you wish you still had such grace?"

Yes, it is nice, my callow young self thought, and it is nice to lay myself down beside such grace. I had no idea how it would feel to age beyond thirty, but I knew that I felt lucky to be partnered with Ellen and to share her company with our friends.

After the holidays I cow-tested, took care of the horses, chickens, and dogs, and sampled the lesbian and feminist novels coming through the surging women-in-print movement that fed and was fed by women's bookstores. For political news, I relied on National Public Radio and a subscription to the *Village Voice*. I listened to KAXE community radio from Grand Rapids while I made my wallets, belts, and horse gear. I spent many hours designing, cutting, dyeing, gluing, sewing, riveting, and braiding as I added inventory to sell at the next summer's art fairs.

Twice I traveled to the Michigan Womyn's Music Festival and pitched my wares in the merchants' tent. I loved and hated much about it. Just to enter the festival land, I had to drive for a day, circumnavigate or ferry across Lake Michigan, wait in a long line of cars, and listen to three or four volunteer workers repeat the same set of instructions. The communally cooked vegetarian stews, boiled in half-barrels over fire pits, tasted bland and unsatisfying to omnivorous me. The cold-water, open-air showers were barely tolerable on hot days, and no one was yet selling coffee, which was practically my life's blood. I'd lost my taste for the internecine feminist political disputes that sometimes flared, but the visual display of lesbian culture, the woman watching, and the music shot to my core and felt both scintillating and indispensable. I particularly remember the five-woman jazz group Alive! changing up rhythms and reaffirming our damaged spirits while their lead singer, Rhiannon, scatted and crooned into the Michigan night, "Woman, you are the spirit healer."

Back in Aitkin County for the fall, I kept on visiting my neighbor Alice at least weekly to deliver fresh milk. After the snow fell, she confided how far behind she was on making her firewood, so I went to help her with the chainsaw that Jane and M'lou had bought me. I followed her into the woods, pulling the saw and gas can on her wooden sled, while she led me to a hillside where she stopped and said, "This was my dad's favorite place." I didn't wonder why. The white trunks of birches slashed the blue sky like lightning bolts as she directed me to a standing dead birch that she wanted felled and cut into stove-sized chunks. I dropped it, sliced it, and helped her stack the pieces on the sled. Then I pulled the load back to her yard.

"You sure do know how to work," she said, following me, and I felt proud to receive such praise from a toughie like her. When we got back to her house, I unloaded the wood and went inside to warm up while she made coffee. Her living room walls were covered with yellowed paper to help keep out drafts. She told me to make myself comfortable, so I rested my feet in my wet wool socks on the skirt of her woodstove. It threw little heat. I couldn't get dry or warm and had my first worried thoughts about whether she should really keep on there. I thought maybe the time had come for her to move to that little house her family had prepared for her, but she told me vehemently that she still wasn't ready to go.

The next spring a farmer on my DHIA route decided to sell his cattle after his wife developed an inflammatory disease and needed to move to a warmer climate. A neighbor of mine, who was also my friend, bought five heifer calves at the auction and then tried to give them to me. I insisted that he let me make monthly payments to him instead. A farmer on my route gave me another heifer that needed medical care and TLC. I brought them all to my Pliny farm, thinking that I might milk them in the barn there after I'd raised them. I'd noticed that people were milking cows in all sorts of barns and sheds along the country roads of northeastern Minnesota. I called Associated Milk Producers, Inc. (AMPI), the big farmer's cooperative creamery, and they sent a man out to talk to me. He said AMPI was loaning money to people like me to buy milking equipment and get started in dairying. Credit was flowing into agriculture. The price of milk had hit an all-time high, and American farmers planned to feed the world.

I watched as three young heterosexual couples bought farms

on my cow-testing route, and when I talked to them they didn't seem to know as much about dairying as I did. When I asked how they got their farms, they told me they'd received low-interest beginning-farmer loans from a federal lending agency called the Farmers Home Administration (FmHA). I started to wonder if I should apply for one of those loans. My utopian dream of a collective farm had given way to a dream of owning a small farm, forty or eighty acres, of my own, but I'd never managed to earn enough money to save for a down payment. I decided that one of those beginning-farmer loans might be my best chance to buy a farm and make a living from it. The cattle and machinery could generate enough income to pay for themselves as well as the land and buildings.

During my six years of cow-testing, I'd watched how the best dairy managers operated, and I'd also noticed some mistakes to avoid. My friends the Rosebergs routinely won the Aitkin County DHIA trophy for the highest-producing dairy herd, and in Carlton County, Marvin and Marlene Mickelson had just taken the same award. Marvin was a slender, graceful man who made the chores look almost effortless when I came to cow-test at their farm. He chainsmoked as he milked, tossing cigarette butts into the wet gutter behind the cows. He sang the cows' praises, and I could see how much pride he took in them, even though his conversation also ran to complaints about repetitious never-ending work. He'd heard about the young-farmer loans and said he might like to sell the place. He wondered if there was some young farmer out there who might want to buy the place fully stocked: cattle, land, and machinery. He definitely caught my interest, and I thought of little else while I tossed before falling to sleep in the Mickelsons' spare bedroom that night.

The next day before milking, I told him and Marlene, "If there's any farm that a person could buy and plan to make a living on it, it's yours. I'd like to try to buy it." They asked a lot of questions and seemed doubtful that I might be able to get a young-farmer's loan approved, but they told me to go ahead and check into it. I didn't blame them for feeling doubtful. I felt doubtful myself. I decided to talk to Bob Roseberg because he was on the Farmers Home Administration board in Aitkin County. He told me that the county board had to approve any farm loan application, and he didn't remember ever approving a loan for a woman or even an unmarried man. As best I could understand the situation, the county boards at that time seemed to be made up mostly of married, heterosexual men who believed that traditional marriage was a necessary stabilizing force in any successful farmer's life. They also knew that a farm bought with a large loan involved tons of labor and little net income, so a wife came in awfully handy. She could clean house, do the laundry, cook the meals, take an off-farm job for extra income, and help in the barn and the fields.

"So would it be better for me to apply alone or with Ellen?" I asked.

"Alone," Bob answered after a diplomatic pause. "Definitely."

Somehow it didn't surprise me that a lesbian wife would not be a point in my favor. On my cow-testing route I talked with the father of one of my dairy farmers. The man had served on another county's FmHA board. After helping with feeding, he stood in the aisle in front of the cows, conversing with me while his son handed me tubes of milk from the milk meters, and I handed him empty replacement tubes back. The old man told me, "They'll never give you that loan."

"Why not?" I asked.

"Because you're not married," he said. "As long as I've been around here, they've never given a loan to a single person."

I remember thinking that such a thing was not only unfair but also most likely illegal—and thinking that it probably happened all the time anyway, since laws made little difference without regulations and a will to enforce them. Ellen and I talked, and we decided that I would apply for the farm loan without her. It was 1980, and she was close to earning her degree. When she did, our plan was that she would look for a job in Duluth so that she could commute to the farm. It was about an hour's drive, and we knew many country people who made a commute like that every day. On the financial side, we decided that I would make the payments on our home and pay for our land taxes, insurance, utilities, and much of our food through the farm. She would provide groceries from town and discretionary money that we could spend on niceties like trips, concerts, and presents for friends and family.

I applied for the loan. I understood from some of the other young farmers that the board had approved their applications without calling them in for an interview, but they wanted to talk to me. So I prepared. I came to the meeting with financial projections and plans. I didn't have to stretch the truth to make the financial projections look good. Instead, I planned conservatively. The Mickelsons' herd produced an average of nineteen thousand pounds of milk per cow. That was far above the state average, but I projected that production would drop two thousand pounds per cow when I took over. I said I knew there'd be a learning curve for any new operator. I also projected that the price of milk would drop two dollars per hundred pounds. No one was predicting the price to drop that low, but everyone knew the government was holding a surplus of dry milk, cheese, and butter and that politicians who believed in free markets and limited government spending saw the surplus as a reason to cut farm price supports. I was trying to err on the side of caution. I also had a list of people who said they would help me with chores if I got sick or needed to travel for any reason. Most of them were women. One of the board members asked, with a pugilistic note in his voice, why there was only one man on my list. Another board member, a First Nations man who had been listening quietly up to this point, jumped in and said with a wry grin, "Tokenism." He broke the tension, and we all laughed. Toward the end of the meeting he told me, "You've proved to me that you can do it."

The third board member said that no one had brought in plans like mine before. Instead, the loan applicants' plans usually looked rosy and unrealistic. He said I had impressed him. I got a letter the next week telling me that the board had approved my loan application for $250,000. That was $100,000 for the cattle and machinery, and $150,000 for the house, buildings, and 286 acres. Now, that would be the price of a middle-class home in many places. At the time, it felt like a fortune to me. It was twenty-five times the value my parents had listed for their house on the financial aid forms they filled out when I applied for scholarships at Macalester.

There was still one big catch, the FmHA county supervisor explained to me. Congress had the power to allocate money for the young-farmer loan program, and the state and federal offices of the FmHA distributed the allocations to county offices. He said there was only a million dollars available for the whole district, and since my quarter-million would take a huge chunk of that, there was no guarantee my loan would ever get funded. At best, the wait would probably be at least a year.

I explained all that to the Mickelsons, and they decided that we should write up a purchase agreement anyway. Marvin wrote in "six yearling heifers" on the line where the earnest money amount was supposed to go. We had agreed in advance that I would put up the heifers for security instead of cash, and the Mickelsons would get them if I couldn't complete the deal. In the meantime, he told me, "You keep them. We don't want your heifers." They wanted to sell their cattle, not acquire more, and I needed to have some skin in the game.

While we waited, I kept on thinking of questions about how the loan process worked. I wrote a legal services group that helped farmers with FmHA loans and learned that the agency was required to set aside part of the loan money that Congress allocated them each year for loans to minority group members and women. I contacted the FmHA supervisor and told him about this loan fund. He said he would look into it.

The next month, when I went to the Mickelsons' farm to cow-test, Marlene told me that Marv had talked to the county supervisor and asked if he thought they should look for someone else to buy the farm. She told me the supervisor said, "Your best chance of getting the money is to sell the farm to Dianna."

Ten months after I applied for the loan, the supervisor notified me that the money had been allocated for my loan. Meanwhile, Ellen had applied for a job as an audiovisual coordinator at a technical college in Duluth, and she got the job. That meant an hour's drive each way for her, but we were ecstatic about being able to live together in a modern house while we pursued the jobs we wanted. We celebrated with her future colleagues over cocktails in Duluth, and her new boss told me with an ironic grin, "Ellen's not excited or anything!"

In the meantime I still lived at Pliny. On the night of the winter solstice, just about one month before our closing date, I approached my friend Alice's place in Solana on my way home from an evening's cow-testing. I saw a pickup parked on the shoulder of the road near the entry to Alice's driveway. Any parked car would have drawn my attention there, and I was startled to see a woman waving for me to stop. When I rolled down my window, I recognized her as a distant neighbor. Her words came out in a torrent: "Alice's house is on fire, and they think she's still in it!" When I looked hard to the left, I saw the orange glow above the treetops. My head must have been too full of dairy farm plans for me to notice it earlier. I parked on the shoulder and walked the narrow driveway with my neighbor. When we made the final curve, we saw an all-out conflagration. The house, the chicken coop, and the outlying sheds were fully ablaze and shooting sparks into the sky. A half-dozen or more people stood around, silhouetted by the flames. There was nothing for me to do but join them and watch the house burn until it collapsed into the cellar. When the walls went down, I saw the skeleton of Alice's iron bed. I'd feared seeing much worse, but I never again saw any sign of my friend.

Great loss and great promise once again collided, and I grieved for her while I packed my things, arranged to have my animals hauled, and looked forward to the beginning of my live-in marriage-of-the-heart with Ellen. Mortality hung heavy with me and made our new life feel all the more precious and desirable.

We had a lot of decisions to make. We'd been discussing for

a long time what to name our farm, and it was time to order our business checks. I'd been advocating for High Roller Holsteins, a sarcastic option meant to tweak the naysayers I'd heard complaining about the "foolish" young farmers who borrowed too much and had to have everything right off the bat "without working for it." Only once I heard an older man point out how times had changed and a young farmer couldn't start with just a wheelbarrow and a couple of cows anymore. "Used to be you could sell your milk anywhere," I heard him tell his friends. "There was a creamery in every town, but now there isn't but one left that will even buy milk in cans."

We wouldn't be selling our milk in cans. Our farm was a Grade A dairy, which meant our milk would be sold for bottling, after the truck from the AMPI cooperative picked it up from our bulk cooling tank. We would interact with milk truck drivers, milk inspectors, and salesmen, and wisely, Ellen wanted to make sure that we didn't offend anyone when naming our farm. So we went with her idea, a gentler version of irony, and called it Happy Hoofer Farm, an allusion to Xaviera Hollander's best-selling memoir of her experiences as an upscale New York call girl and madam, *The Happy Hooker*. To help us celebrate, our friend Margaret drew a small cartoon for us of three Holsteins dancing on their hind legs in a chorus line.

Soon the dairy farm subsumed almost all of my thoughts and energy. The Mickelsons and I had agreed to close our sale on January 20, 1981, Ronald Reagan's first inauguration day. Given his free-market, antigovernment rhetoric in the 1980 campaign, I worried that he might freeze federal farm loans as soon as he took office, and I wanted to get the deal done before he could act. I would worry later about how his agricultural policies might affect the price of milk.

The Mickelsons and I met at my lawyer's office in Carlton to sign the papers and hand over the large check. "Marv cleaned the barn," Marlene volunteered before we parted ways. "He thought it would be nice for you not to have to do it today."

Dianna (right) and Ellen at Happy Hoofer Farm in 1981

I thanked him. I knew I had enough to get used to. Our first evening on the farm, milking went surprisingly well, considering how much I still needed to learn. The milking machines were not the newest technology. They were Surge buckets, five-gallon stainless steel containers with a milking device on top that included a pump, four rubber cups that I placed, one by one, on the cows' tits, and a hose that I plugged into the vacuum line to drive the milkers. The milk flowed into the bucket, and after each cow finished milking, I carried the bucket into the milk room and dumped her milk into a funnel that filtered it into the bulk tank.

There was a rhythm to milking that I found grounding and mindful. I had to perform certain tasks in a certain order and keep moving down the line in a timely fashion. The cows had grown used to the milking order, and most of them started letting down their milk as their time neared. Before putting a milking machine on a cow, I washed her udder and squeezed a little milk from each tit to check for lumps that might be a symptom of infection. A good cow milked about thirty pounds at a time—up to fifty pounds or more for the high producers. If a cow milked more than forty pounds, I had to interrupt her flow, carry the milker to the bulk tank, and empty not just once but twice. In a few weeks, my lower arms bulged like Popeye's.

Night had fallen by the time Ellen finished her hour-long drive home from work. She was tired too but changed clothes and joined me in the barn. When I finished milking, I climbed up into the hayloft and threw down fresh bales, and she helped me spread them in front of the cows before we went into the house. Exhausted, we both slept hard. In the morning, I got up at 5:30, made coffee, drank a couple of cups with Ellen, and walked to the barn. That first morning I swept fresh snow away from the door with the side of my boot before pulling it open and fumbling for the light switch. The cows murmured when the lights came on, and I saw a new calf standing knobby-kneed and trembling in the gutter behind her mother.

I quickly checked and found that the calf was a she—a heifer. She had arrived two weeks early and was covered in amniotic fluid, but she looked strong—a good omen perhaps. I cleaned her as best I could with paper towels and guided her into the aisle in front of her mother, whom I then milked ahead of the rest of the cows so that I could use her milk to feed the calf. A cow's first milk, the colostrum, has a creamy golden look like aged Gouda, and it contains nutrients and antibodies that a calf needs to survive. I fed our new calf from a two-quart bottle while she bobbed and tried to butt me, as she would have done her mother's udder if she'd been born in the pasture. Once I had her fed, I gave the cows the grain they'd been mooing for while waiting. Then at last I was able to go into the milk room and bring out the rest of the milking machines.

Before I got started, Ellen stuck her head in the door and announced, "My car is stuck!"

I went outside, found a grip under her back bumper, and put my back and thighs into the ritualistic northern-state practice of rocking her forward when she goosed the gas, and then letting her roll back until momentum carried her through the snowdrift. We waved to each other as she drove away, and I went back to milking. When I finished, I washed the machines and fed the calves, cows, horses, yearlings, and two-year-old heifers. Everyone bawled and complained because breakfast was so late and the morning was so cold.

After my own breakfast, I scraped the manure from the cows' stalls, replaced the dirty bedding with leftover hay from the feed aisle, ran the barn cleaner, and spread the manure in a nearby hay-field. I could pause then, and I decided to drive into a nearby town to pick up a few groceries at the local co-op store. As I leaned on the counter, chatting with the clerk, my muscles felt like they were about to liquify, and I thought, "How strange that she can't know, looking at me from the outside, how I feel at this moment." I had never felt so totally spent, so challenged, or so ecstatic.

22 Divorce and Dispossession

Haying, milking, feeding, doctoring cattle, and fixing broken equipment filled my days. And then, as the government cut farm support prices, milk and cattle prices dropped across the country, along with those of all other farm commodities, and farm incomes dropped to historic lows compared to the cost of production. By our second year, 1982, a nationwide farm income crisis was growing, and we started paring expenses. Ellen, a neighbor boy, and some of our friends helped in the hayfield, and because there was no money for replacing machinery, I found myself spending more and more time fixing what we already owned, which meant less and less time for the fun things we had planned to do. Fortunately, friends and family still visited, and the Porch Girls, a Duluth acoustic band, came out and played for a women's dance in our calf barn. By 1983, we desperately needed a new hay wagon, and I had to bargain with Ellen to spend some of our discretionary money on it. Neither of us felt happy about it, but I started to understand that I was the only one who felt inextricably bound in place by the farm. I couldn't bring myself to let it go, and as time passed she seemed to wonder more and more why we stayed.

She started coming home from work later in the evenings and complaining more often about the things I could hardly ever do. She made friends in Duluth, like Gerry, who came out with her

Deb (left) and Ellen haying in the early 1980s

lover, Deb, and helped us hay. Ellen also joined a group of pioneering women radio producers, and together they created a women's music and talk program that they called Wise Women Radio. They broadcast the program live once a week from KUMD, a community radio station housed at the University of Minnesota, Duluth.

I loved listening to Wise Women on Sunday evenings. I turned up the volume on the radio in the barn so that I could hear them all the way down the aisle while I fed the cows, milked them, and cleaned their stalls. I also listened to KAXE from Grand Rapids. The women's music movement had really caught on with the programmers on those local community radio stations. I loved hearing Cris Williamson, Margie Adam, Linda Tillery, Holly Near, Bernice Johnson Reagon and her group, Sweet Honey in the Rock, and so many more women on the airwaves at last! The confluence of the community radio movement and the women's music movement opened a space in the commercially dominated radio culture that Shirley and I couldn't quite penetrate when we pitched that demo tape of women's music to the Aitkin radio station's manager.

One winter's day Ellen brought her Wise Women friends to our farm and showed them around. They came out to the barn and walked the aisles and talked to me while I squatted between cows, washed udders, and moved milking machines down the line. They asked questions and passed the time, and I felt bathed in warmth and interest.

"We sure do love Ellen," one of them told me.

"I do too," I said. "She's charming."

"You're pretty charming yourself," the woman said.

I was taken aback and realized that I hadn't really felt charming for a long time but, rather, tired and ragged. At the same time I was proud of my cattle and my work, so maybe that showed through. Few women owned farms, handled large animals and powerful machinery, or took on large amounts of debt without a male partner. The wife of one of the farmers on my cow- testing route told me I was brave when I bought the farm. "Either that or crazy," I joked back, but I did see myself as brave. I'd grown used to operating on the margins, defying expectations, and doing what women didn't usually do. Thanks to my cow-testing job, I'd known what I was getting into. I don't think that was completely true for Ellen.

Before long, she told me that she'd been talking to one of her Wise Women friends who had an open marriage. The friend encouraged Ellen to try it too, and she wondered if we could change the terms of our relationship from monogamy to some more fluid arrangement that would let us experiment with other partners. I saw only danger in the idea. The young woman who'd once thought we didn't own each other and should be free to love whomever we chose had learned through hard experience that people didn't really seem able to share partners without hurting at least one of them. Sex always changed things in unpredictable ways, and I didn't want change just then. I counted on Ellen's love, her company, and the mutuality of our life together.

When I wouldn't agree to an open relationship, she told me that she had already begun an affair with a man in Duluth. She said that she'd meant to keep their relationship casual, but he'd fallen in love with her. He'd cried, she said, and told her how much he needed her, and I knew I hadn't told her anything like that in a long while. When I tried to do it then, things had changed. Maybe my professions of love and need just sounded manipulative when mixed with defensive, angry outbursts, like tearing a towel rack off the wall and throwing it across the room.

She invited me to join her for couples' counseling, and when we sat down in the counseling office, her therapist informed me that the relationship was over. I left in shock, feeling duped, betrayed, outraged, and beneath it all, terrified. From the perspective of age, I see that we were all just trying to be ourselves and find ways to meet our needs. At the time, it was easy to tell myself that my partner had betrayed me doubly by leaving me for a man. I let myself rage about how his male privilege made everything easier for them and gave him social and economic advantages that I could never have or use on her behalf. Suddenly I felt both physically and psychologically inadequate. And then there was the shame of personal and political failure. Her leaving after our six years together seemed to put the lie to the idea that two women could have a fully functioning, lasting relationship.

After she left, I hung on to my farm dream like a life preserver. I didn't waver, even when I found myself overwhelmed and sobbing brokenheartedly while driving a tractor or milking the cows. One evening a neighbor's boy came to buy milk and found me wiping away tears in the barn aisle. His family's response was to stop buying milk from me. My neighbors and family members never talked about my breakup with Ellen. They acted as if nothing had happened, and from their silence I got the idea that they had never taken our relationship seriously in the first place.

My lesbian friends did reach out, and many visited me. Deb drove out from Duluth, and we walked our dogs into the back hayfield and sat on the ground, talking and nearly touching. While our dogs roamed and sniffed, I felt a secret desire arc across the gap between us. She told me later that she did too, but she couldn't let herself go there because her mother had grown up on a dairy farm and had told her never to marry a dairy farmer, "because it's just too hard, dear." Many of my friends lived far away, and before long Deb started a relationship with another woman. I knew it was up to me (as it truly always had been) to pull myself together.

For the next three years, I hung on by doing most of the work myself and piecing together whatever help I could find by bargaining with an assortment of people. A friend of Molly's helped with milking and feeding for a while in exchange for staying in the rooms above the garage space that housed my big John Deere. A local young man helped out and stayed in the spare bedroom of my house. A young woman who worked for the DNR paid rent and boarded with me one summer. During haying, I hired local high school kids, two young women and a few young men, to rake hay

Nancy fixing fence at Happy Hoofer Farm with Faith looking on

and unload hay wagons. Nancy visited and helped build fences. Deb and her new lover, Rose, visited often from Duluth to walk with me, run our dogs, and share meals. Sometimes Deb threw hay bales and helped in the barn, and Rose once cleaned my house. Other dykes came from far and wide to check out my scene after hearing about the farm through the lesbian grapevine or through an ad for a "feminist farmer" that I placed in a dairy farm magazine. I had a recurring dream of a large house filled with lesbian farmers. And then there was the Christian roommate.

I sent a note to be read on KAXE's on-air community bulletin board seeking a farmhand who would work in exchange for meals and a place to stay. The winter of 1983–84 was coming, and I wanted someone who could do simple chores and be there to call 911 if I got hurt outside and didn't show up in the house for a while. A man phoned and then came to talk with me about the job. He was about my age and had a Cat Stevens sort of look and affect that made me think he might work out despite the fact that he didn't know anything about cattle or farming. When I found out that he identified as a born-again Christian, I wondered if he would have a problem with my lesbianism. I know I asked him about it, but I don't precisely recall my question or his answer. For whatever reasons, I decided that we could probably get along, and I went ahead and made an arrangement with him.

He stayed in the spare bedroom, across the hall from mine, and we tried to be friends. The farm was located on the highway between two towns, and we went together to enough basketball games that one of the neighbors asked if I had a boyfriend. After one game we went to the local bar for a drink, and he told me that he thought women were essentially different from men and should act in ways that expressed their feminine nature. I called him a male chauvinist, and after that he started looking glum and tense almost all the time. He complained about the cows' "slow wits" and "big ridiculous bodies" as he curried them. When a news story about the lesbian rights movement came on *All Things Considered*, I perked my ears, and he jumped up and turned off the radio. I didn't dare yell at him or turn it back on. That's when I realized that I felt intimidated and threatened in my own home.

I talked to him about moving on, but he had little money, no car, and nowhere to go, and he seemed to be getting more and more frustrated. Since my bedroom door had no lock, I used an old trick of my mother's, a butcher knife with its blade stuck behind the door casing so that the knife's handle acted like a deadbolt. I hated feeling unsafe, and I thought he must have felt as isolated and unhappy as I did. After some thought, I decided to try introducing him to a neighbor whom I knew also identified as a Christian. When I made the connection, a path opened. They started spending time together, and the neighbor introduced my roommate to a heterosexual couple who ran a Christian camp. They offered him work and a place to live, and our partnership ended amiably. It was my happiest breakup ever—no heartbreak, just fast-forward to the relief of moving on.

In spring 1984, when I attended my creamery's annual meeting in Minneapolis as a delegate from our region, I called a woman I had met through friends and asked if we could get together for coffee or something. April seemed delighted to hear from me. She suggested meeting in the lobby of my hotel and getting lunch at a sushi bar across the street. I'd been reading about this *sushi* for a while, and I wanted to try it. When we got inside, I saw that the chefs stood in a raised kitchen island, surrounded by a narrow moat of running water. We sat on stools around the moat and talked while the chefs prepared different kinds of sushi and placed them on tiny boats that floated around in front of the diners who grabbed whatever looked good as it sailed by.

The experience was new and fresh, and so was April. She had a great sense of humor and an almost breathtaking, outwardly brash aspect to her that she attributed to growing up in Yonkers, New York. Under that shell she had a sweetness and empathy that I found very inviting. She asked me to come by her apartment later, for another meal, a walk, or a maybe a movie on TV. I said right away I would go, and I don't think I was there very long before I told her I wanted to kiss her.

She said with a little laugh, "That would be okay with me. I like you."

I liked her too. Touching and conversation flowed comfortably between us. Soon she visited me at the farm, and we made plans to meet Deb and Rose for dinner at Bob's Chop Suey House. Bob's was in Superior, Wisconsin, which meant a thrilling drive across the high bridge that spanned the channel where the St. Louis River flows into Lake Superior. Bob's had private booths upstairs with curtains we could close for privacy. So we drank wine and ate Chinese food, taking our time, touching if we wanted, and saying whatever came into our heads. Deb said, "Where did you find this woman? She's fun!"

She was, but she wasn't the only fun one. Once, while my ex-lover Nancy was at the farm, April arrived for a short stay. While Nancy and I helped carry her bags, she preceded us into the house. She was wearing those round-toed Mary Jane–style Chinese import shoes that were popular in Minneapolis in the mid-1980s, and as she passed into the entryway while we lagged behind, Nancy took advantage of the moment's opportunity to tease me by whispering, "How do you do it? How do you get girls to come up from the Cities to visit you in their little ballet slippers?"

I had no idea how to answer other than to chuckle and count myself blessed. I never believed I was attractive, even at Rising Moon, when I dropped thirty pounds on the beans-and-rice diet and became a slender boyish dykeling. I could do a good job of acting self-confident, but I have always doubted my own powers.

By 1985, the farm financial crisis had deepened. I saw stories about farm foreclosures, bankruptcies, and rural suicides in the Duluth paper. Evidence of local damage was mounting on the bulletin board at my feed store. There were so many auctions that the sale flyers were stacked and pinned together. Some of my neighbors had already gone out of business, and I found myself needing to carry one bill or another over to the next month almost all the time. The manager of our local gas co-op called one afternoon and asked why I hadn't paid him. I told him there wasn't enough money, and he said, "Well, I'm not going to be the one who gets left out." I had nothing to send him, but I promised to put him at the top of my list the next month. I didn't like doing business that way, and I knew it could not go on.

I went to my FmHA supervisor, and he told me that the only thing he could do for me was to let me sell the farm, providing I could get a big enough down payment from a buyer. I didn't think that was likely, since farmland prices had fallen by nearly half since I bought the farm. Instead of selling I increased the herd by keeping and raising my heifer calves. I also kept using and repairing the old machinery. That meant more and more money for parts, and I had to spend more and more time on repairs and feeding.

That summer, when April came to visit one weekend, she brought a newsletter from a farm group called Groundswell. She said she'd been standing in line for a concert next to a man named Dick Hanson, and he told her about farm protests that were going on in southern Minnesota. He and his lover, Bert Henningson, were out as gay farmers and active in the farm movement, and he gave her the newsletter to take home for me. I remembered that a couple of years earlier I had seen an article in *Newsweek* on AIDS in the heartland, and it had included a photo of a gay couple on their farm field near Glenwood, Minnesota. Those farmers were Bert and Dick. Later, I learned that they were activists on many issues. In the Groundswell newsletter I saw stories and images of farmers speaking up, protesting at foreclosure sales, disrupting auctions, putting up rows of crosses to represent lost farms, and sitting in at banks and in the offices of big quasi-governmental farm lenders like the Production Credit Association and the Federal Land Bank.

Not long after that, a neighbor called to invite me to a meeting. She and her husband had been farmers on my cow-testing route, and they were FmHA borrowers like me. She said that someone called "a farm advocate," a woman from somewhere around St. Cloud, wanted to talk to FmHA borrowers about our rights and options. These particular neighbors had chosen not to be blind but to see Ellen and me for who we were, and I was not surprised that they also chose to see that the Reagan farm policies had put economic forces in motion that could not be blamed solely on the mistakes of individual farmers.

At the meeting I met Sandy, a dairy farmer who told us that she worked for the Farm Advocate Program. She handed out booklets called *The Farmers' Guide to FmHA*. In time, I learned that an attorney named Randi Roth wrote the *Farmers' Guide* during a summer internship with a nonprofit group of lawyers in St. Paul, the Farmers Legal Action Group (FLAG). They educated farmers about their rights, helped elected officials write laws to address the farm crisis, and brought class action lawsuits on behalf of farmers. Another new world was opening up to me. Like the world I had glimpsed at my first gay bar, this one too felt longed-for and dangerous.

Sandy explained that Congress had given FmHA borrowers loan-servicing rights that the Reagan administration refused to use. She said that a legal services lawyer named Sarah Vogel had already sued and won a national class action lawsuit (*Coleman v. Block*) that required the FmHA to defer loan payments if a farmer needed the money to pay necessary farm operating expenses. I thought of my utility bill as she told us how to write a letter to our county supervisor that mentioned the *Coleman* lawsuit and explained why we needed the deferral. She also mentioned that the people who supervised the Farm Advocate Program were looking for a farmer who might want to train to become an advocate in our area. I told her I was interested, and she gave me the phone number of Anne Kanten, a farm organizer and Minnesota's Deputy Commissioner of Agriculture.

I called Anne the next day. In her warm, resonant voice, I heard carefully constructed sentences and thoughtful questions. After a while she said, "Well, maybe this will help." She said she would send a farm advocate named Lou Anne Kling out to meet me and give me some training and "see how it goes." When Lou Anne called me, she asked me to arrange for us to meet with some farmers who needed help. She arrived a week or so later in a big old sedan with a blond-haired woman named Jenny who was also a farm advocate.

I learned from Lou Anne that she had started the farm advocate work on her own. She volunteered to help a neighbor and soon found herself digging into the Code of Federal Regulations that governed FmHA. She told me later that she didn't understand much of the legal language at first, but she just kept on reading and reading until it started making sense. Once she understood how the FmHA was supposed to operate, she found mistakes in the way the local supervisor had handled her neighbor's case, and she was able to help him appeal and keep his farm. After that, word about her spread, and she was soon driving around the state to help farmers who sometimes lined up to see her. She was in her forties, stoutly built, and both sharp and weary around the eyes. She struck me as someone who would be good to have on my side, whether fighting physically or philosophically.

Thanks to Lou Anne, Anne, and the FLAG attorneys, I started to understand more and more about how the farm crisis, the administration's farm policy, and the overall consolidation of wealth fit together. Jim Massey, the director of FLAG, told me that he'd started the work because he wanted to intervene against large economic and political forces that he saw dispossessing farmers and workers alike. When I interviewed him later for an oral history project on the Farm Advocates, he said:

> While the economy supposedly was taking off under Reagan, there were a lot of people who weren't doing so well financially. Farmers were a group of "new poor" as a result of administration policies. What was going on was not just one of those natural swings of the farm economy. It was the beginning of a swing made worse by farm policy.

The FLAG lawyers worked with Lou Anne and the advocates, creating a dynamic feedback loop. Advocates told the lawyers what was happening to farmers and the lawyers lobbied, helped legislators write laws, brought lawsuits, and educated the advocates on laws and regulations that could help. I felt tremendous relief to have found such people.

The evening I met Lou Anne and Jenny, we drove to a neighbor's farm after supper. I watched as Lou Anne showed me how an advocate operated. She listened to my neighbors' situation, explained their rights and responsibilities, and helped them fill out a Farm and Home Plan, the short financial planning document used by FmHA administrators. Afterward, she said that I was hired. She handed me my tools: my own thick volumes of the Code of Federal Regulations that governed FmHA and some copies of the *Farmers' Guide*. She said I would get more training later, along with a modest wage and travel expense reimbursement. The Minnesota Department of Agriculture administered our program, and the state paid us. So I found myself with a part-time job as I did my best to help the people I had known first as my employers, then as my neighbors and colleagues, and then again as my farm advocacy clients. I was also helping myself, of course, as those who care for others nearly always do.

23 Going, Going, Gone

By 1986, cattle prices had dropped nearly by half, and the price of a hundred pounds of milk had dropped below the worst-case scenario I'd imagined when I bought the farm. Farmers around the country sold out in despair and went through bankruptcy and foreclosure—taking many small-town banks and businesses with them. In Carlton County, my FmHA supervisor had deferred a large portion of my loan payments after he received the letter from me invoking the *Coleman* decision, and after months of paying less than the amount due, I knew I'd never be able to get back on top of the accruing balance.

My responsibility for the animals weighed heavily on me. The horses practically took care of themselves in the pasture. I had long since quit riding because I had no time for it and I couldn't afford to get hurt and be unable to take care of the cows. I saw the dairy herd as a unity, a cornucopia, a renewable resource, and a family that had been together a long time—decades—before I took stewardship of them. They earned their own living as well as mine, and I thought they deserved to stay together. I definitely didn't want to be the one who broke that chain of DNA and symbiotic abundance. Even into my sixties, I had recurring dreams of climbing into the hayloft and finding only two or three bales up there, while I listened to the haunting bellows of cattle crying for forage. Thankfully, this never happened in real life. When I ran short of hay, I always managed to buy some and pay for it. I could manage no retirement savings or new clothes for myself, but no one went hungry at Happy Hoofer Farm.

My work with the farm advocates fed my spirit too, by letting me know I could still act as a powerful subject in the world. Every few months we met and learned about topics like financial planning, negotiation skills, mental health resources for farmers, and the laws and rules of agricultural lending. We learned how to find free legal help for farmers and how to get people we thought might be depressed in touch with mental health providers whose services they could afford. We shared stories about stubborn lenders, old-time farmers who presented their advocates with shoeboxes full of unorganized business receipts that were supposed to serve as their financial records, and a proud man who farmed thousands of acres but opened his refrigerator to show his advocate that there was only a bottle of ketchup in it. As we shared our experiences, the stories worked a kind of magic. They showed me a range of troubles and possible responses that kept me from sinking too deeply into my own despair. I could see that my situation wasn't as bad as others, I was not alone, and I had options.

My calendar filled with appointments to help farmers all across northeastern Minnesota. By this time farm activists and rural interest groups had persuaded the Minnesota legislature to pass a law that required lenders who wanted to foreclose on agricultural property to first mediate in good faith with farmers who couldn't pay their debts. Under the new law, lenders and farmers had to go through a formal process with state-trained mediators. I helped farmers prepare for those mediation sessions and accompanied them as their advocate.

When I thought that any of my clients might be heading toward bankruptcy, I tried to find them legal services lawyers who knew farm law and would take their cases for free or reduced rates. These lawyers tended to be brainy, empathetic, and earnest men and women who cared about social justice. In one case a young man from southern Minnesota took the case of one of my farm families. He seemed to have everything going for him, and I was shocked to read in the *Minneapolis Star Tribune* one Sunday morning that he had drowned after going through the ice of a frozen flowage on his snowmobile. It fell to me to call the bank's lawyer and tell him that we needed a postponement of our upcoming mediation session. The man agreed and then asked, somewhat impatiently, "When are we going to meet next?"

I told him I didn't know. I didn't tell him that I couldn't know exactly when, or even how, we would find a new lawyer for my clients. Attorneys willing to study farm credit law in order to expend billable hours helping low-income farmers were precious, few, and far between.

"We can't let this drag on too long, you know," the banker's lawyer added in a voice that seemed so inappropriately insistent and cold, given the circumstances, that I have remembered it all these years. So much for compassion, I thought at the time. He might have seemed a more decent man if I had known him under other circumstances, but the situation put us at odds. When the farm credit mediation law was new, most lenders seemed to view mediation as a lose-win situation that they intended to win by stonewalling, refusing to negotiate, blaming the farmers, and shaming them if possible. That attitude made adversaries, and I suppose I'd been foolish to look for compassion from my adversary. That's what loved ones and allies are for.

In the early winter of 1985, Deb mentioned that an old friend of hers from Girl Scout camp had taken a job in Grand Rapids and lived about an hour's drive from the farm. Deb had told me more than once before that Cedar was the best guitarist she knew (which was saying something, since Deb could both strum and more than hold a tune). Deb said that Cedar would be traveling across northern Minnesota for her work. It might be nice, she thought, if Cedar made a new friend and could stop by when she passed the farm. We made a plan that Deb would invite her to a New Year's Eve party at my house. By the time of the party, the sexual part of my relationship with April had cooled, but no one else knew that we had begun to see ourselves as warm-hearted friends rather than lovers.

We had planned the party around both ends of an evening milking. It was a relaxing and casual affair with food, guitar playing, social drinking, visits back and forth between the house and the barn while I milked, and a joint or two after that slowed the conversation to a quiet flow. Friends came from the Twin Cities, Duluth, and spots in between. In her blue jeans, flannel, and wool, Cedar fit right in. She hung around and talked with me quite a lot while I milked. She said how beautiful the farm was. She didn't mention the cattle or the machinery, just the land. She loved the wild parts of it, the woods, meadows, river, and the way that snow dressed it all in light. She noticed the chickadees, finches, and grosbeaks that came to my feeder, and she spoke rhapsodically about hiking, camping, and snowshoeing. In the house afterward, she played some songs she had written about blue highways, a winter day as cold as "an old brass bra," and loving a woman while Orion transited the sky. She got along well with my friends, and I liked her.

On New Year's morning while I finished up milking, she stood in the barn aisle and confessed her attraction to me. This was an awfully sudden turn of events. I paused with the milking machines pumping on three cows and reached one arm above my head to steady myself on the overhead pipeline that carried milk from the cows to the barn. I told Cedar I liked her too, but I hardly knew her. I needed some time.

She looked crestfallen. After she left for home, I told April about our conversation. She smiled and said, "You're lucky. She's nice."

"Yes," I said. "I know."

Cows and advocacy work kept me busy the next week, though I thought about Cedar a lot. When she visited again, she was complimentary, appreciative, and still in a hurry to court me. I had planned to let some time pass before getting involved with someone new. She rushed me, no doubt, but nothing she said felt overly frightening or needy. Her fundamental kindness shone through, and I saw her hurry as understandably aroused by her anxiety, and charming for that reason, since I understood quite a bit about anxiety after years of living with my own. We went snowshoeing that afternoon in the pasture across the highway from the house, and she leaned over and kissed me. In my surprise, I didn't respond, and the next thing I knew, she had run off. I found myself chasing after her through deep snow, calling her name and feeling like I had to make amends. I hadn't meant to embarrass her. When she finally let me catch her, I explained all that, out of breath, and assured her that I liked her. After that, we started getting to know each other. Some anxieties settled down and others got stirred up. We learned to care for each other through the small steps of keeping things mutual, doing nurturing acts, and talking about our values, plans, and hopes for the future.

At first, she kept the cabin she had rented. She told me she had always dreamed of living in a log cabin, and when I visited her in the snowy woods outside Grand Rapids, I saw that her cabin looked sturdy and splendid, with golden-skinned logs, a loft, and a modern kitchen. Tucked in among the birch and pines and visited by birds and other wildlife that the trees and bird feeder lured near her windows, the cabin was the right home for her. The physical distance between us, and our individual commitments to our work, gave us time to think about how we should go about fitting our lives together. Months later, after her lease on the cabin expired, we were ready for her to move to the farm. From there, she commuted more than an hour to her office, and when she traveled farther for work, she stayed overnight in motels, as she had done before she met me.

She coordinated projects for the Minnesota Environmental Education Board (MEEB), helping citizen volunteers put together programs about local ecology. She'd been working out of Marshall, Minnesota, before she took the northern tier job, and she told me about a man she knew named Bert Henningson. He was the lover of Dick Hanson, the gay farmer who had given April that Groundswell newsletter two years earlier. Bert had been teaching history at the University of Minnesota, Morris, when Cedar met him. She said he was a scholar of agricultural history and economics as well as a MEEB volunteer. Later, I found out that he'd been a conscientious objector during the Vietnam War. I also learned that when Anne Kanten, the farm activist who championed the advocate program, was appointed Deputy Commissioner of Agriculture by Governor Rudy Perpich, she hired Bert to advise her in the Agriculture Department. One day when I was in St. Paul for a training session, I saw him at his desk and stopped to introduce myself. He struck me as a kind, smart, precise man who seemed genuinely glad to hear news of Cedar.

"You know Bert?" Anne asked me as I passed her office afterward, and I told her about my connection to him through "my life partner," which was how I usually referred to my lover when talking to someone who was not gay. Anne just nodded. I saw her as one of the stern and sturdy girls, both physically and ethically. She'd organized rallies for the American Agriculture Movement and lobbied Congress while her son drove one of the family's tractors across the country and down the Washington Mall with a slew of other farmers to protest agricultural policies that hurt family farmers. She'd worked with Bert and Dick for a long time, and I found out that it took a lot more than a lesbian coming out to her to shake Anne up.

The day I met Bert, nothing about him seemed fraught. Over the next year, I heard that he was nursing Dick, who had become acutely sick with AIDS. In 1987, Bert learned that he too was infected with the HIV virus. At a farm advocate training, he told a few of us how sick and weak he felt on his AZT regimen. The antiviral cocktail that has proven so effective against AIDS had not yet been discovered, and many myths about the "gay disease" remained. According to historian Allida Black, Ronald Reagan did not say the word *AIDS* until 1987, which was also the year that Dick died. By then, thirty-seven thousand Americans were in-

Dianna (right) and her mother, Ruth Hunter, during milking at Happy Hoofer Farm

fected with the virus, and twenty-one thousand had died, as Bert would the next year.

In the spring of 1986, Cedar brought Norman Myers, the expert in biodiversity, to speak at an environmental learning center not far from our farm. A month or two later, at a farm advocate training, two of the FLAG lawyers updated us on farm bankruptcy law. They wanted a case study to discuss, so I offered my own situation. We hashed over the facts and the law for a half-hour or more, and I learned that Minnesota allowed a farmer like me to keep $10,000 worth of farm machinery through Chapter 7 bankruptcy (the kind in which the borrower sells out rather than reorganizing). The provision was meant to help a farmer get the fresh start that bankruptcy was designed to provide. I'd grown up thinking of bankruptcy as a shameful act and an admission of failure, and I was surprised to learn that bankruptcy was designed to help people recover from bad financial situations. Bankruptcy's reboot makes it a survival strategy, whether used by billionaire casino owners, corporations acting as if they were people, or a small farmer like me. I came away thinking, for the first time, that

I should consider selling out and filing for Chapter 7, but I wasn't quite ready yet.

That summer my parents visited Cedar and me, along with my aunt and uncle from San Diego. While they were at the farm, Taja gave birth to a colt in the pasture. I hadn't even realized she was pregnant, and I felt ashamed when I thought about the extent of my inattention. The horses had gotten short shrift ever since I took on responsibility for the dairy cows. I had sold Lhasa and her filly when I bought the farm. I never rode anymore, and my spirited mare, Taja, spent her time in a pasture with two maturing colts that I hadn't even found time to halter-train. One of them must have bred her. Luckily, she and her foal thrived.

Meanwhile, a new milk inspector made a visit, and my barn didn't pass inspection. My hired woman and I were in the throes of haying, the machine that cut the hay had broken down, and we had spent hours taking it apart for repairs. I knew that the barn needed whitewashing, but I was hoping to wait until the haying was finished to get at it. The new milk inspector had other ideas. She left a notice that threatened to stop me from selling Grade A milk if I didn't clean up the barn immediately. She stipulated a list of changes she wanted made by the time she returned. As I recall, she gave me less than a week.

As bad as my finances were while selling Grade A milk, I knew they would get even worse if I only had Grade B milk to sell. Grade B milk could be used for making butter and cheese but not for bottling, so it brought a lower price than Grade A. I needed the higher price, but I didn't see how I could find the time to make the improvements the milk inspector wanted while still making hay. She wanted the ceiling in the milk room replaced, the milk room walls repainted, and the interior of the barn whitewashed. To prioritize that work over haying would have cost dearly, because as grass matures its protein content drops, and the cows that eat it milk less. Everything on the farm was connected to everything else, so every job had to be done right and on time, or some other part would suffer. I felt myself in an unbearable bind. I told Cedar and my family that I'd had it. I couldn't take the pressure anymore. I would let the milk inspector bust me to Grade B, and that would ensure that I'd go broke even faster. I would accept failure, file bankruptcy, and sell the farm.

We all went to bed on that glum note, and the next morning after chores my mother's sister took me aside and said, "You know we've been talking, and we decided that we'll all help you. If you're going to go out of business, we think you should go out first class."

Wow! I felt so uplifted by them and, at the same time, ashamed because they were my elders, and I didn't want them to have to do one lick of work on my behalf. I should be doing work for them, I thought, but the farm made worker bees of everyone. Whoever visited ended up chasing cows or helping make hay, or cooking dinner, or, or, or . . . . I told myself this was the last time I would let a guest get sucked into my endless work. Then we got going. My aunt and mom scrubbed the milking equipment and the walls of the milk room. My dad and uncle replaced the milk room ceiling and repainted. My hired woman brought over a whitewash sprayer on loan from her father. She was a dairy farmer herself, or at least the daughter of a farmer who aspired to own and run her own farm some day (which she is now doing). She, Cedar, and I whitewashed the interior of the barn. We sprayed the walls, ceilings, support posts, and beams with a traditional solution of lime, salt, and water that whitened everything and hardened like plaster. The place had never looked so good by the time I was ready to let it go, but I did not change my mind about selling.

Cedar was happy that I'd decided to let go. So was my FmHA county supervisor, I think. He took the news calmly and told me to look for an auctioneer. For me, the loss was so great that I had to play mind tricks to get through it. I concentrated on looking forward to some rest and relief, while in the meantime I got even busier, organizing for the sale. I decided what tractors and equipment to take through the bankruptcy, which I planned to file at a later time. Unfortunately, livestock weren't included in what I could take through Chapter 7, so I had to sell the cattle and horses, along with the rest of my machinery. FmHA would get all of the money earned at the sale. Eventually, the government would get the farm back too, through foreclosure, though that legal process would take more than a year. For the time being, Cedar and I still had a home. After the year passed, we wanted to relocate to some smaller farm. She wanted it to be fully ours, without the history and baggage of Happy Hoofer Farm.

I sold the herd, horses, and machinery at auction on a sunny, seventy-degree day in October 1986. My parents came to help, along with one of Mom's four younger brothers and his wife from Minot. April ran a concession stand for us, while Mom and my aunt cooked brats and schlepped buns and cookies from the kitchen. Deb and Cedar helped carry boxes of farm items from our sheds to the wagons that the auctioneers used as stages. Ellen, my ex who had moved to St. Paul, came and shot photographs and video. A woman who was a stranger took photographs too, and as she focused on my chickens, she said ruefully to me that she wanted to document everything because "this way of life is disappearing. Soon there won't be any more small farms." For me, the day passed in surreal flashes. Unfamiliar images, sounds, and smells mixed with ones I cherished and knew, painfully, that I was experiencing for the last time.

My Dairy Herd Improvement Association records and the reputation of my herd drew competitive buyers, and several of my cows brought more than a thousand dollars. That was a decent amount at the time, since cattle prices had been plummeting throughout the '80s. The cattle seemed to take the sale in stride, thanks to the know-how of the auctioneers. They had set up wisely and brought plenty of help to direct the cows and young stock into the sales ring outside the barn's front door. The phrase *creatures of habit* was very likely coined to describe cattle, though we're the ones who confine them and subject them to routine. Most of them had never gone out the front door before, let alone into a sales ring surrounded by people. I was impressed that they didn't panic. Some of them snorted, balked, and rolled their eyes, but none of them lost their composure completely. The same could be said of me. Regret and sadness would flood me later, along with massive relief and a sense of standing once again at the precipice, still the tarot's Fool blundering into the unknown. I had little idea what I would do next, other than to continue as a farm advocate for a while, but I hoped to write and have more time to cultivate a life of the mind.

As it turned out, with the support of my farm advocate supervisors, Anne Kanten and Lou Anne Kling, I soon coordinated an oral history project in which another writer and I collected the farm advocates' stories. I placed the tapes and transcripts with the Minnesota Historical Society and edited the stories into a book and a series of radio programs featuring the advocates' voices. My book and radio programs reached farmers and farm advocates around the country, and after that I began to publish journalism, poetry, fiction, and creative nonfiction. In 1992, I started graduate work in creative writing at Iowa State University, and in the next few years Cedar and I parted ways, and Deb and I became partners. For the next twenty years, I taught writing and women's and gender studies at four different universities—always in what is now called the "contingent faculty." That means nontenured jobs, often with heavy teaching loads, little or no job security, and low pay, but I was lucky. At the time I started teaching in the academy, the workloads and pay were reasonable (especially compared to dairy farming), and teaching and interacting with smart and challenging students and colleagues fed my intellect and spirit. After everything I've experienced, I still see through the eyes of a working-class girl, and I can't help but mention that my last two positions offered renewable contracts, health insurance, and enough pay to cover expenses and save for retirement. In my last job I earned a defined-benefit pension, an almost extinct perk these days. Because of it, I was able to retire in 2012. The following year I started work on this memoir.

As I wrote, I found that one moment during the farm auction called to me with particular clarity. Taja and her colt went up for sale together since he was still a suckling. I had resigned myself to letting them go, my beautiful Red One and her lookalike son, but when the bidding started, I saw Deb raise her hand. A neighbor wanted them too, and he and Deb bid each other up to a hundred and twenty-five dollars. Deb was in at that price, and he was out.

"Do I hear a hundred and thirty?" The auctioneer asked. "A hundred and thirty? A hundred and thirty? I'm bid a hundred and twenty-five. Going once. Going twice. Sold right over there for a hundred and twenty-five!"

It was a lot of money in those days, but Deb just smiled and told me that she was giving them back to me. "You were losing everything else. I didn't think you should have to lose your pets, too," she said after the sale. Decades later, when we looked back on that day as a legally married couple who had been together for twenty-two years, she said, "You must have known that was an act of love."

Yes, I did, but what kind of love, and how would we live it? Weren't those always the questions?

A few days after the sale, Cedar and I took a drive to visit my old friends Haven and Verna Damar, the owners of Del Lago. We phoned ahead, and Verna had her homemade bread and home-grown honey waiting on the table when we arrived. Our talk turned to piloting planes, since Cedar's dad was soon to retire as an airline captain. I'd never associated planes with Haven and Verna before Cedar told them how her dad had parlayed his assignment as an airplane mechanic during World War II into pilot training and then a captain's job for American Airlines after the war.

"I could have done that," Haven said.

"You could have?" I asked.

"Yes," he said. "I was a pilot."

"What did you fly?" I asked him.

"Bombers," he said and stood up, without looking at us.

Life's crazy connections struck again. My mom had helped build B-17s for Boeing in Seattle during the war. As Haven walked away from the table, I noticed that his hair had lost its blond color and had gone entirely platinum, as had Verna's. He still had that soldierly posture, but I thought his gaze had stopped zeroing in as piercingly as I remembered from that first day I met him, when I stood uncomfortably under it at Del Lago. He walked into the next room and stared at a framed print that depicted a squad of American bombers, flak exploding around them while their own bombs and shadows fell across some European town. Suddenly I thought I understood where the calm, cold eye and steady hand of the custom butcher had come from, and why Haven might have chosen to get down from the sky and go home to what he knew and loved before the war.

He told us he'd been offered a deal like the one Cedar's dad took. The airlines sent recruiters to hire men like him. At the time airline captains didn't earn much, Cedar told me—nothing like the hundred-thousand-dollar-a-year salaries that senior captains commanded just before her father retired.

Haven surprised me very much when he said with what sounded like genuine regret, "I should have done it."

I suspect it was only a passing thought, even if possibly a recurring one. I'd always seen him as a perfectly happy man in control of his circumstances. But then I hadn't yet given up on the myth that any of us can control much of anything, even though I probably should have learned it growing up among people who had lived through the Great Depression and the most violent war in human history. I don't see the World War II generation as greater than any other. Most of them followed rules and valued conformity when they might have asked more questions, but the ones I knew had human decency, belief in the public good, and revulsion to crassness and violence. I've learned from them that the past is never really past, and life seems to just get more complicated as we go on. New questions put the run on old answers, and new levels of meaning emerge just to be even further complicated by facts. Like the film version of Patricia Highsmith's character Carol Aird, I see that I've never really known what I was doing.

The best I can say for myself is that some horse of dreams has carried me this far. Call it luck, hard work, or resilience. I sometimes feel like one of those inflatable clown toys that I envied when other kids got them in the '50s. You punched them in the nose, and they flipped backwards and popped right back up. "Sand in your bottom," my friend Lisyli called it when I talked to her recently. Most of us back-to-the-land lesbians had it. The sand in my bottom helped me get through the Cuban Missile Crisis, the violent springs of 1968 and '70, coming out, and (so far) patriarchy, homophobia, the backlash against feminism, and the long cold wars against socialists, small-time farmers, student activists, lesbians, and everyone queer enough not to be afraid to stand apart, in one way or another, from the mainstream materialistic culture that is the real culture of death.

Our lesbian back-to-the-land experiments gave us some new remedies to try. They carried us forward from everything we needed to leave behind, even if we sometimes got hurt while trying out our ideas. For some of us, Haidiya Farm, Rising Moon, Del Lago, and Pliny were the few good things in a lifetime of struggle. For me, they are still the ideals that point the way toward a collective home, a loving sisterhood, and a way of living that replenishes rather than depletes.

I'm coming close now to finishing my seventh decade. I'm still a lesbian, still a feminist, still a farmer of flowers, roots, herbs, apples, and berries in the urban gardens and green spaces that I share with Deb. Most of my back-to-the-land friends are living out land dreams in one way or another: Shirley with gardens, fruit trees, and a log house she built with other women; Summer with a truck that looks like her old Chevy Mabel; Nancy on a farm with a red barn, a tractor, and a well-equipped workshop; Cedar building a cabin on twenty wild acres beside a wild and scenic river; Ellen in retirement from providing urban gardening services; Marea raising hybrid daylilies that she sells online; Martha, Patricia, and Molly on land that they garden and enjoy.

My lesbian back-to-the-land story is just one of many, no other of which is exactly like mine or anyone else's. We followed our dreams of independence and freedom. We cared for each other's well-being and growth, and we made new lives as self-defined women in a patriarchal world. Complete liberation, unconditional love, and long-term collective living may have slipped through our fingers, but at least we tried to be true to ourselves. Does everyone do that? If not, I don't know why not. We have to love ourselves and live with courage. After Willa Cather's protagonist Lucy Gayheart loses one sweetheart to drowning and another to miscommunication and paralyzing shame, she falls into a deep depression. Her turning point comes in a flash of insight: "What if—what if Life itself were the sweetheart?"

Yes, what if.

Life itself keeps rushing forward. I have loved it always, and I remain astounded at how substantial and captivating it feels as we move forward through it, on the cusp of being and becoming, in those infinitesimal moments before it all passes into story and history.

Acknowledgments

Many thanks to the readers who commented on my memoir before it was published, especially to my primary reader, Pamela Mittlefehldt; to my copy editor at the University of Minnesota Press, Louisa Castner; and to Martha Benewicz, Karen Browne, Shirley Duke, Christine Jenkins, Susan King, Carol Langer, Molly McCarthy, Nancy Sanders, Marea Sweeten, Mary Turck, and Ellen Wold. Thanks for research help to Lisa Vecoli, curator of the Tretter Collection in GLBT Studies at the University of Minnesota, Twin Cities and to Ellen Holdt-Werle, archivist and special collections librarian in the DeWitt Wallace Library at Macalester College.

The following women provided photographs or shared archival material and stories: Judith Bagan, Carol Batteen, Martha Benewicz, M'lou Brubaker, Lisyli Hardin, Eunice Hunseth, Susan King, Meadow Muska, April Posner, Jane Stedman, and Shary Zoff. My greatest gratitude goes to Deb Anderson, my reader, confidante, and lawfully wedded paramour. The events described in this memoir actually happened, and I conveyed them as accurately as I could, given the scope, strengths, and vagaries of memory. Whenever possible, I checked my own memories against the written record and against the memories of those who shared my women's land journey. Many of the names used in this book are real, and all of the characters represent real people. In some cases I used pseudonyms out of deference to people I couldn't contact and to those who had concerns about being publicly identified. The names Ari, Theia, Marj, Summer, Trent, Maya, Otter, young Schmidt, the O'Hares, the Hardys, Tracy, Barrett, Sadie, Sierra, Marl, Fred, Rod, Rochelle, and Gerry are pseudonyms.

An earlier version of "The Great Man and the Dead Cow" was published on the Lake Superior Writers' website. Early drafts of that chapter as well as "MAD, MAD, MAD, MAD World," "Women, Horses, and Other Embodied Spirits," and "Del Lago" (some under earlier titles) were read for broadcast for the KUMD Radio "Women's Words" series. They are archived for listening at the KUMD website.

This memoir is dedicated to all of the lesbians who went back to the land looking for replenishment and liberation.

Resources

For readers who would like to follow a research thread or simply explore further, here is information about selected sources mentioned in *Wild Mares*.

Bechdel, Alison. *Fun Home: A Family Tragicomic*. Boston: First Mariner Books, 2007.

Boston Women's Health Book Collective. *Our Bodies, Ourselves: A New Edition for a New Era*. New York: Simon and Schuster, 2005.

———. *Women and Their Bodies*. Boston: Boston Women's Health Book Collective, 1970.

Cather, Willa. *Lucy Gayheart*. New York: Vintage, 1995.

Cheney, Joyce, ed. *Lesbian Land*. Minneapolis: Word Weavers, 1985.

Ehrenreich, Barbara, and Deirdre English. *Witches, Midwives, and Nurses: A History of Women Healers*. New York: Feminist Press at the City University of New York, 2010.

Gordimer, Nadine. *Telling Times: Writing and Living, 1954–2008*. New York: W. W. Norton, 2010.

Hersh, Seymour M. "Letter from Vietnam. The Scene of the Crime: A Reporter's Journey to My Lai and the Secrets of the Past." *New Yorker,* March 30, 2015, 56–61.

Lerner, Gerda. *A Death of One's Own.* Madison: University of Wisconsin Press, 1985.

Lorde, Audre. "Uses of the Erotic: The Erotic as Power." In *Sister Outsider: Essays and Speeches.* Berkeley, Calif.: Crossing Press, 2007.

Martin, Del, and Phyllis Lyon. *Lesbian/Woman.* Volcano, Calif.: Volcano Press, 1991.

McConnell, Kathy. "Rising Moon: The End or the Beginning?" *Gold Flower: A Twin Cities Newspaper for Women* 4, no. 9 (September 1975): 3 and 15.

Morgan, Robin, ed. *Sisterhood Is Powerful: An Anthology of Writings from the Women's Liberation Movement.* New York: Random House, 1970.

Radicalesbians. *Woman-Identified Woman.* Somerville, Mass.: New England Free Press, 1970.

Redstockings Collective. "The Redstockings Manifesto." In *Gender Issues and Sexuality: Essential Primary Sources,* ed. K. Lee Lerner, Brenda Wilmoth, and Adrienne Wilmoth. Detroit: Thomson Gale, 2006.

Renault, Mary. *The Last of the Wine.* New York: Vintage, 2001.

The Report of the President's Commission on Campus Unrest. Washington, D.C.: Government Printing Office, 1970.

Rosenfeld, Seth. *Subversives: The FBI's War on Student Radicals and Reagan's Rise to Power.* New York: Farrar, Straus and Giroux, 2012.

Stanton, Elizabeth Cady. "Solitude of Self." In *Feminism: The Essential Historical Writings,* ed. Miriam Schneir. New York: Vintage, 1994. 157–62.

Wings, Mary. *Dyke Shorts.* Dyke Shorts Comics, 1978.

Illustration Credits

Dianna Hunter is author of the book and radio series *Breaking Hard Ground: Stories of the Minnesota Farm Advocates*. She taught writing and women's and gender studies at four universities, including the University of Wisconsin–Superior, where she was a lecturer and director until she retired in 2012.